The "How To" Grants Manual

The "How To" Grants Manual

Successful Grantseeking Techniques for Obtaining Public and Private Grants

Third Edition

by
David G. Bauer
"

AMERICAN COUNCIL ON EDUCATION ★
ORYX PRESS ★
Series on Higher Education
1995

The rare Arabian Oryx is believed to have inspired the myth of the unicorn. This desert antelope became virtually extinct in the early 1960s. At that time several groups of international conservationists arranged to have 9 animals sent to the Phoenix Zoo to be the nucleus of a captive breeding herd. Today the Oryx population is over 1000, and nearly 500 have been returned to reserves in the Middle East.

Copyright © 1995 by the American Council on Education and The Oryx Press
Published by The Oryx Press
4041 North Central at Indian School Road
Phoenix, Arizona 85012-3397
Published simultaneously in Canada

Printed and bound in the United States of America

∞ The paper used in this publication meets the minimum requirements of American National Standard for Information Science—Permanence of Paper for Printed Library Materials, ANSI Z39.48, 1984.

Library of Congress Cataloging-in-Publication Data

Bauer, David G.
    The "how to" grants manual : successful grantseeking techniques
for obtaining public and private grants / by David G. Bauer. —3rd
ed.
        p. cm. — (American Council on Education/Oryx Press series on
higher education)
    Includes bibliographical references and index.
    ISBN 0-89774-851-4
    1. Fund raising. 2. Grants-in-aid. 3. Nonprofit organizations.
I. Title. II. Series.
HG177.B38 1995
658.15'224—dc20

95-1437
CIP

CONTENTS

• • • • • • • • • • •

PREFACE

· · · · · · · · · · ·

The third edition of The "How To" Grants Manual is a compilation of 25 years of effort to systematize the grantseeking process for nonprofit agencies in the United States. Having instructed over 15,000 grantseekers in hundreds of seminars, I am sensitive to the need to actively manage grantseeking. Whether you are a first-time grantseeker, a veteran, or a director of a grants office of 20, this manual is intended to help you improve the investment return of your grants effort.

The "How To" Grants Manual will increase your knowledge of the competitive grants marketplace and show you how to locate and secure grant funds. It also outlines a systematic approach for organizing proposal efforts that will save you hours of precious time and increase your monetary return by thousands of dollars. By applying the techniques presented in this manual, you will increase your success rate while projecting a more professional image to funding sources.

The third edition includes suggestions that readers have shared with me since the book's last edition, recent changes in the area of corporate philanthropy, and guidance on developing new types of relationships that result in money. Information on using computer databases and electronic retrieval and searching systems (including the Internet), more worksheets, and time-saving sample letters are also provided.

The arrangement of the manual follows the recommended grantseeking pattern. Part 1, "Getting Ready to Seek Grant Support for Your Organization," will show you how to view your proposal from the perspective of the potential grantor. Part 2, "Government Funding Sources," is devoted to understanding the federal grants process and includes strategies for improving the quality of your federal proposal. Part 3, "Private Funding Sources," takes a comprehensive look at the foundation and corporate grants marketplace. Part 3 assists the grantseeker in researching and selecting private funding sources and preparing a letter proposal to a foundation or corporation. The focus in both parts 2 and 3 is on how to select prospective grantors and increase your chances of success through pre-proposal contact. You will learn how to create a tailored approach designed to meet the grantor's needs as well as those of your organization.

No matter what your level of grantseeking expertise, this book will help promote *your* system for grants success. While this manual does not come with a guarantee, surveys of its users consistently demonstrate success rates of 70 to 80 percent.

A software package entitled Grant Winner is available to help you organize the grantseeking techniques outlined in this manual. You may want to refer to the ordering information at the end of the book.

In order to reduce the time spent on researching possible funding sources for projects involving higher education, I suggest you read the companion piece to this manual, *The Complete Grants Sourcebook for Higher Education* (Phoenix: American Council on Education/Oryx Press, third edition forthcoming, 1995). If you are involved in evaluating and improving your organization's grants effort, you will find the book *Administering Grants, Contracts, and Funds* (Phoenix: American Council on Education/Oryx Press, 1989) particularly helpful. If you are interested in instructing others in grantseeking, you may find the videotape training program *Winning Grants* invaluable. (For ordering information, see the list of resources available from Bauer Associates at the end of the book.)

Special thanks must be given to the American Council on Education, the SUNY Institute of Technology Utica/Rome, and the University of Rochester School of Medicine, Department of Pediatrics, for providing me with opportunities to develop many of the techniques shared in this manual.

INTRODUCTION

• • • • • • • • • •

Why seek grants? My answer to this question is similar to Willie Sutton's response when asked why he robbed banks—because that's where the money is! Successful grantseeking is a rewarding process because it results in money; however, the money is not the end in itself. The benefits that our society and world derive from the grantseeking efforts of over 500,000 501(c)3 nonprofit organizations are the rewarding end.

As long as there are needs and interests that require more support than nonprofit organizations can provide through their normal allocation processes, there will be a demand for grant funds. And as long as there are wealthy individuals and profitable companies looking for ways to impart their values and demonstrate their concerns, as well as governments willing to fund scientific research and efforts to find new and better solutions to social problems, there will be grantseekers.

For many faculty members at universities and research centers, grantseeking is a necessity. The ability to attract grant funding is a requirement for their continued appointment and tenure. Many faculty members, however, continue seeking grants even after they have secured their position. Why? They pursue grant funding for many of the same reasons that those of you in nonacademic fields do, and it's not for money!

Do grantseekers get paid extra to write proposals? No. Most nonprofits (including universities and research centers) do not pay their staff extra for writing proposals. In fact, they do not even provide release time or reduced work loads to help individuals who are seeking grants. The legal and ethical requirements that govern grantseeking do not allow proposal developers or consultants to be paid a percentage of the awarded grant, making the question of why individuals pursue grant funding even more of a mystery. The quest for a grant in the nonprofit world is equivalent to efforts in the for-profit world that are associated with superior performance and superachievers. In fact, findings in studies on motivation and achievement in the for-profit world are similar to those documented in a study by Sharol Jacobson and Mary Elizabeth O'Brien on the satisfying and stressful experiences of first-time federal grantees.[1] Some of the satisfying experiences reported by the respondents in this study included:

- praise and personal recognition
- satisfaction from working with a research team
- satisfaction from immersion in research
- satisfaction from commitment of subjects
- salary, space, travel, and equipment
- speaking opportunities
- opportunity to review proposals
- familiarity with federal agency personnel
- recognition in university publications
- increased awareness of research among students and colleagues
- increased responsiveness from campus research officials

Grantseekers want and deserve recognition and support from their organization and peers for dedicating their spare time and extra efforts to the pursuit of grant funding. While payment for successful grantseeking is illegal and unethical, recognition and appreciation are acceptable anytime.

This book contains many suggestions to help you integrate grantseeking into your busy professional life. Initially, you may think that some of the suggestions will direct you away from that special project that brought you to the grants marketplace, but this is not the case. All of the suggestions are aimed at helping you develop a wider perspective from which to view your project so that you can increase your chances for funding.

To those individuals and organizations who have made this world a better place through the use of the grants mechanism, I thank you. To you, the grantseeker who is trying to improve our collective lot, I applaud your efforts and dedicate this book to providing you with the best techniques I know for locating funds while using your time most efficiently.

REFERENCE

1. Sharol F. Jacobson and Mary Elizabeth O'Brien, "Satisfying and Stressful Experiences of First-Time Federal Grantees," IMAGE: *Journal of Nursing Scholarship* 24, no. 1 (Spring 1992): 45–49.

The "How To" Grants Manual

PART 1

·········

Getting Ready to Seek Grant Support for Your Organization

CHAPTER 1

• • • • • • • • •

How to Move from an Idea to a Funded Project

Developing a Proactive Grants System

Many grantseekers take a reactive approach to the task of proposal development. They develop their project first, often in great detail, and then search for a grantor to fund it. The search often results in locating a funding opportunity with an impending application deadline. The time constraint forces the grantseeker into a *reactive* mode that precludes being able to develop insight into the hidden agenda of the grantor, does not allow for pre-proposal contact, and makes it virtually impossible to prepare a proposal that is tailored to the grantor. Because of these factors, reactive grantseeking is fraught with rejection, as well as negative attitudes. To avoid these problems, grantseeking should be viewed as a quest to develop a *relationship* with a grantor who values the same outcomes that your proposal suggests, not as an opportunity to locate funding for what *you* want to do.

Proactive grantseeking is based on researching prospective grantors in order to match their grant interests with your projects and ideas. In many cases, reactive grantseekers and proactive grantseekers invest the same amount of time developing their proposals. What is different is *when* and *how* they invest their time and how these variables influence their success rate. Proactive grantseekers put in small amounts of time *throughout* the grantseeking process. The analogy to the age-old story of the rabbit and the turtle applies here. The reactive grantseeker (rabbit) makes a Herculean attempt at developing a proposal, racing against time (and the deadline), only to lose to the proactive grantseeker (turtle) who has been plodding along the grants trail using an energy-efficient and ultimately successful strategy.

The first step in taking a proactive approach to grantseeking is for you to extricate yourself from the notion that your proposal's approach is the only (or at least the best) way to move ahead. In reality, there are many approaches that could result in the changes your proposal suggests. By neglecting to develop several approaches to discuss with the potential grantor during pre-proposal contact, grantseekers limit their ability to uncover any preferences or hidden agendas that the grantor may have. Those grantseekers who have fixed ideas about their projects and exactly how they will be carried out miss the opportunity to learn what the grantor is really looking for. In addition, their proposals often suffer from a narrow viewpoint, focusing on what they want instead of the needs of the prospective grantor. This myopic approach can be contrasted with the equally ill-fated general approach. General proposals are designed to fit any possible grantor's guidelines. Whether myopic or general, proposals resulting from these approaches are easily recognizable because of a preponderance of statements beginning with "We want," "We need," and so on.

Unfortunately, this self-focus has been aided by the use of computers for grants database searches. In many cases the overzealous and self-focused grantseeker will secure a computer printout of all the grantors who have funded projects even remotely related to theirs and then send the same proposal to every grantor on the list. What these grantseekers overlook is that the shot-gun approach results in high rates of rejection and negative positioning with funding sources.

Whenever your proposals (or those of your nonprofit organization) result in failure, you risk positioning your organization in a negative manner. Of course, grantseeking will always result in a certain percentage of rejection. That is bound to happen. But how much rejection can you, the grantseeker, and your organization afford before the very appearance of your name on a proposal elicits a negative reaction from grantors? What is the success rate you need to achieve to avoid negative positioning? Anything less than a 50 percent success rate could result in negative positioning. A 70 or 80 percent failure rate could not possibly create a positive image for you or your organization.

Many grantseekers resort to a "one proposal fits all grantors" strategy because they run out of time and mistakenly believe that the "shotgun" approach will be time efficient. Time efficiency means nothing, however, when proposal after proposal is rejected. In my early attempts at grantseeking I quickly learned that the best strategy for winning grants was to tailor each and every proposal to the perspective of the potential grantor. I remembered a theory I learned as a psychology major and applied it to grantseeking. Twenty-five years later, I can say unequivocally that this theory has helped me develop millions of dollars in successful projects and research for nonprofit organizations. I share this theory with you to help you approach grantseeking from the grantor's perspective and to provide you with the basis for developing a tailored proposal to each grantor.

Leon Festinger developed the theory of cognitive dissonance[1] to explain how individuals learn and assimilate information. In brief, Festinger states that each of us sees, hears, and remembers what we already believe to be true. When we are presented with information that is contrary to what we believe to be true, dissonance or static is created in our information-receiving systems. To reduce this static, we discount the information. While Festinger was interested in how individuals learn, the theory of cognitive dissonance also applies to how grants are awarded.

By expanding Festinger's theory, I developed the "values glasses theory" and the concept of values-based grantseeking. Those who review proposals and decide which are to be funded and which are to be rejected read each proposal submitted to them through the lenses of their values glasses. In essence, these lenses are filters based on what the individual believes to be true. Naturally, we hold our beliefs and values in high esteem and seek to maintain a balance between our values and our actions. When a grantseeker submits a proposal that differs significantly from what grantors or reviewers believe to be true, dissonance or static is created. Since it is much easier for the grantor or reviewers to discount the proposal than alter their beliefs, the proposal is rejected.

Many unsuccessful grantseekers write their proposals from their point of view, using their own beliefs and vocabulary, instead of from the grantor's viewpoint. This approach invariably results in rejection unless luck prevails and they happen to locate a grantor with values glasses similar to theirs.

Successful grantseekers avoid jeopardizing their chances at being funded by being sensitive to the values of the grantor. They do not pander to the reviewer, or wrap a wolf in sheep's clothing, but their approach to proposal preparation does reflect their knowledge of the grantor. In my opinion, this approach demonstrates respect for the grantor's values.

To be truly successful, your proactive grants system should be based upon meeting the needs of the grantor, your organization, and you, the proposal developer. You need not invest more time in the process than the reactive grantseeker; you just need to invest your time more wisely. Instead of a 72-hour, last-minute, Herculean proposal effort, invest 10 hours per month for seven months. This will give you plenty of time to research the grantor, make pre-proposal contact, and construct a tailored proposal—all without the stress of a last-minute effort!

REFERENCE

1. Leon Festinger, *A Theory of Cognitive Dissonance* (Stanford, CA: Stanford University Press, 1962).

CHAPTER 2

Developing and Documenting the Need

Searching the Relevant Literature

Reports from federal, foundation, and corporate grantors suggest that one of the most frequent errors in proposal development is the lack of substantiation of the problem that the proposed project is seeking to solve. Grantors have reported that 50 percent of proposals are eliminated from competition because they lack a well-developed statement of need. Whether you are developing a research proposal or a model demonstration project, you must document that there is a gap between what exists now and what ought to, or could, be.

Failure to document need most often results from the self-focus of the proposal writer. Committed proposal writers frequently believe that grantors are as motivated as they are to solve a particular problem, so they move directly to presenting the project/solution before ever establishing the need for a solution. Do not assume that the grantor knows the need in your field. Even if the proposal reader is an expert, your efforts to describe the most relevant advances demonstrate *your* expertise and command of the most current data and provide the motivation for the grantor to reduce that gap.

To begin developing the need statement for your proposal, answer the following questions:

- What is the problem that requires a solution?
- What will happen if this needs area is not addressed?
- What is the gap between what exists now and what ought to be or would be if the knowledge existed to solve the problem?

- Why should grant funds be used *now* to solve the problem and reduce the gap?

Why one proposal is selected for funding over others is a function of several factors, but one of the most important considerations is how well the proposal documents the urgency of the problem. There is no doubt that you will enhance your "fundability," or ability to attract funds for your project, by providing the funding source with a well-documented need. Whether you are proposing a research study, a model, or a demonstration project, you must demonstrate a command of the current literature in the field of interest.

Researchers may focus on studies to document need, while those seeking project grants may look beyond facts and statistics to case studies. In either instance, needs documentation should be gathered before contacting a funding source or writing a proposal.

There are six basic needs assessment approaches:

1. Key informant: Quotes from people who know about the problem or are experts in the field.
2. Community forum: Public meetings to get testimony on the problem.
3. Case studies: Examples of clients in a need population.
4. Statistical analysis: Use of data from public records.
5. Survey: Random selection of population to answer questions related to the need.
6. Studies: Literature search of published documents on the subject.

The needs assessment table and needs assessment worksheet (see table 2.1 and exhibit 2.1) will help you decide which approach to adopt for your project. Corporate and foundation grantors may respond best to case studies or examples of the human side of the need, while government funders usually prefer a needs statement based on facts and studies. By having a variety of needs assessment techniques at your disposal, you will enhance your ability to tailor your proposal to a specific grantor.

You may find that you need to attract a small foundation or corporate grant initially to fund the collection of data for your needs assessment. If this is so, locate a funding source that will value the fact that its modest investment will allow you to develop an excellent needs statement and ultimately make it possible for you to attract larger grants from other funding sources for conducting your project. See chapters 19 and 20 for information on how to locate potential funding sources for small needs assessment grants.

Some funding sources refer to a proposal's needs statement as a search of the relevant literature. In this case, you must perform a thorough search of the studies and articles in your field and present a selection of citations to the literature in your proposal. The literature must document both the urgency of the problem and your command of the current knowledge in the field. The key

TABLE 2.1

NEEDS ASSESSMENT TABLE

Type of Approach	Advantages	Disadvantages
Key Informant—Solicit information from individuals whose testimony or description of what exists for the client population or state of affairs is credible because of their experience and/or expertise. Includes elected officials, agency heads (police chiefs, juvenile delinquency case workers, parole officers, etc.). Funders may value their opinions/insights.	· Easy to design. · Costs very little. · You control input by what you ask and whom. · Excellent way to position your organization with important people (shows you're working on common problems/concerns).	· Most funding sources know you have selected and included comments from those individuals sympathetic to your cause. You may be leaving out parts of the population who have not been visible and caused problems that were noticed and commented on.
Community Forum—Host or sponsor public meetings. You publicize the opportunity to present views of the populace and invite key individuals to speak. Funder may like the grassroots image this creates.	· Easy to arrange. · Costs very little. · Increases your visibility in the community. · Promotes active involvement of the populace.	· Site of forum has profound effect on amount and type of representation. · You can lose control of the group and have a small vocal minority slant results or turn meeting into a forum for complaints.
Case Studies—An excellent approach to assist the funder in appreciating what representative members of the client population are up against. Select individuals from the needs population or client group and provide an analytical, realistic description of their problem/situation, their need for your services, etc.	· Easy to arrange. · Costs very little. · Increases sensitivity to the client's "real world." · Very moving and motivating.	· Your selection of a "typical" client may be biased and represent a minority of cases. · You must describe one "real" person—not a composite of several. The anonymity of the person must be ensured.

TABLE 2.1

NEEDS ASSESSMENT TABLE *(continued)*

Type of Approach	Advantages	Disadvantages
Statistical Analysis—Most funders like to see a few well-chosen statistics. With this approach you utilize existing data to develop a statistical picture of the needs population: · Census data/records · Govt. studies/reports · Reports and research articles	· There is an abundance of studies and data. · Little cost to access data. · Allows for flexibility in drawing and developing conclusions. · Analysis of data is catalytic in producing more projects and proposals as staff "sees" the need.	· Can be very time-consuming. · Bias of staff shows up in studies quoted. · Feelings on funder's part that you can prove anything with statistics. · If original data have questionable validity, your extrapolation will be inaccurate.
Survey—Very commonly used approach to gathering data on the needs population, this approach is useful even when the survey is carried out with volunteers and has limited statistical validity. Accurate surveys may entail control groups, random samples, and computers and statistical analysis. However, acknowledgment by you that the results of your survey cannot be extrapolated beyond the sample group will prove more than adequate in most situations.	· High credibility with funders. · Excellent flexibility in design of survey to get at problem areas and document exactly what you want to document. · Demonstrates local needs. · Provides proof of your concern for the problem well in advance of proposal preparation. · Small sample size and identified needs population provide for an inexpensive means of assessment.	· Takes time to do survey properly. · Small sample size and nonrandom sample make it impossible to extrapolate to the entire needs population.
Studies—Citing of relevant research in the field or area of need. This is a commonly used approach to document the gap between what is and what ought to be for research projects. However, it can also be used for model projects. The literature search should focus on articles, books, and papers that resulted from a controlled study or use of a scientific approach to increasing information.	· Citing studies demonstrates the proposal developer's thoroughness and expertise in the area and command of the subject data. · Studies provide an unbiased approach to documentation of need.	· Unless properly organized, the literature search may seem disjointed and overwhelming to the reader. · Time-consuming.

What information do we need to document the problem?	Which approaches to needs assessment are best for us and/or preferred by the funder?
	Key Informant: _____
	Community Forum: _____
	Case Studies: _____
	Statistical Analysis: _____
	Survey: _____
	Studies: _____

Data to be gathered	How data will be gathered	Who will do it	Date due	Cost	Consortium agencies involved

NEEDS ASSESSMENT WORKSHEET

EXHIBIT 2.1

to being able to develop this portion of your proposal successfully is to consistently read the journals and major publications in your field. Whether you set aside a specific time each week to review the publications or perform a computerized search of relevant literature in the field, you must include references in your proposal that present a clear, concise, and current picture of the problem. Gather many references, but include only the best ones, and be careful not to include too many. A large number of references could overwhelm the reader and cloud or confuse the real issue or problem.

Be aware that you could cause dissonance in readers by citing references, researchers, or data that the readers do not favor. While the readers' reaction to specific information is not totally in your control, the more you know about the values and background of the reviewers and decision makers, the better able you will be to avoid this problem.

Whether the potential grantor understands the importance of addressing the problem and ultimately enacts your solution is a function of how compelling your needs documentation is. After you, the grantseeker, document a need, ask yourself the following question: Would you dedicate your own money to closing this gap between what we know now and what we could know or do?

CHAPTER 3

. . . .

Finding Time to Write
Grant Proposals
Organizing a Proposal Development
Workbook

Most grantseekers prepare proposals in their spare time. After working with nonprofit organizations for 25 years to increase staff involvement in grantseeking, I have determined that the two major obstacles to grantseeking are finding the time to get involved and developing a proactive approach.

Many creative and well-intentioned grantseekers develop innovative approaches to solving problems. They can often cite the literature that documents their command of the current state of knowledge in the field, but they have a problem putting the need and their idea together in a proposal. When asked why, they often say they cannot find the time.

The steps necessary to produce a grant application are logical and follow a definite order. Many people are overwhelmed by their perception of the work involved. Because of this, they procrastinate and avoid approaching proposal development until it is too late to do an adequate job.

Allen Lakein was one of the early leaders in time management. In his book *How to Get Control of Your Time and Your Life,* Lakein presents a technique that you can use to get your grant writing process under control and organized.[1] His "Swiss cheese" concept suggests dividing a difficult task into smaller, less overwhelming parts. Lakein's example of a mouse confronted by the job of carrying away a huge piece of cheese is analogous to a grantseeker presented with the prospect of creating a grant proposal. Both the mouse and the grantseeker feel overwhelmed! To avoid this feeling, Lakein suggests that the mouse should divide the big piece of cheese into smaller parts. By eating small pieces of cheese at a time, making the cheese into "Swiss cheese," the mouse can divide the task into manageable parts so that the final task of carrying the cheese away is less onerous.

I have applied this concept to grantseeking and created a set of tabs for making a "Swiss cheese" book, referred to professionally as the proposal development workbook (see exhibit 3.1). Suggestions for tabs are given later in this section, or sets of tabs are available for purchase from Bauer Associates. I have divided the task of developing a proposal into 25 steps. By addressing each step in the grantseeking process, you, the proposal developer, can organize your approach, control the process, and lower your anxiety level. By nibbling at your proposal a piece at a time, you will not be overwhelmed by the process and you will ultimately save time and increase your success rate.

I have found the "Swiss cheese" concept a great help in making the grants process more understandable and manageable. In fact, I suggest that you construct a proposal development workbook for each of the major problem areas for which your organization is planning to seek grant funding.

For example, imagine that your nonprofit organization is working with senior citizens. You might construct four proposal development workbooks: one for the elderly and transportation, one for the elderly and health, one for the elderly and nutrition, and one for the elderly and recreation. Each proposal development workbook would be placed in a three-ring binder with each tab acting as a divider for one of the tasks involved in developing a full-scale proposal. When you read a research article on nutrition and the senior citizen, you would make a copy of the article, abstract, or summary and place the copy under the tab for "Documenting Need." To avoid making this section of your workbook too voluminous, place the summary or abstract of the article in your workbook instead of the entire article, but be sure to include a reference as to where the entire article has been filed.

When politicians or community leaders visit your organization and express their concern for the elderly, you could ask them for a letter of support for your group's work and whether they would be willing to serve on your advisory committee. Copies of their letters of support would be filed under the tab labeled "Advisory Committees and Advocacy," as would their names, addresses, and telephone numbers.

As you can see, proposal development workbooks act as files for proposal ideas. Most potential funding sources would be very impressed by a prospective grantee who responds to a question by referring to a proposal development workbook instead of fumbling through a tattered pile of file folders and loose pages of notes.

One grantseeker using this process called our office to tell us how helpful her proposal development workbook was during a visit with a funding source. When asked why the funding source should give the money to her organiza-

INTRODUCTION TO YOUR
PROPOSAL DEVELOPMENT WORKBOOK
(SWISS CHEESE BOOK)

The grants mechanism is one method to unlock the world's largest reserve of collective and specific genius and pits that reserve against the multitude of problems that plague the modern world.

By supplying monies to solve a problem, funding sources benefit from competition amongst the best minds and groups to seek those funds, and apply their methodology to the test of reality.

Funding sources exist because individuals have created them by acts of commission that represent various motivations and bias views of what the needs are. Each funding source has a certain perspective on what it wants for its money — a perspective based on its values and how it interprets its charge as a granting entity. Each funding source (corporation, foundation or government agency) has NEED to invest the money entrusted to it in ways that reflect on how they view the goals of the organization.

You, as a grant seeker, have a NEED for financial resources to support projects aimed to address certain problems. The key to successful grant seeking is matching up your particular need for financial resources with the need of funding sources to invest their financial resources and produce the desired results. This approach requires "homework" before you write your proposal. Many grant seekers begin their grants process with a proposal. Successful grant seekers know that the writing of the proposal occurs much later in the process — after you know what the funding source wants.

Your grant Proposal Development Workbook is your Swiss Cheese Book. The steps involved in preparing for and producing a grant application or proposal are simple and follow a definite order. The design of this notebook is based upon a systematic approach to grant seeking described by David G. Bauer in his *"How To" Grants Manual.*

The "Swiss Cheese" Concept

Many people seeking grants find the process complex and difficult to deal with. They get overwhelmed with the enormity of the total task. They frequently either delay starting the application process until it is too late to do an adequate job or they avoid applying at all.

One way of looking at the task of getting ready and applying for grants is taken from a book developed by Allen Lakein, entitled *How to Get Control of Your Time and Your Life.* A mouse confronted with a large piece of cheese does not attempt to eat it or move it in one large piece. It will eat holes in the cheese or take it in pieces — a little at a time. The same applies to grant seeking: TAKE EACH PART AND APPROACH IT A LITTLE AT A TIME.

PROPOSAL DEVELOPMENT WORKBOOK

EXHIBIT 3.1

tion instead of one of the hundreds of other applicants, she opened her proposal development workbook to the tab on uniquenesses and presented a list of 50 reasons why her organization was uniquely suited to carry out the proposed project, with the top five reasons circled. The grantor was quite impressed.

The proposal development workbook is one step in the process of making your grants effort more cost- and time-efficient. If you thought that proposal preparation was a Herculean task—a last minute, 48-hour miracle—think again. You will find that the application of the "Swiss cheese" concept and the development of proposal development workbooks will provide you with an organized approach to proposal preparation, an approach that makes effective use of your time. In addition, this approach will help you improve your organization's image with funding sources (known as "positioning" in marketing talk) by enabling you to present your organization as an honest, organized, well-planned agency.

Those grantseekers who prepare proposals overnight run the risk of damaging their organization's image in the eyes of funding sources. One hastily written proposal with budget transpositions and typographical errors can affect your organization's image for many years.

The construction of proposal development workbooks is a proactive process that can work for you and your organization. Once this approach is initiated, I am sure that you will find it invaluable for promoting the development of project ideas, locating funding sources, and writing proposals.

Review the list of suggested proposal development tabs after you have read this manual. You may want to eliminate some areas to tailor the concept to your organization. The following are suggested tabs:

- Introduction
- Documenting Need
- Organizing the Process
- Developing Ideas
- Redefining Ideas
- Uniquenesses
- Advisory Committees and Advocacy
- Choosing the Marketplace

In addition, you will want tabs to organize the research and contacts in the marketplace you choose. For government funding sources, consider the following additional tabs:

- Researching Government Marketplace
- Characteristics: Government Grants
- Contacting Government Sources
- Planning Federal Proposals
- Improving Federal Proposals

- Submission: Public Sources
- Decision: Public Sources
- Follow-Up: Government Sources

For private funding sources, you may also include the following tabs:

- Differences: Public versus Private Sources
- Recording Research
- Foundation Research Tools
- Researching Corporate Grants
- Contacting Private Sources
- Letter Proposal
- Submission: Private Sources
- Decision: Private Sources
- Follow-Up: Private Sources

The following chapters include worksheets, letters, and forms that could be placed behind each of the tabs in your proposal development workbook. These materials are also available on the software program Grant Winner. (For ordering information see the list of resources available from Bauer Associates at the end of the book.)

Grantseekers can also create a computer file for each of their proposal development tabs. While some may prefer to do this, a computer disk may be difficult to use with a potential funding source during a visit. You will still need a hard copy of your proposal development workbook. In addition, some proposal developers may find that arranging hard copies of certain sections of their workbook, like the studies to be included under the "Documenting Need" tab, will help them develop their approach.

REFERENCE

1. Allen Lakein, *How to Get Control of Your Time and Your Life* (New York: American Library, 1974).

CHAPTER 4

· · · · · · · · ·

Developing Grant-Winning Ideas

From Research to Model Projects

The underlying theme of this manual is that when you ask a funding source for grant support you must look at your organization and your request from the funding source's perspective. This concept supports the "golden rule of grantseeking"—he or she who has the gold—rules. The least the prospective grantee can do is try to determine what the grantor values, likes, and dislikes, avoiding those areas that are potentially negative and highlighting those that appeal to the grantor's interests and make the prospective grantee look competent.

The process outlined in this chapter recommends that you develop several alternative approaches to the problem you have documented. There is usually more than one way to perform your research or develop your model project. To increase your chances of selecting the "right" approach for inclusion, you should be able to discuss more than one way of solving the problem with the prospective funding source before submitting your proposal. Even the briefest pre-proposal contact could give you the insight necessary to tailor your approach to the funding source. In addition, discussing several approaches with the prospective funding source before selecting one for your proposal will increase your credibility and demonstrate that your favored approach is based on careful analysis, not the personal biases and preferences of you or your staff.

The worksheets in this chapter will help you

- generate ideas by brainstorming your approaches with colleagues and key individuals on your grants advisory committee

- develop a system to summarize your best ideas and assess organizational commitment to the project
- conduct a cost-benefit analysis of your best ideas that highlights the differences, strengths, and weaknesses of each approach

BRAINSTORMING

One of the best techniques for developing sound proposals and alternative solutions to problems is to brainstorm proposal ideas with staff and peers. Inviting others to share in idea generation taps the collective genius of the group and builds support for your proposal. In fact, the brainstorming process can even promote the feeling that your project is "everyone's" project, so that colleagues and volunteers will be more willing and eager to work at night and on weekends to meet the deadline.

Many researchers are reluctant to share their approach to researching a problem because they fear that their idea will be stolen. In the majority of cases this fear is unwarranted. Most colleagues can be trusted, and discussing proposal ideas and solutions with them can help eliminate the development of narrow, self-focused grant ideas.

Brainstorming is a simple technique for quickly generating a long list of creative ideas. To obtain maximum benefit from the process:

1. Break your participants into groups of five to eight.
2. Appoint a neutral group leader to facilitate the process (encouraging and prodding other members, checking the time).
3. Appoint a recorder.
4. Set a time limit (10 minutes will be plenty).
5. State one question or problem (e.g., reducing the number of high school dropouts, increasing school attendance, keeping pregnant teenagers in school, increasing student interest in certain subject areas).
6. Ask group members to generate and present as many possible solutions to the problem as they can within the time limit.
7. Encourage group members to "piggyback" on each other's ideas (suggesting a new idea that adds to one already given).
8. Record all answers, combining those that are similar.
9. Avoid any evaluation or discussion of ideas until the process is over; this rule is crucial for productive brainstorming. The recorder can ask to have an idea repeated but should allow no comments, negative or positive (e.g., "We can't do that!" "That's stupid!" or "I love your thinking.") by others.

PRE-PROPOSAL SUMMARY AND APPROVAL FORM

The pre-proposal summary and approval form (see exhibit 4.1) could be sub-titled "Brainstorming/Wish List Summary Form." When you have an idea you would like to seek funding for, fill out this form before writing your full-scale proposal. Then have the form reviewed by your proposal review committee, staff, or administrators and returned to you with their criticisms and suggestions. Make sure the form is reviewed by those people who must sign the final proposal. The purpose of the pre-proposal summary and approval form is to elicit comments from your organization's leaders and to have them endorse your solution. The form actually provides a vehicle to test the acceptance of your idea or project with your superiors. This is important because they should agree on the use of institutional resources before you invest hours of your time on proposal development. There are many benefits to using the pre-proposal summary and approval form:

- Projects can be quickly summarized, so more ideas for projects are generated.
- The increase in the number of ideas lends itself to an increase in the number of fundable projects.
- By generating a number of ideas you may enhance your ability to see the advantages of combining several good ideas into one great one. Comments from those reviewing the form may also lead the proposal writer in this direction.
- Because at this point in the proposal development process project designers have not invested a great deal of time in writing a proposal for their idea, they are less defensive when their project summary is criticized and suggested improvements are easier to make.

Many organizations find it useful to make two-sided copies of the pre-proposal summary and approval form and distribute them to their staff. Using the form can be beneficial when proposals must be approved before they are submitted.The pre-proposal summary and approval form can be used to make sure that the individuals who are required to sign your proposal at submittal time know (in advance) that the proposed project is coming. I recommend that you have key people comment on the areas they question or may object to in the right-hand margin of the form. Then ask them to initial the form, giving their consent or approval to proceed. This ensures that the time, money, and resources spent in your proposal preparation process will not be met with a negative response internally and result in failure to have your proposal signed when ready for submittal.

This pre-proposal summary and review process also allows decision makers to comment on important issues and requirements relative to:

- matching funds commitment
- space, equipment, personnel, and resource allocations

	Comments	Signature
Problem Area: _____		
Possible Solution: _____		
_____		
1. Total Estimated Dollar Cost: $_____		

	Comments	Signature
2. Matching/In-Kind Commitment: $_____		
3. Estimated Time Needed for Proposal Process: _____		
Pre-Proposal Contact Date(s): _____		
Proposal Submission Date: _____		
Project Start-Up Date: _____		
4. Individual(s) in Charge—Project Director: _____		
_____		
Co-workers: _____		
_____		
5. How This Project Relates to the Mission or Goal of Our		
Organization: _____		
_____		
_____		
_____		
6. Summarize the Objectives:		
7. Summarize the Methods:		
8. Estimate of Non-Personnel Resources Needed		
Travel: _____		
Supplies: _____		
Printing: _____		
Equipment: _____		
Other: _____		
9. Estimated Equipment Costs: _____		
10. Facilities Needed: _____		
_____		
_____		
Square Feet: _____		
Desired Location: _____		
Special Considerations: _____		
11. Project Personnel Needed		
Title Salary Range Name (If Known)		
_____		
_____		

PRE-PROPOSAL SUMMARY AND APPROVAL FORM

EXHIBIT 4.1

- coordination of pre-proposal contact and access to funding sources
- organizational mission and plans

The explanation of how this project relates to the mission or purpose of your organization is of critical importance. Funding sources are wary of groups that write proposals simply to "get" money. You may want to look over the discussion of case statements in chapter 6 to develop the relationship between your project and the reason your organization exists. Some organizations give prospective grantseekers a copy of their case statement or mission statement when they disseminate pre-proposal review forms and explain the organization's grantseeking process.

The pre-proposal summary and approval form also becomes a valuable way of coordinating contact with funding sources. Many grantseeking organizations find themselves unknowingly discredited by unauthorized staff contact with grantors. While these contacts are usually made by zealous, well-intentioned staff members, the mistakes they may make and the first impression they may leave are potentially indelible sources of embarrassment. Many grantors allow organizations to submit only one proposal per funding cycle. They do not want to be put in the position of choosing another organizations' priorities. To maintain a flawless reputation, be stringent about the communication and coordination of your grants strategy from the very onset of grantseeking.

COST-BENEFIT ANALYSIS WORKSHEET

An important aspect of any fundable idea is its economic feasibility. Funding sources want to know that you have chosen methods that will produce the best results for the least amount of money. The cost-benefit analysis worksheet (see exhibit 4.2) will help you demonstrate economic accountability.

Column One

Place brief descriptions of each approach you are considering in column one. For example, a project to feed senior citizens could range from a meals-on-wheels program, to group meals, to a food cooperative for the elderly. Choose two or three possible approaches that will meet the goals of the project from your brainstormed list of ideas.

Column Two

Record the estimated price or cost of each idea or set of methods in column two. This figure can be taken off of your pre-proposal summary and approval form and is intended to be an estimate of the cost of the approach, not a final budget. One way to ensure variety in the approaches and in the amount of

1 Summary of Idea and Methodology	2 Cost	3 No. of Persons Served	4 Cost per Person Served	5 Positive Points	6 Negative Points	7 Rating

COST-BENEFIT ANALYSIS WORKSHEET

EXHIBIT 4.2

funds required is to select the approach you favor and determine how you would have to alter it if you could have only one-half of the amount requested.

Column Three

Use this column to estimate the number of people who will be affected by a particular approach. Remember to roll out the benefits over several years and over the life of the equipment.

Column Four

Enter the estimated cost per person or client served. This is essential since funding sources are apprehensive about sponsoring projects that possess an unrealistic cost per individual served. Projects with a high cost per person are considered a waste of money by many funders, so grantseekers may have great difficulty securing continued or follow-up funding for such projects.

Column Five

Summarize the advantages of each idea or set of methods in this column. By having this information on hand, some funders may actually consider support- ing a more costly approach because they can see how the outlined advantages outweigh the expense.

Column Six

In this column outline the disadvantages or drawbacks to each approach. This demonstrates your honesty, which will increase both your credibility with funders and their confidence in you. Funders know that each approach has pitfalls or variables that must be controlled.

Column Seven

The seventh column is used to rate each approach. Your objective is to present the problem and several alternative solutions while allowing funding sources to:

- feel confident that you have analyzed the situation carefully
- observe your flexibility and see the pros and cons of each approach
- identify the approach they favor (giving you the advantage of knowing which approach is most likely to result in funding)

You may prefer not to place your own preferences on the cost-benefit analysis worksheet, but rather to rate the approaches based upon the funder's comments.

Use this worksheet each time you refine your project ideas and bring completed cost-benefit analysis worksheets to preliminary meetings with funding officials. They will be impressed by the fact that you considered their financial interest while designing your project.

Remember that many grant officials are executives of profit-making companies. They are very sensitive about maintaining cost efficiency in all of the investments they make. Take this into account when refining your project ideas; it will help you win more grants.

Your grantseeking efforts are more likely to receive support and to provide a basis for matching funds and in-kind contributions when you apprise your administration of your entrepreneurial grants efforts and seek their endorsement.

CHAPTER 5

. . . .

Redefining Proposal Ideas to Find More Funding Sources

Many grantseekers have a myopic view of their proposal idea. They have tunnel vision and define their idea narrowly. What these grantseekers fail to see is that they could make their project appeal to many more funding sources by just broadening their perspective.

To expand your funding horizons, think of your project in as many ways as possible. This will help you uncover potential funding sources that may not be obvious when you think of your project in only one way. Consider your project or research in terms of at least the following four categories to determine how you could change or alter your idea so that it appeals to different grantors:

1. Subject area: What subject areas can you relate your project/research to?
2. Constituency group: What constituencies or target groups could benefit from the project/research?
3. Type of grant: Could your proposal be considered a needs assessment? Pilot project? Model project? Research?
4. Project location: What are the geographic boundaries of your project as currently conceived? Could they be expanded to attract more or different funding sources?

Carefully examine each of these categories. Each time you look at your project from another subject area, constituency group, grant type, or geographic boundary, you may uncover additional funding sources interested in supporting your work.

Review the following worksheet on redefining your project (see exhibit 5.1). Put a check mark next to the subcategories that might apply to your project, and use the space provided to explain how your project could be related to these subcategories. The subject areas and constituency groups you identify will become key words in your search for potential funding sources. You will use these key words when working with computer databases as well as the indexes in grants research books such as *The Foundation Directory*. The more key words you use, the more potential funders you will uncover. By expanding your universe of funders and selecting your best choices for pre-proposal contact, you will have a better chance of locating the grantor who is most likely to be attracted to your proposal.

Those grantseekers who thought this book would immediately lead them to one grantor for their narrowly defined project may be experiencing a bit of frustration. Yes, I am suggesting that you redefine your project to increase your number of potential grantors, but do not despair. I can assure you that the steps you take now to redefine your project will pay dividends when you begin your search to locate the best possible funding source for your project.

---

1. List the words that describe the subject area your project/research is directly related to.

   _____   _____
   _____   _____
   _____   _____

2. What changes could you make in your project/research that would allow you to relate it to other subject areas?

   _____
   _____
   _____

3. The following nonexhaustive list of subject areas is designed to encourage you to explore other possible areas for which you may find grant funds. (By changing your focus and/or including other beneficiary groups, you can redefine your project and make it applicable to more interest areas.)

REDEFINING YOUR PROJECT

EXHIBIT 5.1

Education
__ Preschool
__ Elementary
__ Middle/Junior High
__ High School

Education—Specific Subject Areas
__ Dropout Prevention
__ Adult
__ Special
__ Vocational
__ College/University
__ Gifted & Talented
__ Remedial
__ Literacy
__ Reading
__ Math
__ Science

__ _____
__ _____
__ _____

Humanities

Art
__ Art History

__ _____
__ _____

Music
__ Classical

__ _____
__ _____

Museum
__ American History

__ _____
__ _____

Theater
__ Shakespearean

__ _____
__ _____

Other

__ _____
__ _____

Sciences/Technology

Physical Science

__ _____
__ _____
__ _____

Life Science

__ _____
__ _____
__ _____

Engineering Science

__ _____
__ _____
__ _____

Computer Science

__ _____
__ _____
__ _____

Other

__ _____
__ _____

REDEFINING YOUR PROJECT *(continued)*

EXHIBIT 5.1

Business/Corporate
__ Employment Training/Development
__ Product Development
__ Patents
__ Economic Development
__ Employment
__ _____
__ _____
__ _____
__ _____

Constituency Groups
__ Youth/Children   Minorities
__ Gangs   __ Native American
__ Elderly/Aged   __ Hispanic
__ _____   __ Black
__ _____   __ Asian
__ _____   __ _____
__ _____   __ _____
__ _____   __ _____

Health   *Environment*
__ Disability   __ Agriculture
__ Blindness   __ Conservation
__ Deafness   __ _____
__ _____   __ _____
__ _____   __ _____
__ _____

                             Housing
                             __ Construction
                             __ Low Income
                             __ _____
                             __ _____
                             __ _____

4. Location: Many funders view your project's fundability in terms of how it affects
   the geographic area of concern. Place a check mark next to the areas your project/
   research could have a significant impact on.
   __ City/Community   __ Region
   __ County/Borough/Parish   __ Nation
   __ State   __ International

REDEFINING YOUR PROJECT *(continued)*

EXHIBIT 5.1

27

5. Type of Grant: Review your project in relation to the different types of grant funds.

__ Model/Demonstration Project
__ Research Project
__ Needs Assessment Grant
__ Planning Grant
__ Equipment Grant
__ Training Grant
__ Construction
__ Discretionary

__ _____
__ _____
__ _____

What could you do to change your project to attract another type of grant fund?

_____

_____

_____

You can also change your proposal's focus by adding "partners" who will share in the proposed work. List other organizations whose involvement would add depth to your project and increase your credibility with the funding source.

Partner	*Advantage*
_____	_____
_____	_____
_____	_____

REDEFINING YOUR PROJECT *(continued)*

EXHIBIT 5.1

CHAPTER 6

. . . .

Why Grant Funds to You and Your Organization?

Capitalizing on Your Capabilities

Many grantseekers lose sight of the fact that funding sources must select a few grant winners from many applicants. The successful grantee must stand out from the rest of the competition. Therefore, it is important for you to project an image that puts you a cut above the rest. One way to do this is to demonstrate to the funding source that you are different from the others in your field and that because of these differences you are their best choice for funding.

Grantseekers often have difficulty articulating why a grantor should choose them over others. Many grantseekers see themselves as just another college, hospital, school district, association, or nonprofit organization. A closer look, however, inevitably yields a number of very positive differences between them and others. A little time spent on developing a list of your organization's special qualities or uniquenesses will go a long way toward convincing a grantor that yours is the right organization to fund.

Start by examining what you do differently from the others and then look at how you do it. Consider your staff, location, buildings, and special areas of interest. In some cases, being similar to other organizations could even be presented as a feature that makes you particularly suited for funding. For example, if your organization is similar to many others in the United States, you might suggest to the funding source that your proposal be viewed as a pilot project that could be replicated throughout the country.

UNIQUENESS EXERCISE

Use the following brainstorming exercise to develop a list of your organization's unique features. This exercise will add a little excitement and flavor to meetings and can be done with a variety of groups such as staff, volunteers, clients, board members, and grants advisory committee members. Keep the information you develop in your proposal development workbook, where it will be ready for use in proposals, endorsement letters, and pre-proposal contact.

Please note that you may encounter some initial reluctance to this exercise because some individuals think it promotes bragging. However, these same individuals probably believe that humility and occasional begging will move grantors to take pity on your organization and fund your proposals. They are wrong! From the grantor's point of view, the humble approach does not highlight the reasons a prospective grantee should be funded.

To combat this problem, just remind all those participating in the exercise of its positive results. After the exercise, you will have a list of factors that make your organization unique, from which you will be able to select those uniquenesses that may appeal to a particular funding source. Also, the exercise will refocus those participating in the activity on the positive attributes of your organization and away from the negative.

1. Distribute the uniquenesses worksheet (see exhibit 6.1) to the group, remind the group of the rules for brainstorming (outlined in chapter 4), and set a time limit for brainstorming.
2. Use question one or two from the worksheet, and record the group's answers.
3. Give each individual 10 points, and ask each to rank the group's answers from a potential grantor's perspective. Each person should allocate his or her 10 points over the entire list.
4. Add the totals for each answer, and you will have a weighted list.

If you do this exercise with several different groups, combine all of the lists and distribute the combined list to all of the groups. All the group members will then be aware of your organization's unique qualities.

Use the final list to select uniquenesses that will convince funders that their money will go further with you than with any other prospective grantee. For example, a particular funding source may be impressed with your total number of years of staff experience, central location of buildings, special equipment, and broad needs populations and geographic coverage.

Your uniquenesses list will also prove valuable in

- recruiting and training staff, board members, and volunteers
- developing case statements
- using other fund-raising techniques such as direct mail and wills and bequests

Our organization has many unique qualities. These positive qualities can be used to convince funding sources that they are investing wisely when they grant our organization money.

This exercise will result in a combined list of qualities that make us stand out from the competition for grant funds.

Your leader will tell you whether to answer question one or two and when to begin recording your responses.

1. What makes our organization good at what we do?

_____

_____

_____

_____

2. Why would a funding source give a grant to us instead of some other organization in our field? (What makes us a good investment? What are the advantages of funding us?)

_____

_____

_____

_____

UNIQUENESSES WORKSHEET

EXHIBIT 6.1

Do not forget to include yourself, the proposal initiator, project director, or principal investigator, as a uniqueness. Your previous work, publications, collaborative efforts, awards, and recognition are important components of your organization's overall uniqueness.

One culminating activity is to have half of your group role-play a grantor and the other half role-play a prospective grantee. Review one of the problems or needs your organization is planning to address and your organization's proposed solution. Then have the individuals playing the grantor ask those playing the prospective grantee why the grantseeker's organization should be the one selected to implement the proposed solution. Have the grantee group start by saying, "Our organization is uniquely suited to implement this solution because . . ."

USING YOUR ORGANIZATION'S CASE STATEMENT TO SUPPORT YOUR PROPOSAL

Your case statement is another key ingredient in convincing the grantor that your organization should be selected for funding. When you submit your application for funding, your approach should be based on the following three important factors:

1. There is a compelling need for the project.
2. Your organization is uniquely suited to carry out the project.
3. The project supports your organization's stated purpose or mission.

The third factor is especially important. Your case statement should demonstrate your organization's predetermined concern for the project area. If yours is a joint or consortia proposal, the mission or case statements of all the participating organizations should provide a documentable concern for the problem you will address. In short, your case statement should give the funding source written documentation that the purpose of your organization (its reason for existing), your project, and the grantor's values and concerns are a perfect match.

Elements of a Case Statement

Your case statement should consist of how and why your organization got started, what your organization is doing today, and where your organization is going in the future.

How and Why Your Organization Got Started. Explain the original societal problems or needs that resulted in the formation of your organization. Most funding sources will find societal need today more important than the number of years your organization has been in existence. In fact, some funding sources actually have the greatest doubts about those nonprofit organizations that have been around the longest. These funders believe that such organizations generally are bureaucratic, have a tendency to lose sight of their mission, and have more "dead wood" on their payrolls than "younger" nonprofit organizations.

What Your Organization Is Doing Today. Describe your organization's activities. What are its current priorities, programs, resources, and uniquenesses? Who are its clients? How has the passage of time affected its original mission and reason for being?

Where Your Organization Is Going in the Future. Since funding sources look at their support as an investment, they want to be sure they invest in organizations that will be around when their funding runs out. In other words, they want the organizations they invest in to have a 5-year, 10-year, or even longer plan for operation. By demonstrating to funding sources that your organization has a long-range plan and the ability to secure future funding, you will show grantors that you are worthy of their funding and that the project they invest in will continue to benefit people for many years to come.

Use the case statement worksheet (see exhibit 6.2) to determine what should be included in your case statement. If you already have a case statement, review it to see whether it needs updating or tailoring to the grants marketplace. If your existing statement is long, use the case statement worksheet to help you edit it to one concise page.

Remember, most potential grantors are more interested in how funding your proposal will move both of your organizations (theirs and yours) toward each of your missions than in your actual project methods. Funding sources consistently work to separate applicants who sought them out simply as a source of money from applicants who can demonstrate that the direction

1. How and Why Your Organization Got Started: _____
   Year: _____   Primary Movers/Founders: _____
   Original Mission: _____

2. *Today*
   Changes from the Original Mission: _____
   _____
   _____

   Societal Need Changes: _____
   _____
   _____

   Current Priorities: _____
   _____
   _____

   Clients: _____
   Staff: _____
   Buildings: _____

3. *Future* —Where Your Organization Will Be Five Years from Now:
   Changes in Mission: _____
   _____
   _____

   Changes in Need: _____
   _____
   _____

   Changes in Facilities and Staff: _____
   _____
   _____

4. Opportunities that Exist or Will Exist to Move Your Organization
   Toward Its Plans/Goals:
   • _____
   • _____

CASE STATEMENT WORKSHEET

EXHIBIT 6.2

outlined in their proposal is predetermined and an important component of their organization's overall mission.

The importance of relating your proposal to your organization's mission cannot be overemphasized. Before soliciting a potential grantor, be sure to ask yourself whether you are going to the funder just because you heard it had money and you want some, or because your proposal can serve the missions you both value.

CHAPTER 7

. . . .

Involving Volunteers through Advisory Committees and Advocacy

One of the most important resources in a successful grants effort is the involvement of volunteers. When grantors are faced with volunteers who believe so strongly in a project that they are willing to work to further it with no personal benefit, the parent organization's credibility is greatly enhanced.

Involving others in increasing your potential to attract funding suggests that *who* you know may be more valuable than *what* you know and how you write your proposal. But this is not true. A poorly developed idea and proposal will need much more than "friends" and the suggestions presented here. If you have a great idea or proposal, however, it is your responsibility to take advantage of every possible edge in your quest for funding. This includes involving individuals who can help ensure that your proposal receives the attention it deserves.

While this may sound like politics, hold your condemnation just one more minute. The politics of grantseeking is a fascinating area that spells M-O-N-E-Y for those who master the art. Do not be frightened or disgusted by the word *politics*. The politics of grantseeking is a very understandable process that enables individuals to become advocates for what they value and believe in.

Those people who know your organization and identify with your cause or mission deserve to know how they can be of service to you and the cause or field you represent. When asked to become advocates for your project, individuals are free to say no or that they are too busy, but you should not make this decision for them by assuming that they would not want to be involved. There is no harm in asking, and you will be surprised by how many individuals welcome your invitation.

Consider exploring the area of advocacy and how you can help others help you. The worksheets in this chapter will assist you in determining who your advocates are and how they can best serve you. You will probably discover that there are more supporters for your project than you realized.

GRANTS ADVISORY COMMITTEES

One highly effective method for involving volunteers in your grants quest is to develop a grants advisory committee focused on the need or problem your grant proposal will address. Think of this committee as an informal affiliation of individuals you invite to take part in attracting grant funds to the problem area you have chosen. These individuals will be surveyed to determine their willingness to supply resources, as well as play an advocacy role. For example, while working for a university-affiliated hospital, I initiated a grants advisory committee on health promotion and wellness for children and another on research for children's diseases.

Invite fellow professionals, individuals from other organizations and the community, and corporate members who are interested in the area you have identified. By inviting a cross section of individuals to join your committee, you develop a wider base from which to draw support. Ask yourself who would care if you developed grants resources to solve a particular problem. Develop a list of individuals, groups, and organizations you think would volunteer a little of their time to be instrumental in making progress in the problem area. Be sure to include:

- individuals who might know foundation, government, or corporate grantors
- colleagues who may have previously prepared a proposal for the grantor you will be approaching or who may have acted as grant reviewers

Also consider current and past employees, board of trustees members, and former clients.

GRANT RESOURCES

After you have identified individuals or groups who would be interested in seeing change in the area identified, make a list of skills and resources that would be helpful in developing your proposal. Match these with the types of individuals who might possess them. Your list of skills and resources may give you some ideas about who you should recruit for your grants advisory committee. Consider the skills and resources and the types of individuals that could be useful in

- preparing your proposal (writers, experts in evaluation design or statistics, individuals with skills in the areas of computer programming, printing, graphics, or photocopying)
- making pre-proposal contact (individuals with sales and marketing skills, people who travel frequently, volunteers who could provide long-distance phone support)
- developing consortia or cooperative relationships and subcontracts (individuals who belong to other nonprofit groups with similar concerns)

Review the grants resources inventory (see exhibit 7.1) for those resources and skills your volunteers may be able to provide.

HOW TO INCORPORATE ADVOCATES TO INCREASE GRANTS SUCCESS

Specific activities to consider in relation to advocacy roles of individuals on your list are:

- writing endorsement letters
- talking to funding sources for you and setting up appointments
- providing expertise in particular areas (finance, marketing, and so on)
- accompanying you to meetings with potential funders or even visiting a funding source without you

Use the advocate planning sheet (see exhibit 7.2) to organize your approach.

Endorsement Letters

One very effective way to use advocates is to request that they write endorsement letters related to your organization's credibility and accomplishments. Without guidance, however, many advocates will develop endorsement letters that focus on inappropriate aspects of your project or organization. To prevent this, spell out what you are looking for. Provide advocates with a draft endorsement letter that suggests what you would like them to consider including in their letters, such as:

- pertinent facts or statistics that you may then quote or use in your proposal
- the length of time they have worked with you and/or your organization (e.g., number of hours, consortia or cooperative work relationships)
- a summary of their committee work and their major accomplishments

Please indicate the resource areas you would be willing to help with. At the end of
the list, provide more detailed information. In addition, if you are willing to meet
with funding sources, please list the geographic areas you travel to frequently.

_____ Evaluation of Projects
_____ Computer Equipment
_____ Computer Programming
_____ Layout and Design Work
_____ Printing
_____ Budgeting, Accounting, Developing Cash Flow, Auditing
_____ Audiovisual Assistance (equipment, videotaping, etc.)
_____ Purchasing Assistance
_____ Long Distance Telephone Calls
_____ Travel
_____ Writing/Editing
_____ Searching for Funding Sources
_____ Other Equipment/Materials
_____ Other

Description of Resources: _____
_____
_____
_____
_____

Areas Frequently Visited: _____
_____
_____
_____

GRANTS RESOURCES INVENTORY
EXHIBIT 7.1

Advocates should almost be able to retype your draft on their stationery and
sign it. If the grantor has any special requirements concerning endorsement
letters, make sure they are followed.

Contacts

Another way to involve your advocates is to present them with the names of
grantors that are most likely to be interested in your proposal and ask whether
they know any of the grantors' key individuals, such as board members.
Although this approach is reactive in nature, it may be necessary if your

Project Title: _____ Project Director: _____

Select from the following list the ways you can use advocates to advance your project.

- Endorsement letters
- Testimonials
- Letters of introduction

- Set appointments
- Accompany you to see funding sources
- Go see funders for you

Techniques for This Project	Advocate to Be Used	Who Will Contact Advocate and When	Desired Outcome	Date Completed

ADVOCACY PLANNING SHEET

EXHIBIT 7.2

advocates are reluctant to reveal all of their contacts and are holding back to see how serious you are in researching potential grantors.

The proactive approach to using advocates involves asking your supporters to trust you with a comprehensive list of their contacts. This includes asking your grants advisory committee members to reflect on their ability to contact a variety of potential grantors that may be helpful in your grants effort. To take a proactive approach, follow these steps:

1. Explain the advocacy concept to the individuals you have identified and how the information they provide will be used. Ask each participant to complete an advocacy/webbing worksheet (see exhibit 7.3) and return it to you. Some organizations find they have better results in introducing the advocacy concept when they relate the concept to a major project of the organization that has widespread support.

2. Distribute the advocacy/webbing worksheet to the individuals you have identified as possible advocates. This may be done in a group or individually.

3. Input the advocacy information you collect from the completed worksheets in your computer or file it.

4. When a match between a potential funder and an advocate is made, call your advocate and discuss the possibility of having him or her arrange a meeting for you with the funding source. Ask the advocate to attend the meeting with you to add credibility to your presentation.

Keep all completed advocacy/webbing worksheets on file and update them periodically. This is a good activity for volunteers. Be aware, however, that care should be taken to safeguard advocacy data. Advocacy data should be considered personal information that is privileged; you must not allow open access to the data or you will be violating your advocates' trust. Using a large central computing facility to store this information greatly reduces security. Instead, use a small personal computer system, and store a copy of your program in a safe place. This approach will ensure the privacy of this confidential information. An inexpensive software program designed especially for storing and using advocacy information entitled Winning Links is available from Bauer Associates. (For ordering information, see the list of resources available from Bauer Associates at the end of the book.)

If possible, computerize your advocacy information using Winning Links. When a potential funding source is identified, search your advocacy database to determine whether any of your advocates have a relationship to the potential funding source. You may have an advocate who

- is a member of both your organization and the funding source's board
- can arrange an appointment to get you in to talk to the funder
- can write a letter to a "friend" on the funding source's board
- has worked for the grantor or been a reviewer for the funder's grant program

---

Our organization's ability to attract grant funds is increased substantially if we can talk informally with a funding official (or board member) before we submit our formal proposal. However, it is sometimes difficult to make pre-proposal contact without having a link to the funding source. We need your help. By completing this worksheet, you will identify any links that you may have with potential grantors and possibly open up an oasis of opportunities for our organization.

If you have a link with a funding source that our research indicates may be interested in supporting one of our projects, we will contact you to explain the project and discuss possible ways you could help us. For example, you could write an endorsement letter, arrange an appointment, or accompany us to see the funding source. Even a simple phone call could result in our proposal actually being read

---

ADVOCACY/WEBBING WORKSHEET

EXHIBIT 7.3

and not just being left in a pile. No matter what the case may be, you can rest assured that we will obtain your complete approval before any action is taken and that we will never use your name or link without your consent.

Links to foundations, corporations, and government funding sources are worth hundreds of thousands of dollars per year and your assistance can ultimately help us continue our vital mission. Thank you for your cooperation.

Your Name: _____ Phone No.: _____
Address: _____

1. What foundation or corporate boards are you or your spouse on?

2. Do you know anyone who is on a foundation or corporate board? If so, whom and what board?

3. Does your spouse know anyone on a foundation or corporate board? If so, whom and what board?

4. Have you served on any government committees? If so, please list.

5. Do you know any government funding contacts? If so, please list.

6. Please list any fraternal groups, social clubs, and/or service organizations to which you or your spouse belong.

ADVOCACY/WEBBING WORKSHEET *(continued)*

EXHIBIT 7.3

Community Support

Advocacy can also play a valuable role in developing and documenting community support for your project. Some funding sources require that you demonstrate community support in the form of advisory committee resolutions and copies of the minutes of meetings. It is important to start the process of applying for a grant early so that deadlines do not interfere with your ability to document your advisory committee's involvement and valuable work.

To deal creatively with the area of community support:

- put together a proposal development workbook (see chapter 3) to focus on your problem area
- organize an advisory committee to examine the problem area
- involve the advisory committee in brainstorming project ideas, examining needs assessment techniques, writing letters of endorsement, and providing links to funders

Review the worksheet on developing community support (see exhibit 7.4) to help you determine how to use community support to increase your fundability.

Organize your supporters and maximize your chances for success by working through and with your volunteers. Involve those individuals who can be of service to your cause, from enhancing your resources to helping identify links to funders.

Project Title: _____ Project Director: _____

Date: _____

#	Techniques	Applicability to This Project	Who Will Call Meeting	Members of Committee	Dates
1	Use advisory committee to brainstorm uniquenesses of your organization (chapter 6).				
2	Use advisory committee to work on setting up needs assessment.				
3	Use advisory committee to brainstorm project ideas.				
4	Use your committee to develop a public relations package and produce it (printers, media reps.), including newspaper coverage for your organization (press releases, interviews) and television coverage (public service announcements, talk shows).				
5	Have an artist perform or have an open house for key people* in the community.				

*Public officials, congresspeople, potential advocates, and others.

How to Develop Community Support Worksheet

EXHIBIT 7.4

CHAPTER 8

. . . .

Choosing the Correct Marketplace

Proactive grantseeking involves assessing your grants potential, selecting the basic marketplace (government, foundation, or corporate) for your proposal idea, and researching the best prospects within the chosen marketplace.

Many prospective and oftentimes overzealous grantseekers launch their efforts to research possible grantors too quickly. To maximize your grants potential, you must do the kind of planning described in the preceding chapters. Developing a proposal effort that will promote a professional image of your organization requires an approach to research that has the following characteristics:

- Reflects a win-win attitude. Your research must be in-depth enough to ensure that your project will meet the funding source's interests, needs, and values while moving your organization toward its mission and providing benefits to your clientele or field of interest. In this case the funder wins, your organization wins, and your clients win.
- Provides you with the confidence to present yourself as worthy of funding. You have taken the time to find the "right" funder by doing your research, and this will become apparent to the prospective grantor. The funder will hear the confidence in your voice and see it in your proposal.

After you have redefined your project, begin to narrow down your search for the correct funding source. How do you know which funding marketplace is the "right" one for your project? Each marketplace has different types of funding sources and distinct funding characteristics. Certain factors predetermine how a funding source will "view the world," so you must match your proposal idea with those grantors most likely to find your proposal appealing.

Start by reviewing the distinct characteristics of each marketplace. After you select the right marketplace for your project, you may start researching individual funding sources within that marketplace.

GENERAL GRANTS MARKETPLACE INFORMATION

I have administered a grants marketplace quiz as a pre-test assessment instrument to over 10,000 grantseekers since 1975. These grantseekers attended one of my training seminars and, therefore, were not randomly selected and may not represent all grantseekers. However, they do vary widely in grants expertise and background. What is interesting and surprising is that more incorrect answers are given to the quiz today than 19 years ago. Why is this, when today's grantseekers are exposed to an abundance of information about grants and funding sources through the general media, professional journals, newsletters, and conferences? I believe that news sources may in fact contribute to current misconceptions about the grants marketplace.

Grantseekers, and those they work for, read announcements about nonprofit groups that attract large, above-average grant awards, but the awards that make the news are usually exceptions to the rule. These awards unfortunately are often interpreted by well-meaning, motivated grantseekers and their administrators as the norm or average. Nonprofit leaders use these large awards to shape their view of the marketplace. Judging the marketplace by what makes the headlines thus creates and reinforces misconceptions about grant giving and influences expectations about the level of grant support from each sector of the marketplace. As a result, many grantseekers end up basing their strategic decision making on fantasy rather than fact.

To choose the correct marketplace for your proposal, you need to base your choice on knowledge. The two main sources of support for nonprofit organizations and their grant requests are government and private philanthropy.

In the late 1970s, the Filer Commission Report estimated that government grant support was equal to support from private philanthropy (grants from foundations and corporations, bequests, and individual giving). This figure was estimated to be about $40 billion from each marketplace. Since that time, the marketplace has changed significantly.

- Federal funding through grants declined from a 1980 high of $40 billion, to a 1984 low of between $22 billion and $25 billion, to a 1987 level of $30 billion, to a 1994 high of $80 billion.
- Private philanthropy grew from a 1979 level of $43.69 billion to a 1993 level of $126.2 billion. What most grantseekers fail to realize, however, is that only 12 percent of the $126 billion in the private marketplace is disbursed through the grants mechanism by foundations and corporations.

Grantseekers must look beyond these figures to determine what these changes really mean and how to adapt their grantseeking strategies.

In the public arena, the decrease in government grant funding in the mid-1980s created an initial overreaction on the part of nonprofit organizations. Because many grantseekers knew that government funding was cut, they did not even bother to apply for government funds, and the applications for government grants declined substantially. The same phenomena may now be at work in the mid-1990s. Well-publicized cuts in a few government programs may result in a reduction in applications to federal sources and an increase in foundation and corporate requests as grantseekers overreact once again. But government grant support for nonprofit organizations is still $80 billion, or five times greater than private grant support. While federal grant support has not kept pace with the rate of inflation since 1980, it is still much greater than foundation and corporate grant totals combined.

Although private philanthropic support of nonprofit organizations encompasses individual giving, gifts made through bequests, and foundation and corporate giving, these components have not shared equally in the increase from $40 billion to $126 billion. Corporate grant funding has actually lost ground, while individual donations have grown. Individuals seldom award grants, however. The actual percentage of private funds distributed through the grants mechanism has remained relatively stable over the years and is much less than most individuals realize. In fact, the total grants marketplace for corporate and foundation grants has only grown from $9.67 billion in 1986 to approximately $15 billion in 1994.

Many executive directors, presidents, and board members of nonprofit organizations do not know or understand the marketplace facts. When your organization's leaders base their resource-development strategies on misconceptions about the marketplace, you, the grantseeker, may not receive the resources you need for a successful grantseeking effort. Remember, sound grantseeking strategies reflect a knowledge and understanding of the grants marketplace, not wishful thinking.

THE GOVERNMENT MARKETPLACE

Seek federal funds first! The marketplace facts have already substantiated the basis for this deduction. The federal government is the largest single grantor in the world ($80 billion in 1994). Foundations and corporations grant approximately $15 billion annually, and some of these grantors will fund only those grantseekers who have exhausted the possibility of a federal grant. In other words, foundations and corporations know who has the most grant funds to give away and may only consider requests from those who have been rejected by or have discussed their projects with federal grantors.

Historical Perspective

The federal government has used the grants mechanism in one way or another since the United States was founded. The term *land grant college* refers to the federal government's early attempts to encourage states to develop a system of higher education that would link education and agriculture. The federal government developed much of its current role as a grantor during the post-- Korean War period. The Russian accomplishment in space, *Sputnik,* encouraged the U.S. government to make grants available to foster education and research.

Use of the government grants mechanism increased with the Kennedy and Johnson administrations. Most grants under the New Frontier and Great Society programs were administered on the federal level. Early grant programs supported projects and research related to specific problems. For example, when national concern centered on the social issues of the 1960s, the grants mechanism was employed to encourage research and develop model projects that focused on the disadvantaged, the elderly, minority groups, people with disabilities, and so on. In the 1970s the grants mechanism was used to support advances in health care and to address such problems as drug and alcohol abuse, smoking, and cancer. Grants such as these, aimed at specific categories or problem areas, came to be known as categorical grants.

In the 1970s, however, there began a growing trend toward local, regional, and state distribution of federal government grant dollars. This trend was based on federalism, or the belief that local and state governments know best what they need. This "New Federalism," or revenue-sharing perspective, moved the grants marketplace from categorical grants, in which the federal government allocated funding to selected categories, to formula and block grants, which allowed the state and local governments to combine categorical funding and pool federal funds to address problems. The Reagan administration encouraged this trend by signaling a decline in government's use of the grants mechanism to initiate, direct, and sustain change in American society.

First, the Reagan administration called for a reduction of $40 billion in domestic grants. Although there were repeated attempts to virtually eliminate grants altogether, Congress did not allow cuts below the $20 billion to $22 billion level. However, grant funds were cut almost in half.

Second, the Reagan administration attacked the categorical grants funding mechanism. The administration's philosophy of "the government governs best which governs least" could not support a categorical grants system controlled by Washington bureaucrats. Instead, the Reagan administration capitalized on "New Federalism" concepts and growing conservatism to institute the most dramatic change in the history of the U.S. grants mechanism—the block grant.

Block Grants

The block grant concept was founded on the premise that it was not the purview of the federal government to force the states to follow categorical grant program priorities. The categorical programs were "blocked," or synthesized into groups of related programs, and the funds were sent directly to the states. The states could set their priorities and "grant" the federal funds to high-priority areas and projects.

The block grant movement caused mass confusion in the grants world because grantseekers had to figure out who had the funds and what would be funded. In most cases the states received more decision-making power but less money than they did under categorical grants. The block grant mechanism allowed the federal government to reduce staff formerly used to administer categorical grant programs. Decreases in staff were limited, however, because the federal government still had to direct the research component of categorical programs to avoid duplication and to coordinate research efforts.

Because of the federal government's continued involvement in the administration of grants, along with Congress's desire to deal with problems in education, employment, and crime, the late 1980s marked the decline of the block grant mania of the early Reagan years. The use of categorical funding mechanisms increased. Virtually all of the new grant programs introduced after 1986–87 were categorical grants, and most grant experts agree that this trend will continue.

Project, Categorical, and Research Grants

Project, categorical, and research grants are designed to promote proposals within defined areas of interest. These grant opportunities address a specific area with which a federal program is concerned, such as drug abuse, dropout prevention, nutrition for the elderly, or research on certain types of diseases. The government, through hearings and appropriation of money, selects the problem to be corrected, and prospective grantees design approaches to solve or reduce the problem, or to increase knowledge in the area through research.

Project and research grants are awarded by various agencies under congressionally authorized programs. Ideally, grants are awarded to the organizations (and individuals) whose proposals most clearly match the announced program guidelines. Most federal grant programs use nongovernment review panels (often referred to as peer review panels) to evaluate the projects. Peer review helps ensure that the "best" proposals are selected for funding. Because project design is left to the grantseekers, there is room for a wide variety of creative solutions, making the project grants approach very popular among grantseekers.

Government granting agencies usually require grantseekers to complete long applications. As categorical grants have increased, each federal agency that controls funds has developed its own grants system. Grants applications and the administration of grants differ in format from agency to agency. Generally, the applications are tedious, complicated, and time-consuming to complete They can make it very challenging to tailor your proposal content to meet the needs of the granting agency as well as your own needs. There is usually a three- to six-month review process, which may include a staff review by federal agency personnel and a peer review. Successful grantees are required to submit frequent reports, maintain accurate project records, and, in some cases, agree to federal audits and site visits by government staff.

To be successful in research and project grants, grantseekers must be mindful of the constant changes in emphasis and appropriations. Hidden agendas and shifts in focus result from the funding agency's prerogative to interpret and be sensitive to changes in the field of interest.

Formula Grants

The term *formula grants* refers to granting programs under which funds are allocated according to a set of criteria (or a formula). The criteria for allocation of these grant funds may be census data, unemployment figures, number of individuals below the poverty level, number of people with disabilities, and the like, for a state, city, or region. Formula grant programs are generally specific to a problem area or geographic region and have historically been used to support training programs in the fields of health, criminal justice, and employment.

The formula grant funds may pass through an intermediary, such as a state, city, or county government or a commission, before reaching the nonprofit grantee. The formula grants mechanism is another example of the "New Federalism" that started developing in the early 1970s. While the general rules for formula grants are developed at the federal level, the rules are open to interpretation, and local input can significantly alter the federal programs. To encourage local control and input into how federal funds are spent, the formula grants mechanism requires a mandated review by local elected officials.

Contracts

No discussion of federal support to nonprofit organizations would be complete without a discussion of government contracts. In recent years the differences between a grant and a contract have become harder to discern. Indeed, after hours of negotiation with a federal agency on your grant, you may end up having to finalize your budget with a contract officer.

In theory, the basic difference between a grant and a contract is that a contract outlines precisely what the government wants done. You are supplied with detailed specifications and the contract is awarded on a lowest-bid basis. With a contract, there is decidedly less flexibility in creating the approach to the problem. To be successful in this arena, you must be able to convince the federal contracting agency that you can perform the contract at an acceptable level of competency and at the lowest bid. Contracts are also publicized or advertised in different ways than grants. Grant opportunities are published in the *Catalog of Federal Domestic Assistance* (see chapter 9, exhibit 9.3), while contracts are advertised in a daily government publication known as *Commerce Business Daily* (see chapter 9, exhibit 9.5).

There are several types of contracts, including fixed cost, cost reimbursable, and those that allow the contractor to add additional costs incurred during the contract. The grants statistics quoted in this chapter do not include government contracts monies. The variety, number, and dollar value of government contracts are staggering and go far beyond the $80 billion cited earlier. Scandals over inflated prices for parts in government contracts highlight the problems in administering contract bids and are leading to changes aimed at simplifying government purchasing and reducing paperwork.

Contracts have been increasingly pursued by nonprofit groups in recent years. The contracts "game," however, requires a successful track record and documentable expertise. The best way to break into this marketplace is to identify a successful bidder and ask whether you can work for them as a subcontractor. This way, you gain experience, confidence, and contacts.

Many nonprofit groups have found that they can reduce the problems they routinely encounter in bidding on contracts by developing separate profit and nonprofit agencies for dealing with such issues as security agreements, academic freedom, patents, and copyrights.

Shifts away from domestic grant program funds have led some nonprofit organizations to look at Defense Department contract opportunities for implementation of their programs and research. But please note that bidding on government contracts is a task for the experienced grantseeker only.

STATE GOVERNMENT GRANTS

It is difficult to estimate how many grant dollars are awarded through individual state program initiatives. Many of the federal government grantseeking techniques in this book also apply to accessing state grant funds. Many states develop their own initiatives in the social welfare and health areas, and few states deal in research funding. Most state grant funds are federal funds that must pass through the state to you, the grantseeker.

There are some advantages to state control of grants. Because states distribute federal block and formula grants, these grants are easier to access. They require less long-distance travel and allow you to use your state and local politicians to make your case heard. These advantages are counterbalanced, however, by the fact that some states develop their own priorities for federal funds. States may add additional restrictions and use a review system made up of state bureaucrats and political appointees. Although states have their own monies, granting programs, and rules, if they distribute grant monies obtained from the federal government, they must guarantee that the eventual recipient of those funds will follow all federal rules and circulars.

THE FOUNDATION MARKETPLACE

There are approximately 35,765 private foundations in the United States with $170 billion in assets. These foundations made awards totaling $9.2 billion in 1993. Though these figures may seem staggering to the novice grantseeker, there is some consolation in the fact that only 1.3 percent of all foundations gave 48 percent of all the grants and had 66.2 percent of all the assets.

News coverage of large grant awards made by the bigger foundations leads to misconceptions about the marketplace. Many grantseekers and their boards would be shocked to learn that there were only 145 grant awards in excess of $2.5 million in 1993 and fewer than 60,000 awards for more than $10,000 each. Grantseekers hear about the big grants and may not want to deal with the reality that only a small number of all foundations—approximately 460—have a relatively high grant size (from tens of thousands into the millions). The 35,305 or so other foundations have a much lower average grant size, but collectively award the hundreds of thousands of grants that make up the remaining 52 percent of the foundation grants marketplace.

Foundations increased their grant giving by 6.6 percent in 1993. This increase was due to the overall increase in foundation assets of 8 percent in 1992. Foundations by law must give away 5 percent of the market value of their assets each year or pay a tax. Most do not have a plan for what to do if they experience a dramatic increase in their stock portfolios, so the Internal Revenue Service allows a grace period of one year to adjust to the compulsory 5 percent payout.

Whether your nonprofit organization is a research institute or a small community agency, you need to know the basic facts about the foundation marketplace. Not only are the grant award sizes very different from what you may expect, so are the purposes for which foundations grant money.

Most grantseekers mistakenly believe that foundations grant the majority of their funds for building and renovation projects (capital grants). This is not true. While the average size of capital grants is large and likely to make the news, less than 25 percent of foundation grants support this area. In contrast, 43.2 percent of foundation funds go toward projects, and 11.2 percent toward research. In fact, project and research grants represent the majority of foundation funding. Because the award size in these areas is considerably less than for building and renovation, publicity surrounding these awards is limited.

Knowledge of the foundation marketplace requires that grantseekers be more flexible in their approach to funding. For example, just because your organization would like to acquire computer equipment does not mean you should apply for an equipment grant. The outright granting of foundation funds to purchase computer equipment accounts for only .7 percent of foundation funds. You will be more likely to obtain the desired equipment by attracting foundation grant support through a model project or research proposal that proposes to make a difference in the foundation's stated areas of interest and by including the computer equipment in the proposal as a necessary means to the desired outcome.

Researchers should take note of the potential of foundation funding as a means to developing the preliminary data and publications that are essential for winning a federally funded research proposal. Prospective federal grantees need preliminary data to substantiate their approach. With partial foundation funding, you can develop preliminary data and possibly publish an article to position you for acquiring a federal grant.

One other important consideration is that foundation grants can provide a source of matching funds. While only a small percentage of foundation funds are awarded for matching contributions, the mere possibility of pursuing a grant for this purpose can be significant to those organizations that find that matching requirements place some valuable federal sources out of their reach.

Selecting the right foundation marketplace and requesting an appropriate grant size from a potential funder require knowledge of the types of foundations and their specific characteristics. The five basic classifications of foundations are:

1. Community
2. National general purpose
3. Special purpose
4. Family
5. Corporate

Community Foundations

Community foundations, a group of several hundred foundations, represent the newest and fastest growing area in the foundation marketplace. The main purpose of community foundations is to provide a grants mechanism to address problems and interests that affect the geographic area the foundation was created to serve.

Community foundations use a variety of geographic parameters to define *community.* Some use state boundaries, while others use city boundaries. In either case, community foundations are easy to identify because their name denotes the area they serve (e.g., San Diego Foundation, Cleveland Foundation, North Dakota Foundation, Oregon Foundation).

Most community foundations have no connection with United Way fund drives and usually are not in competition with their neighboring United Way—supported organizations. In actuality, community foundations are frequent grantors to agencies supported by the United Way. While both groups seek to enrich the community and address its problems, the community foundation usually builds its funding base through bequests. Local citizens make a bequest to the community foundation to ensure that the interest proceeds from the bequest stay in the community. Donors may even restrict grants to their specific areas of interest. This method of fund-raising is very different from the United Way approach of payroll deductions, cash contributions, and corporate solicitation. In some communities the United Way has begun to incorporate a more aggressive bequests program to build an endowment fund. In these communities, conflicts may arise as both the community foundation and the United Way seek the same donors.

The assets of community foundations are growing daily. The primary beneficiary of community foundation grants is the health area, followed by social welfare, education, and arts and culture. Community foundations are concerned with what works and are more interested in supporting the replication of successful projects than in taking chances with experimental approaches or research.

Most community foundations have been initiated by public-spirited citizens who leave money in a bequest to the foundation for specific types of local projects. Since the monies may be held separately according to donor interests or for general purposes, these foundations are classified as public charities. Community foundations exist to deal with local needs. They will fund causes that other foundations would not think of funding.

If your organization's purposes relate to local need, community foundations may even be willing to fund your organization to cover last year's deficit if it means keeping you in business to serve your target population. You can even acquire funding from your community foundation for a needs assessment if you approach the foundation with the rationale that a good needs assessment will result in attracting monies from other sources. In other words, you must convince a community foundation that a needs assessment grant will help you produce a higher quality proposal and will ultimately be responsible for all other funds that you generate.

If you are not sure whether there is a community foundation in your area, write or call:

The Council on Foundations
1828 L Street, N.W., Suite 2200
Washington, DC 20036
(202) 467-0427

If you find that there is not a community foundation in your area, invite some community leaders and wealthy, long-standing citizens together to consider initiating one. As a matter of fact, you can even get a grant to start a community foundation. You will never be sorry. Your community will benefit and you will gain another prospective funding source for your proposals.

National General Purpose Foundations

When asked to name a national general purpose foundation, most people would give the name of a large foundation like the Rockefeller Foundation or Ford Foundation. Although large foundations like these number less than 100, they have two-thirds of all assets among the 34,000 foundations and account for over 50 percent of the grant dollars.

To be designated as a national general purpose foundation, a foundation does not need to fit a hard-and-fast definition. *National general purpose* refers to the foundation's scope and type of granting pattern. Foundations in this group have a philanthropic interest in several subject areas and make grants for proposals that will have a broad-scale impact across the United States and, more recently, the world. They prefer model, creative, innovative projects that other groups can replicate to solve similar problems. Since national general purpose foundations like to promote change, they do not usually fund deficits, operating income, or the many necessary but not highly visible or creative functions of organizations.

Special Purpose Foundations

Several hundred foundations fall into the special purpose category. How *special purpose* is defined could increase this number by thousands. For our purposes, special purpose foundations include those foundations whose funding record consistently supports a specific area of concern and whose funding represents a significant contribution in that specific area. For example, the Robert Wood Johnson Foundation is a special purpose foundation focusing on the area of health. These foundations are well financed by unusually large asset bases.

The key to success in this marketplace is to match your project with the special purpose foundation's specific area of interest. Your grant request will be evaluated according to the potential impact your project will have on the foundation's special area of concern.

Family Foundations

There are over 30,000 foundations in this category. Because their granting patterns represent the values of the family members whose interests have been memorialized by the creation of the foundations, granting patterns of family foundations vary widely from foundation to foundation. Most family foundations do have well-defined geographic preferences and specific interests, so they may seem to act as small-scale, special purpose foundations. True special purpose foundations, however, represent large-scale efforts and long-term commitments to a field, while family foundations change their giving patterns and funding priorities frequently.

The family foundation is the type of foundation most susceptible to the influence of board members, friends, and popular causes. In fact, linking your organization to friends of a family foundation will ensure that your proposal at least receives attention. Since many family foundations periodically change their priorities, it is helpful to have a contact who keeps you informed of the foundation's current funding interests. Even when you have a link to the board and access to the foundation, you must research the foundation thoroughly to keep abreast of changes in interests and commitment.

Corporate Foundations

Corporate foundations, a group of over 2,000 grantors, account for only $1.5 billion of the $6 billion that corporations report as tax-deductible contributions on their tax returns. Corporate foundations have been paying out more than their respective parent companies have been depositing for over 10 years. Except for in 1986, corporate assets have had to be used to maintain this corporate giving pattern.

The main distinction between corporate foundations and other corporate philanthropy vehicles is that corporate foundations must follow the same federal rules that the other four types of foundations must follow. The establishment of a foundation for public good requires that all foundations list the benefactors of their grants and make their tax returns available for public viewing. This requirement can become a problem for corporations when their corporate stockholders object to the types of organizations or specific projects that the corporate foundation supports. In addition, the public scrutiny to which the corporate foundation is subject allows for social activists and leaders of particular causes to research a company's giving pattern and arrange for demonstrations, which could result in negative public relations. To avoid such problems, many corporations only make noncontroversial grants through their foundation; they make all other grants through a corporate grants program that does not require public disclosure.

The main reason for initiating a corporate foundation is to stabilize a corporation's philanthropy program. Corporate foundations lead to a more uniform and stable approach to corporate social philanthropy than giving programs that rely solely on a percentage of company profits. Programs tied to company profits are subject to the "seesaw" effect, because profits can vary widely from year to year.

Since corporate foundations are an extension of a profit-making company, they tend to view the world and your proposal as any corporation would. They must see a benefit in all of the projects they fund. Many of these foundations fund grants only in communities where their parent corporations have factories or a special interest. For the most part, every grant made by a corporate foundation must benefit either the corporation or its workers or enhance the corporation's ability to attract high-quality personnel to the community.

CORPORATE PHILANTHROPY

There are over 2.3 million for-profit corporations in the United States, and many misconceptions about their giving patterns exist. A small percentage of corporate grants are well publicized, so grantseekers think there are many more corporate grants than there really are and that the grants are large. In actuality, a minority of corporations make grants.

- Corporate contributions (noncorporate foundation) account for $4.5 billion or ¾ or all corporate grants.
- Only 35 percent of all corporations make tax-deductible contributions to nonprofit organizations.
- Of those corporations that do contribute, less than 10 percent give grants of over $500 a year.

You must do extensive research before applying for a grant from a corporation. This will help you avoid the embarrassment of asking for a grant from a corporation that has never given one or has never given one of the size you are requesting.

Although corporations contributed over $6 billion to nonprofit organizations in 1993, tax-deductible corporate contributions reported have shown little growth in recent years. In fact, when inflation is factored in, these contributions have declined. The most widely accepted index used to measure corporate philanthropy is the percentage of pretax income donated to nonprofit organizations as a tax deduction. Consider that in 1992 pretax income donated by corporations was 1.5 percent, while in 1993 the amount donated declined to 1.3 percent. Corporate profits, however, increased in 1992 and 1993 by 9 percent and 14 percent respectively. In the past, corporate profits were directly related to corporate philanthropy, but this is no longer true. In 1992 and 1993, profits increased while corporate giving decreased. Clearly there are forces acting on this source of grant funds that need to be explored.

First, many companies are cutting employees and are under pressure to show the greatest dividends and returns. Second, employee loyalty and community image are not as great a concern to corporations as they have been in the past. Mergers and acquisitions have removed corporations from their original ties with the community. Significant decreases in corporate investments have been particularly apparent in merged companies with corporate headquarters in Europe, Asia, and Australia.

Even in a nongrowth environment, however, corporate giving (nonfoundation grants) supports a philanthropic effort amounting to $4.5 billion of the $6 billion cited. Why do corporations give tax-exempt gifts of money and products? Some give out of feelings of social philanthropic responsibility. Others give to help themselves improve relationships with employees, the community, and unions or to gain marketplace advantages through product research opportunities and the positioning of products in lucrative marketplaces.

Corporate giving is usually a "this-for-that" exchange. Corporations do not usually *give away* money; they *invest* it.

- Education receives 35 percent of corporate contributions. (Education provides trained workers for the companies and raises the purchasing power of the population.)
- Health and welfare receive 25 to 30 percent. (Health and welfare provide direct benefits to employees and have the potential to lower health costs and services.)
- Civic and community affairs receive 10 percent. (By investing in these areas, corporations provide visible support to communities.)
- Culture and the arts receive 10 percent. (These areas create and sustain quality of life.)

Many corporations' giving patterns are related to the geographic concerns of their workers and factories. You can learn far more about the profitability of the publicly held corporations in your area and their contributions potential by purchasing a share or two of their stock than by buying expensive resource books on corporate philanthropy. Begin your search for corporate grants by asking your chamber of commerce for a list of corporations in your area. From this list, identify those companies that might be interested in your project because it could benefit their workers or product development. Then purchase shares of their stock and watch how much information will be sent to you. In no time at all you will learn about their parent firms, officers, proxy statements, and dividends.

To approach corporate funding sources, you must relate your request to

- their attainment of corporate goals (e.g., programs that will provide manpower training or increase the availability of resources)
- employee or management benefits (e.g., health programs, cultural programs, recreation facilities)
- improvement of the environment around the corporation (e.g., programs that affect transportation, communication, or ecology)
- improved corporate image (e.g., programs that will give the corporation a better reputation in the community)

When you evaluate your potential for getting corporate grants, determine what the "returns on the investment" are, and emphasize these in your presentations to corporate funding officials.

Do not automatically assume that all corporations want to be publicly recognized for their grants. In some cases, what they really want is anonymity. A survey by the Conference Board of 410 corporations that granted $2.25 billion to nonprofit organizations uncovered $100 million that the companies did not even claim as tax deductions. Although it is not clear what motivates corporations to award grants they do not claim as tax deductions or receive public recognition for, grantseekers should be careful about assuming they know why corporations make grants.

Another interesting aspect of corporate philanthropy is what might be called the "school of fish syndrome." Corporations do not like to be the first to fund a project because there is an element of risk involved. They are afraid to leave the protection of the "school" and are extremely sensitive to what their competition is doing. This can work in favor of the successful grantseeker. Once one corporation gives you a grant, others will tend to follow. In addition, if a corporation gives grants to another organization in your field, your chances of getting a grant from a competing corporation increase. Corporations do not want to be first to take a chance, but, then again, they do not want to get left behind. Risk reduction by association, however, may be on the decline as corporations seek new types of arrangements with nonprofit organizations.

CORPORATE CONTRACTS: THE "NEW" SOURCE OF CORPORATE SUPPORT

Many corporations support nonprofit organizations through contracts, some of which are viewed as marketing agreements or business ventures. While these contracts are not taken as tax write-offs or deductions, they can be viewed as an extension of the "this-for-that" principle that characterizes the tax-deductible corporate grant. Billions of dollars flow from corporations to nonprofit organizations through marketing budgets rather than philanthropy programs. This is particularly true in cases where corporate support in cash or products can be viewed as self-serving and as a marketing or sales expense by the IRS instead of a tax-deductible grant.

This new form of corporate involvement is not accounted for on tax returns and is just now being surveyed and reported in nonprofit newsletters and journals. Like corporate philanthropy, corporate contracts are not subject to public information laws and scrutiny, so the amount of money distributed through this mechanism is unknown. I personally have worked with several nonprofit organizations to secure corporate support and have found that many ultimately received their payment from the budgets of marketing departments. In some cases, they were awarded funds from the corporation's foundation as well.

Nonprofit employees find it difficult to understand why a company would fund a proposal with corporate funds and not take a deduction on its corporate tax return. We forget that any money *spent* by a company on research, testing, and marketing is 100-percent deductible as a business expense and lowers the company's net earnings, before taxes anyway.

Compared to foundations and government granting agencies, corporations have very unstructured application procedures. Personal contact, crucial to the success of any grant solicitation or contract agreement, is especially important here. Procuring corporate support almost always involves personal contact, followed by a businesslike proposal and negotiation with decision-making executives. You must appeal to the business sense of every corporate official you contact and always clearly demonstrate how support of your proposal will benefit his or her firm.

SUMMARY OF THE GRANTS MARKETPLACE

Now you have a basic idea of the types of funding sources that make up the grants marketplace and the amount of grant support contributed by each. You know that the best strategy is to approach the federal grants area first. You must play the odds that favor this $80 billion marketplace and also explore the possibility of state and block grants. The greater the potential for developing a model that applies to a large area or a great number of people, the more interest you will generate from federal and state funding sources. After you have exhausted your funding potential with government sources, move to the private sector marketplace.

The $15 billion in grants from foundations and corporations provide a distant second to the government's $80 billion, but the variety of project interests and ease of proposal preparation are definite pluses. After reviewing foundation and corporate opportunities, move to associations, service clubs, and other nonprofit groups for support.

THE GRANTS SUPPORT TABLE

The grants support table (see table 8.1) will give you an idea of the strengths and weaknesses of your project in relation to the various funding sources and will help you choose the correct marketplace for your project.

Record your project title and a brief description on the top of the table. Then evaluate how closely your project meets the criteria for each of the funding sources.

Criterion A: The Need

What is the need for your project or research? On whom will it have an impact? How large is the target population? Can the needs population be defined as "special"?

Criterion B: Project Methods/Approach

The information provided in this section is for general use only. There will always be exceptions to the categories presented here, but funding sources generally prefer a specific approach or type of project. For example, some grantors like to fund replication grants, while others prefer research proposals.

Criterion C: Friends/Contacts/Links with Funders

Having friends, contacts, and others who can talk with a funding official or board member or set up an appointment for you is valuable in all grantseeking, but is particularly critical when you are applying close to home.

Criterion D: Grants Experience

Your organization's grants track record is an important credibility builder with state and federal funding sources, corporations, and national foundations. You can still attract funding from community and family foundations, however, even if your organization does not have a track record. Having a solid board whose names are recognized by grantors will help you.

Criterion E: Personal Contact with Officers or Board Members

Personal contact is important with community, national, special purpose, and family foundations, and essential with corporate, state, and federal sources.

TABLE 8.1

GRANTS SUPPORT TABLE

Project Title: _____

Project Description: _____

Criteria	Community Foundation	National Foundation	Special Purpose Foundation	Family Foundation	Corporate Source	State Source	Federal Source
A The Need	Local needs only	National needs, widespread	Need in their specialty	Geographic concerns usually	Needs of workers or products and marketing concerns	Local and statewide need	National need
B Project Methods/ Approach	No experiments; interested in time-tested, proven approaches that can be replicated	Unique, cost-effective, research, model and demonstration	Viewed as special to this area, projects, models, research	Depends on what the Board likes and has funded in the past	Proven safe project methods, unique research protocols related to corporate interests	Replication and model approaches	Mostly model, innovative and research
C Friends/ Contacts/Links with Funders	Very important, local contacts	Important	Important, especially in field of interest	Very important, gives you hidden agenda	Very important, give money to those they trust	Important to have endorsement/ support of bureaucrats, politicians	Same as state

TABLE 8.1

Grants Support Table (continued)

Criteria	Community Foundation	National Foundation	Special Purpose Foundation	Family Foundation	Corporate Source	State Source	Federal Source
D Grants Experience	Credibility and need can overcome lack of experience	Important, likes to work with grantees who are proven	Not as important as potential contribution to field	Not critical, will overlook experience in favor of making a difference	Important, expert experience	Credibility in your state important	Credibility important, as are experience of project director or P.I., publications, and past grants
E Personal Contact with Officials of Board	Very important, especially with board members	Important with staff and program officials	Important with staff and program officials	Important with board members	Essential to contact corporate officials and involve their workers	Essential to contact program officers	Same as state

PART

2

· · · · · · · · ·

Government Funding
Sources

CHAPTER 9

Researching the Government Marketplace

Public funding, or government funding, comprises:

- Federal funds: Grants and contracts received directly from federal agencies.
- State funds: Funds from (a) state grant programs that distribute funds generated from state revenues other than federal revenue-sharing monies and (b) state grant programs that distribute federal grants funds.
- County, borough, and city funds: Funds, consisting of everything from parking-meter monies to dollars passed down from the state and federal government, for grants to specific geographic areas.

APPROACHING FEDERAL FUNDING SOURCES

Federal granting programs are created by Congress through the enactment of public laws and the appropriation of funds. The actual disbursement of these funds follows a systematic progression based on publicly announced rules. Many grantseekers are unaware of how this federal funding system works and, therefore, are unable to take advantage of rules published early in the funding process.

When you do not know the system, you are forced to react to a Request for Proposals (RFP) announcement and develop your proposal in a few short weeks. Grantseekers who know the system, however, can develop a proactive approach to seeking funds that alerts them to a deadline four to six months in advance.

Use the pre-proposal summary and approval form in chapter 4 (see exhibit 4.1) to begin your search for funding. Because almost all federal funding documents use key words and subject areas to categorize granting programs, your worksheet on redefining your project (see chapter 5, exhibit 5.1) will be useful in your research.

FEDERAL GRANTS RESEARCH FORM

Gathering the information necessary to choose your best federal grant prospect requires persistence. You must make personal contacts, gather data, and analyze the data. Without careful attention to detail, the information you were sure you would remember can easily get lost. As one grantseeker reported in a grants seminar, "The only way I can extort my unusually high salary from my boss is to keep all the research and contacts in my head. Nothing is written down, and my board prays that nothing will ever happen to me!" This is not a good idea because all those contacts and bits of information could be lost.

The federal grants research form (see exhibit 9.1) will allow you to keep track of the grant programs you investigate and will prevent your contacts and projects from being lost if anything happens to you. Copy this form and pass out a sufficient number of copies to your grants researchers so that your data gathering will be consistent and complete.

The key to providing your organization with federal funding is a combination of determination, hard work, and homework. The homework consists of systematic research, record keeping, and follow-up.

As you look at examples of the resources available on funding opportunities, you will see that the information necessary to complete the federal grants research form is readily available. Do not stop with the first few funding sources that sound or look good. Remember, your goal is to locate the best funding source for your project. Complete your research, then review and rate those funding sources you have identified using the federal funding source evaluation worksheet in chapter 10 (see exhibit 10.2).

FEDERAL RESEARCH TOOLS

How do you research and track these funds? The federal research tools worksheet (see exhibit 9.2) outlines some of the more useful resources for locating government funds.

For (*Your Project Reference or Title*): _____

CFDA No. _____ **Deadline Date(s):** _____

Program Title: _____ **Gov't. Agency:** _____

Create a file for each program you are researching and place all information you gather on this program in the file. Use this Federal Grants Research Form to

- keep a record of the information you have gathered
- maintain a log of all telephone and face-to-face contacts made with the government agency
- log all correspondence sent to and received from the agency

Agency Address: _____ **Agency Director:** _____

Telephone Number: _____ **Program Director:** _____

Fax Number: _____ **Name/Title of Contact Person:** _____

Place a check mark next to the information you have gathered and placed in the file.

- ❑ Program description from *CFDA*
- ❑ Letter requesting to be put on mailing list
- ❑ List of last year's grantees
    - ❑ Sent for   ❑ Received
- ❑ List of last year's reviewers
    - ❑ Sent for   ❑ Received
- ❑ Application package   Expected availability date _____
    - ❑ Sent for   ❑ Received
- ❑ Comments on rules/final rules from *Federal Register*
- ❑ Notice of rules for evaluation from *Federal Register*
- ❑ Grant Scoring System—Point allocation for each section
    - Source: _____
- ❑ Sample funded proposal
- ❑ Federal Funding Source Staff Profile (exhibit 10.5)
- ❑ Written summary of each contact made

FEDERAL GRANTS RESEARCH FORM

EXHIBIT 9.1

Name	Description	Where to get it	Cost	Where to use it locally
Catalog of Federal Domestic Assistance (202) 783-3238	The official information on all government programs created by law. However, does not mean funds have been appropriated (see sample entry).	Supt. of Documents U.S. Government Printing Office Washington, DC 20402	$50/year	
Federal Assistance Programs Retrieval System (FAPRS) (202) 708-5126	A retrieval system that uses key words to match with federal granting programs to give the *CFDA* programs that are related to the desired grants area.	Federal Domestic Assistance Catalog Staff GSA/IRMS/ WKU 300 7th Street, S.W. Reporters Bldg., Room 101 Washington, DC 20407 Or call your congressperson.	Ask your congress-person how to do an *FAPRS* search. He or she may do it for you at no cost.	
Federal Register (202) 783-3238	Official news publication for the federal government; makes public all meetings, announcements of granting programs, regulations, and deadlines (see sample entry).	Supt. of Documents U.S. Government Printing Office Washington, DC 20402	$490/year	
U.S. Government Manual (202) 783-3238	Official handbook of the federal government. Describes all federal agencies and gives names of officials.	Supt. of Documents U.S. Government Printing Office Washington, DC 20402 Or call your congressperson.	$30/year	

FEDERAL RESEARCH TOOLS WORKSHEET

EXHIBIT 9.2

Name	Description	Where to get it	Cost	Where to use it locally
Federal Executive Directory (202) 333-8620	Includes names, addresses, and phone numbers of federal government agencies and key personnel.	Federal Executive Directory 1058 Thomas Jefferson St., N.W. Washington, DC 20007	$197/year	
Commerce Business Daily (202) 783-3238	The mechanism to announce the accepting of bids on government contracts (see sample entry).	Supt. of Documents U.S. Government Printing Office Washington, DC 20402	$275/year	
Congressional Record (202) 783-3238	Day-to-day proceedings of the Senate and House of Representatives; includes all written information for the record (all grant program money appropriated by Congress).	Supt. of Documents U.S. Government Printing Office Washington, DC 20402	$20/soft cover $30/hard cover	
Listing of Government Depository Libraries (202) 783-3238	Locations of public and university libraries that receive government publications like the *CFDA*.	Chief of the Library Dept. of Public Documents U.S. Government Printing Office Washington, DC 20402		
Agency Newsletters and Publications, RFPs, and Guidelines	Many federal agencies publish newsletters to inform you about the availability of funds and program accomplishments. You may also request application materials, guidelines, and so on.		usually free	

FEDERAL RESEARCH TOOLS WORKSHEET *(continued)*

EXHIBIT 9.2

Catalog of Federal Domestic Assistance (CFDA)

The *Catalog of Federal Domestic Assistance (CFDA)*, which is published by the federal government, lists the 1,100 granting programs that disseminate approximately $80 billion in grants annually. The catalog is provided free of charge to at least two federal depository libraries in every congressional district. Consider locating and using one of these copies instead of purchasing your own copy. The *CFDA* is available in hard-copy format and in an electronic edition.

***How to Use the* CFDA.** First, familiarize yourself with the indexes in the *CFDA*. The following indexes are included:

- Agency program index: Although difficult to use, gives you codes for types of assistance each agency program provides.
- Applicant eligibility index: Allows you to look up a program to see whether you are eligible to apply. Because you must already know of the program to use this index, it is not a great help in identifying sources.
- Deadline index: Enables you to look up the deadline dates for programs to see whether the programs have a multiple deadline system.
- Functional index: Groups programs into 20 broad functional categories, such as agriculture and education, and 176 subcategories.
- Popular name index: Lists programs by their commonly used names (the names most often referred to by agencies and applicants). Check the popular name index when you cannot find a federal program listed under the name you have for it.
- Subject index: The most commonly used index, since most people express their interests according to subject.

Compare your key words and redefinition sheets to entries in the popular name index and the subject index, and select those programs that you believe will be interested in your project idea. Briefly outline the sources on your federal grants research forms. Be sure to write down the *CFDA* number that references the program.

***Reading the* CFDA.** A sample *CFDA* entry (see exhibit 9.3) has been included to show the information provided in this valuable resource. In the sample, *CFDA* Number 84.215, The Secretary's Fund for Innovation in Education, reader aids have been placed in the left margin. These numbers will not appear in the *CFDA* document.

1. Federal agency: This is the branch of the government administering the program, which is not much help to you except as general knowledge or for looking up programs and agencies in the *United States Government Manual*.

2. Authorization: You need this information to fill out some program applications or to look up the testimony and laws creating the funding (for the "hard-core" researcher and grantseeker only).

3. Objectives: Compare these general program objectives to your project. Do not give up if you are off the mark slightly; contact with the funding source may uncover new programs, changes, or hidden agendas.

4. Types of assistance: Review and record the general type of support from this source, and then compare the information to your project definition.

5. Eligibility requirements: Be sure your organization is designated as a legal recipient. If it is not, find an organization of the type designated and apply as a consortium or under a cooperative agreement.

6. Application and award process: Review this information and record it on your federal grants research form. Do not let the deadline data bother you. If the award cycle has passed, you should still contact the agency and position yourself for the following year by asking for copies of old applications and a list of current grantees and by requesting to be a reviewer.

7. Assistance considerations: Record information on any match you are required to provide. This will be useful in evaluating funding sources. Matching requirements may eliminate some funding sources from your consideration. In addition, assistance considerations will help you develop your project planner (see chapter 11). When you know about matching requirements in advance, you can identify what resources your organization will be required to provide.

8. Financial information: This section gives you an idea of what funds the agency program may have received, but do not take the information here as the last word. One entry I recently reviewed said the funding agency had $3 million for research. When contacted, the agency had over $30 million to disseminate under the program described and similar ones in the *CFDA*. Refer to the entry and evaluate it.

9. Regulations, guidelines, and literature: Record and send for any information you can get on the funder.

10. Information contacts: Record and use to begin contacting funders as outlined in this book. Note the name and phone number of the contact person. While the contact person or number may have changed, you at least will have a place to start.

11. Related programs: Some *CFDA* entries include suggestions of other programs that are similar or related to your area of interest. While these suggestions are usually obvious and you may have already uncovered the programs in your research, review this section for leads.

84.215 THE SECRETARY'S FUND FOR INNOVATION IN EDUCATION (FIE)

FEDERAL AGENCY: OFFICE OF ASSISTANT SECRETARY FOR EDUCATIONAL RESEARCH AND IMPROVEMENT, DEPARTMENT OF EDUCATION

AUTHORIZATION: Elementary and Secondary Education Act of 1965, Title IV, Part F, 20 U.S.C. 3151-3157.

OBJECTIVES: To conduct programs and projects that show promise of identifying and disseminating innovative educational approaches.

TYPES OF ASSISTANCE: Project Grants.

USES AND USE RESTRICTIONS: Funds may be used to support a wide range of projects under the FIE general authority for programs the Innovation in Education Program and the specific program authorities: computer-based instruction; and comprehensive school health education programs.

ELIGIBILITY REQUIREMENTS:
Applicant Eligibility: State educational agencies, local educational agencies, institutions of higher education, public and private organizations and institutions may apply. Under the comprehensive school health education program only State educational agencies (SEAs) local education agencies (LEAs), or SEAs or LEAs in collaboration with other entities of their choice may apply.
Beneficiary Eligibility: State educational agencies, local educational agencies, institutions of higher education, public and private organizations and institutions will benefit.
Credentials/Documentation: None.

APPLICATION AND AWARD PROCESS:
Preapplication Coordination: Preapplications are not required for this program. Applicants for computer-based instruction projects must comply with statutory preapplication planning requirements. This program is eligible for coverage under E.O. 12372, "Intergovernmental Review of Federal Programs." An applicant should consult the office or official designated as the single point of contact in his or her State for more information on the process that State requires to be followed in applying for assistance, if the State has selected the program for review.
Application Procedure: Described in application notices published annually in the Federal Register. Contact the headquarters office listed below for application packages containing the announcement, application, and assurance forms and for further information about Fund for Innovation in Education programs.
Award Procedure: The Assistant Secretary for Educational Research and Improvement approves the selection of applications for negotiation. The selection of applications is competitive, based on staff and nonfederal, peer review according to the selection criteria contained in the Education Department General Administrative Regulations (EDGAR) at 34 CFR 75.210 and the annual application notice published in the Federal Register.
Deadlines: Announced in an application published annually in the Federal Register. Contact the headquarters office for further information about Fund for Innovation in Education programs.
Range of Approval/Disapproval Time: Approximately six months.
Appeals: None.
Renewals: Awards are made annually. Following an initial, competitively selected award of up to twelve months, two additional one year non-competing continuation awards may be made for a maximum of three years.

ASSISTANCE CONSIDERATIONS:
Formula and Matching Requirements: None.
Length and Time Phasing of Assistance: Awards are made annually. Following an initial, competitively selected award of up to twelve months, two additional one-year non-competing continuation awards may be made, for a total maximum term of three years.

POST ASSISTANCE REQUIREMENTS:
Reports: Annual progress and financial reports as required by EDGAR unless otherwise required in the award document.
Audits: In accordance with the Education Department General Administration Regulations in the Appendix to 34 CFR 80, State and local governments that receive financial assistance of $100,000 or more within the State's fiscal year shall have an audit made for that year. State and local governments that receive between $25,000 and $100,000 within the State's fiscal year shall have an audit made in accordance with the Appendix to Part 80, or in accordance with Federal laws and regulations governing the programs in which they participate.
Records: As required by EDGAR.

FINANCIAL INFORMATION:
Account Identification: 91-1100-2-1-503.
Obligations: (Grants) FY 93 $28,007,730; FY 94 est $36,963,000; and FY 95 est $35,000,000.
Range and Average of Financial Assistance: The anticipated range is between $50,000 to $500,000, depending on availability of funds.

PROGRAM ACCOMPLISHMENTS: In fiscal year 1993, the comprehensive School Health Education program received 108 applications and funded 11 projects. The Innovation in Education program received 737 applications for funding under a general competition and made 10 awards. Under a second competition for State curriculum frameworks, 14 projects were funded from 71 applications. The Computer-Based Instruction program received 477 applications and funded 13.

REGULATIONS, GUIDELINES, AND LITERATURE: Education Department General Administrative Regulations, 34 CFR 74, 75, 77, 78,79,80, 81, 82, 85, 86.

INFORMATION CONTACTS:
Regional or Local Office: Not applicable.
Headquarters Office: FIRST Office, Office of Educational Research and Improvement, Department of Education, 555 New Jersey Avenue, NW., Washington, DC 20208-5524. Telephone: (202) 219-1496. Use the same number for FTS.

RELATED PROGRAMS: None.

EXAMPLES OF FUNDED PROJECTS: Under the general competition, projects provided a variety of innovative approaches to help students in elementary or secondary school reach high standards of academic achievement in one or more of the core subjects of mathematics, science, history, the arts, civics, geography, foreign languages, and English. Under the State curriculum frameworks competition, awards were given to two projects for English, two for geography, three for the arts and seven awards for projects that were multidisciplinary. Under the Computer-Based Instruction Competition most projects were to train teachers to utilize and integrate state-of-the-art computer technology in the teaching of mathematics, science, history, and foreign language.

CRITERIA FOR SELECTING PROPOSALS: (1) Meeting the purposes of the authorizing statute; (2) extent of need for the project; (3) plan of operation; (4) quality of key personnel; (5) budget and cost-effectiveness; (6) evaluation plan; and (7) adequacy of resources. For detailed criteria, see the regulations.

SAMPLE *CFDA* ENTRY

EXHIBIT 9.3

12. Criteria for selecting proposals: Review and record the information here. Criteria are frequently listed with no regard to their order of importance and lack any reference to the point values that they will be given in the review. Therefore, you should also obtain the rules from the *Federal Register,* the agency publication, or a past reviewer.

After reviewing the *CFDA* entries, select the best government funding program for your project. Contact the federal agency by using the contact person listed under "Information Contacts."

Federal Assistance Programs Retrieval System

The enhanced version of *Federal Assistance Programs Retrieval System (FAPRS)* is a computerized question-and-answer system designed to provide rapid access to *CFDA* program information. The system includes information on federal programs that meet the developmental needs of the applicant and for which the applicant meets basic eligibility criteria.

Program information provided by *FAPRS* is determined from input supplied by the requester. Input required includes the name and population of the state, county, city, town, or federally designated American Indian tribal government for which program information is requested; the type of applicant (e.g., state or local government, federally designated American Indian organization, nonprofit organization, small business, or individual); the type of assistance under which programs are administered (e.g., grants or loans); and the specific functional categories and subcategories of interest. Based upon the information supplied by the requester, the output provided by *FAPRS* consists of one or more of the following:

- a list of program numbers and titles
- the full text of selected programs
- specific sections of the program text

As originally developed by the Department of Agriculture, *FAPRS* was designed to aid small isolated rural communities that were unfamiliar with federal assistance programs or unable to locate federal aid programs with the greatest funding potential. The following features have been incorporated into the new *FAPRS* system:

1. Expanded functional categories and subcategories: As listed in the functional index and the *CFDA*, the enhanced version of *FAPRS* uses 20 functional categories and 176 subcategories to specify areas of interest.
2. Expanded applicant eligibility specifications: The eligibility specifications now include 12 government-related and 10 nongovernment-related applicant types.
3. Specifications of the type of assistance desired as one of the search criteria: At present, the *CFDA* lists up to 15 types of assistance provided by federal programs.
4. Display of definitions for functional subcategories, applicant types, and types of assistance.
5. The ability to select specific sections of *CFDA* text to be displayed.
6. Formatted display of federal circulars outlining the rules applicable to each program.

States have designated access points where *FAPRS* searches may be requested. In addition, bulletins on *FAPRS* are available from the system to inform users of the addition or deletion of programs, changes to program numbers from one edition of the *CFDA* to the next, and enhancements and changes to the system. For further information on *FAPRS,* the location of the nearest state access point, or a list of the time-sharing companies from which interested persons may arrange for direct access to the system, write to the Office of Management and Budget, Budget Review Division, Federal Program Information Branch, Washington, DC 20503. Your congressperson will be able to assist you in finding out where you can obtain an *FAPRS* search in your area.

Other Computer Databases

The *CFDA* can also be accessed through several other computer databases. Your choice of which database to use for locating those federal grants programs most suitable to your project depends on

- what database access your grants advisory committee members subscribe to
- what database connections your organization may currently have online through your library, grants office, or development office
- how much time and resources are at your disposal for setting up a grants searching system
- your ability to access a communication device, telephone line, etc.

The Internet

Originally, this worldwide network of access to computer networks was limited to colleges, university researchers, and their federal sponsors. It is now available to anyone with a computer and an Internet service provider. Much of the federal grant information is posted on bulletin boards and in news groups, and it is expected that federal agencies will continue to increase their use of electronic tools. Grantseekers can also contact program officers with specific questions via e-mail.

In higher education, access to the Internet is provided by the college or university that maintains the Internet server. The server, which may be referred to as a "node," is a mainframe computer where many individual account holders are found. Since smaller organizations may not have a mainframe computer, they can join a commercial Internet server such as CompuServe or America Online. Delphi is another Internet provider offering full access to e-mail, telnet, FTP, and gopher. You can reach Delphi by calling (800) 695-4005. Before enrolling with any server, be sure to check program limitations and costs.

You will find numerous books about the Internet in your local bookstore's computer section. *The Internet Companion: A Beginner's Guide to Global Networking* (Addison-Wesley, 1993) and *The Whole Internet: User's Guide and Catalog* (O'Reilly and Associates, Inc., 1992) are just two among many. *Internet Access Providers: An International Resource Directory* will help you locate Internet servers. (Published by Meckler Company, June 1994; call (800) 632-5537 for more information.)

Once you have access to the Internet and a node at which you can collect information, you can search the *CFDA* and the *Federal Register* on your computer. For example, say you are interested in procuring a grant for computer laboratory equipment. By conducting a *CFDA* or *Federal Register* search on the Internet, you would find that several National Science Foundation (NSF) programs support the purchasing of computer laboratory equipment.

Your next step would be to log into the NSF computer using one of the many gopher programs offered by most Internet providers. The various gopher programs present the user with a menu of public access services worldwide. These programs allow the user to browse and select lists of services without knowing the telenet addresses of the service providers. Once in the remote system, the user is presented with a list of the available services to choose from. If a useful file is found, the user can use the gopher to download it directly without using complicated file transfer procedures. Each gopher menu leads to another.

Depending on what gopher software you are using, you would find the NSF gopher by selecting "other gophers around the world" from the main gopher menu.* A list would be presented, and you would select "North America" and "USA." From the next list that comes up, you would select "General" and scroll through it until you found the NSF gopher. Once you call up the NSF "home page," you have several items to choose from including

- About STIS (the name of the NSF computer system)
- Search NSF Publications
- NSF Publications

To find the information for our example, looking for grants to purchase computer laboratory equipment, select "Search NSF Publications." At the prompt, you would type "computer laboratory equipment." Once you have identified the files you want, you can download them directly to your computer using the gopher.

Your organization or one of your advocates may already have access to the Internet. Recently, while working with a public school district in rural Texas, I discovered that every teacher in the state had the option of accessing the Internet for a $5.00 per person annual fee, but many were unaware of this

---

*Editor's note: Different gopher programs may have different options from the ones discussed here. For instance, some Internet software will allow you to go directly to the gopher by typing the address, in this case: STIS.NSF.GOV. Users should practice with their particular programs.

opportunity. Before you pay a service fee, be certain that you have not over-looked your existing access possibilities or those of your advocates.

Sponsored Project Information Network (SPIN)

InfoEd, a New York–based company, produces and distributes the Sponsored Project Information Network (SPIN). SPIN is a database originally developed by the Research Foundation of the State University of New York (SUNY) to provide grants information on all federal programs and some foundations and corporations.

The *CFDA* is available through this fee-based system. One advantage of SPIN is that you can subscribe via a user-friendly dial-up service. You can reach InfoEd by calling (800) 727-6427.

The GRANTS Database

Produced by Oryx Press, *The GRANTS Database* includes information on more than 8,900 current funding sources, covers all major disciplines and sub-ject areas, and includes grants from private and commercial organizations as well as federal, state, and local governments. Essential information is pro-vided on each source, including program name, program description, sponsor's address and telephone number, requirements and restrictions, funding amount, deadline date, and renewal information. For further information, call the Oryx Press at (800) 279-6799.

The *GRANTS Database* is available on CD-ROM from Knight-Ridder In-formation Services. *KR Information OnDisc: The GRANTS Database* pro-vides the user with the complete *GRANTS Database,* updated bimonthly, and several convenient search methods. Call Knight-Ridder Information Services at (800) 334-2564 for more information.

Users can also access *The GRANTS Database* online through Knight-Ridder. Knight-Ridder gives the user access to thousands of continually updated funding sources, plus helpful new search capabilities. For information about online subscriptions to Knight-Ridder call (800) 982-5838.

GrantSearch CFDA

Produced by Capitol Publications, *GrantSearch CFDA* is an electronic edition of the *Catalog of Federal Domestic Assistance* and includes the full text of all federal grant programs included in the *CFDA.* The material has been built into a special personal-computer format called an information data-base or infobase. All you need to do is load the disks into your hard drive and search for the information you desire. There are no fee-per-minute or addi-tional charges to be concerned with. An updated disk with all of the latest entry changes can be purchased annually. For more information, call (703) 683-4100.

Federal Register

The *Federal Register* is the newspaper of the federal government. To make legal notices on a great variety of federal issues official, the government must publish notices in the *Federal Register*. The hard copy of this government publication is provided free of charge to the two federal depository libraries in your congressional district. Locate your nearest source.

The creation of new government granting programs and the rules governing both new and old government granting programs must be published in the *Federal Register*. Rules to evaluate proposals are also printed in the *Federal Register*. The following points will help you read the sample pages from the *Federal Register* in exhibit 9.4.

1. Purposes, prices, and information on how to access the *Federal Register*'s online database.
2. Contents: Provides a detailed account of what is in a particular volume of the *Federal Register*. The information is listed alphabetically by department or agency name. For example, in this volume the Education Department is announcing notices related to vocational and academic learning integration program demonstration projects.
3. Reader Aids: Describes services and gives phone numbers for services. Of particular significance is the "Fax-on-Demand" section. Those grantseekers who do not have easy access to a print copy or online services can request a fax of the volume and page numbers that apply to programs they are interested in. (Note: The government sponsors classes around the United States on how to read and understand the *Federal Register*. Call (202) 523-4534 to find the nearest class and plan to attend.)
4. Note the following points in this example from the Department of Education:
   - Note to Applicants—You could write your proposal on August 1, because this is the same application information that will appear in the request for proposal (RFP) package that will be mailed out later.
   - Purpose of Program—Provides valuable insight into what the program is interested in funding and refines information from the *CFDA*.
   - Eligible Applicants—Check to make sure your organization is still eligible to apply for these funds, because changes from the information provided in the *CFDA* are announced here.

8-1-94
Vol. 59   No. 146
Pages 38875-39246

Monday
August 1, 1994

federal register

SAMPLE OF THE *FEDERAL REGISTER*

EXHIBIT 9.4

Federal Register / Vol. 59, No. 146 / Monday, August 1, 1994

FEDERAL REGISTER Published daily, Monday through Friday, (not published on Saturdays, Sundays, or on official holidays), by the Office of the Federal Register, National Archives and Records Administration, Washington, DC 20408, under the Federal Register Act (49 Stat. 500, as amended; 44 U.S.C. Ch. 15) and the regulations of the Administrative Committee of the Federal Register (1 CFR Ch. I). Distribution is made only by the Superintendent of Documents, U.S. Government Printing Office, Washington, DC 20402.

The Federal Register provides a uniform system for making available to the public regulations and legal notices issued by Federal agencies. These include Presidential proclamations and Executive Orders and Federal agency documents having general applicability and legal effect, documents required to be published by act of Congress and other Federal agency documents of public interest. Documents are on file for public inspection in the Office of the Federal Register the day before they are published, unless earlier filing is requested by the issuing agency.

The seal of the National Archives and Records Administration authenticates this issue of the Federal Register as the official serial publication established under the Federal Register Act. 44 U.S.C. 1507 provides that the contents of the Federal Register shall be judicially noticed.

The Federal Register is published in paper, 24x microfiche and as an online database through GPO Access, a service of the U.S. Government Printing Office. The online database is updated by 6 a.m. each day the Federal Register is published. The database includes both text and graphics from Volume 59, Number 1 (January 2, 1994) forward. It is available on a Wide Area Information Server (WAIS) through the Internet and via asynchronous dial-in. The annual subscription fee for a single workstation is $375. Six-month subscriptions are available for $200 and one month of access can be purchased for $35. Discounts are available for multiple-workstation subscriptions. To subscribe, Internet users should telnet to wais.access.gpo.gov and login as newuser (all lower case); no password is required. Dial in users should use communications software and modem to call (202) 512-1661 and login as wais (all lower case); no password is required; at the second login prompt, login as newuser (all lower case); no password is required. Follow the instructions on the screen to register for a subscription for the Federal Register Online via GPO Access. For assistance, contact the GPO Access User Support Team by sending Internet e-mail to help@eids05.eids.gpo.gov, or a fax to (202) 512-1262, or by calling (202) 512-1530 between 7 a.m. and 5 p.m. Eastern time, Monday through Friday, except Federal holidays.

The annual subscription price for the Federal Register paper edition is $444, or $490 for a combined Federal Register, Federal Register Index and List of CFR Sections Affected (LSA) subscription; the microfiche edition of the Federal Register including the Federal Register Index and LSA is $403. Six month subscriptions are available for one-half the annual rate. The charge for individual copies in paper form is $6.00 for each issue, or $6.00 for each group of pages as actually bound; or $1.50 for each issue in microfiche form. All prices include regular domestic postage and handling. International customers please add 25% for foreign handling. Remit check or money order, made payable to the Superintendent of Documents, or charge to your GPO Deposit Account, VISA or MasterCard. Mail to: New Orders, Superintendent of Documents, P.O. Box 371954, Pittsburgh, PA 15250-7954.

There are no restrictions on the republication of material appearing in the Federal Register.

How To Cite This Publication: Use the volume number and the page number. Example: 59 FR 12345.

SUBSCRIPTIONS AND COPIES

PUBLIC

Subscriptions:
Paper or fiche — 202-512-1800
Assistance with public subscriptions — 512-1806

Online:
Telnet wais.access.gpo.gov, login as newuser <enter>, no password <enter>; or use a modem to call (202) 512-1661, login as wais, no password <enter>, at the second login as newuser <enter>, no password <enter>.
Assistance with online subscriptions — 202-512-1530

Single copies/back copies:
Paper or fiche — 512-1800
Assistance with public single copies — 512-1803

FEDERAL AGENCIES

Subscriptions:
Paper or fiche — 523-5243
Assistance with Federal agency subscriptions — 523-5243

For other telephone numbers, see the Reader Aids section at the end of this issue.

Printed on recycled paper containing 100% post consumer waste

SAMPLE OF THE FEDERAL REGISTER (continued)

EXHIBIT 9.4

Contents

Federal Register

Vol. 59, No. 146

Monday, August 1, 1994

SAMPLE OF THE *FEDERAL REGISTER* (continued)

EXHIBIT 9.4

Reader Aids

Federal Register

Vol. 59, No. 146

Monday, August 1, 1994

INFORMATION AND ASSISTANCE

Federal Register

Index, finding aids & general information	202–523–5227
Public inspection announcement line	523–5215
Corrections to published documents	523–5237
Document drafting information	523–3187
Machine readable documents	523–3447

Code of Federal Regulations

Index, finding aids & general information	523–5227
Printing schedules	523–3419

Laws

Public Laws Update Service (numbers, dates, etc.)	523–6641
Additional information	523–5230

Presidential Documents

Executive orders and proclamations	523–5230
Public Papers of the Presidents	523–5230
Weekly Compilation of Presidential Documents	523–5230

The United States Government Manual

General information	523–5230

Other Services

Data base and machine readable specifications	523–3447
Guide to Record Retention Requirements	523–3187
Legal staff	523–4534
Privacy Act Compilation	523–3187
Public Laws Update Service (PLUS)	523–6641
TDD for the hearing impaired	523–5229

ELECTRONIC BULLETIN BOARD

Free **Electronic Bulletin Board** service for Public Law numbers, Federal Register finding aids, and list of documents on public inspection.　202–275–0920

FAX-ON-DEMAND

The daily Federal Register Table of Contents and the list of documents on public inspection are available on the National Archives fax-on-demand system. You must call from a fax machine. There is no charge for the service except for long distance telephone charges.　301–713–6905

FEDERAL REGISTER PAGES AND DATES, AUGUST

38875–39246

CFR PARTS AFFECTED DURING AUGUST

At the end of each month, the Office of the Federal Register publishes separately a List of CFR Sections Affected (LSA), which lists parts and sections affected by documents published since the revision date of each title.

LIST OF PUBLIC LAWS

Note: No public bills which have become law were received by the Office of the Federal Register for inclusion in today's **List of Public Laws.**

Last List July 27, 1994

SAMPLE OF THE *FEDERAL REGISTER* (continued)

EXHIBIT 9.4

DEPARTMENT OF EDUCATION

[CFDA No.: 84.248]

Demonstration Projects for the Integration of Vocational and Academic Learning Program; Notice Inviting Applications for New Awards for Fiscal Year (FY) 1995

Note to Applicants: This notice is a complete application package. Together with the statute authorizing the program and applicable regulations governing the program, including the Education Department General Administrative Regulations (EDGAR), the notice contains all of the information, application forms, and instructions needed to apply for a grant under this competition.

Purpose of Program: The Demonstration Projects for the Integration of Vocational and Academic Learning Program provides financial assistance to projects that develop, implement, and operate programs using different models of curricula that integrate vocational and academic learning. The Secretary wishes to highlight for potential applicants that this program can help to further the National Education Goals. Specifically, the integration of vocational and academic learning directly supports the National Education Goal that, by the year 2000, every adult American will be literate and will possess the knowledge and skills necessary to compete in a global economy and exercise the rights and responsibilities of citizenship.

Eligible Applicants: Institutions of higher education, area vocational educational schools, secondary schools funded by the Bureau of Indian Affairs, State boards of vocational education, public or private nonprofit organizations, local educational agencies, and consortia composed of these entities.

Deadline for Transmittal of Applications: September 16, 1994.

Deadline for Intergovernmental Review: November 15, 1994.

Available Funds: $6,000,000 to $7,000,000 for the first 12 months. Funding for the second, third, and fourth years is subject to the availability of funds and to a grantee meeting the requirements in 34 CFR 75.253.

Estimated Range of Awards: $300,000–$500,000 (funding for the first 12 months).

Estimated Average Size of Awards: $365,000 (funding for the first 12 months).

Estimated Number of Awards: 15–19.

Note: The Department is not bound by any c :timates in this notice.

Project Period: Up to 48 months (four 12-month grant cycles).

Applicable Regulations: (a) The Education Department General Administrative Regulations (EDGAR) as follows:

(1) 34 CFR 74 (Administration of Grants to Institutions of Higher Education, Hospitals and Nonprofit Organizations).

(2) 34 CFR Part 75 (Direct Grant Programs).

(3) 34 CFR Part 77 (Definitions that Apply to Department Regulations).

(4) 34 CFR Part 79 (Intergovernmental Review of Department of Education Programs and Activities).

(5) 34 CFR Part 80 (Uniform Administrative Requirements for Grants and Cooperative Agreements to State and Local Governments).

(6) 34 CFR Part 81 (General Education Provisions Act—Enforcement).

(7) 34 CFR Part 82 (New Restrictions on Lobbying).

(8) 34 CFR Part 85 (Governmentwide Debarment and Suspension (Nonprocurement) and Governmentwide Requirements for Drug-Free Workplace (Grants)).

(9) 34 CFR Part 86 (Drug-Free Schools and Campuses).

(b) The regulations for this program in 34 CFR Parts 400 and 425.

Invitational Priorities

Under 34 CFR 75.105(c)(1), the Secretary is particularly interested in applications that focus primarily on one or more of the following areas. However, an application that meets these invitational priorities does not receive competitive or absolute preference over the applications.

(a) Demonstrating strong ties with the State's school-to-work activities through the integration of academic and vocational skills at work-based learning sites.

(b) Demonstrating strong ties with the business and industry skill standards projects funded by the Departments of Education and Labor through the identification and use of concrete world-of-work examples to teach abstract concepts and principles.

(c) Including both vocational and academic faculty and employers in the design of integrated curricula and courses that are targeted at the secondary and postsecondary levels of instruction.

(d) Involving the education community and employers in providing inservice training for teachers of vocational education students and administrators in the planning, implementation, and operation of integrated curricula or programs.

(e) Disseminating information and materials regarding effective strategies for integrating vocational and academic learning to national audiences.

(f) Evaluating programs that integrate vocational and academic learning through the use of experimental and control group samples.

Selection Criteria

The Secretary uses the following selection criteria to evaluate applications for new grants under this competition. The maximum score for all of these criteria is 100 points. The maximum score for each criterion is indicated in parentheses. For this competition, the Secretary assigns the fifteen points, reserved in 34 CFR 425.20(b), as follows:

Program factors (34 CFR 425.21(a). Five points are added to this criterion for a possible total of 15 points.

Educational significance (34 CFR 425.21(b)). Ten points are added to this criterion for a possible total of 20 points.

(a) *Program factors* (15 points) The Secretary reviews each application to assess the quality of the proposed project, including—

(1) The extent to which the project involves creative or innovative methods for integrating vocational and academic learning; and

(2) The quality of the services that the project will provide to—

(i) Individuals who are members of special populations;

(ii) Vocational students in secondary schools and at postsecondary institutions;

(iii) Individuals enrolled in adult programs; or

(iv) Single parents, displaced homemakers, and single pregnant women.

(b) *Educational significance* (20 points) The Secretary reviews each application to determine the extent to which the applicant—

(1) Bases the proposed project on successful model vocational education programs that include components similar to the components required by this program, as evidenced by empirical data from those programs in such factors as—

(i) Student performance and achievement;

(ii) High school graduation;

(iii) Placement of students in jobs, including military service; and

(iv) Successful transfer of students to a variety of postsecondary education programs;

(2) Proposes project objectives that contribute to the improvement of education; and

(3) Proposes to use unique and innovative techniques that address the

SMALL OF THE *FEDERAL REGISTER* (continued)

EXHIBIT 9.4

need to integrate vocational and academic learning, and produce benefits that are of national significance.

(c) *Plan of operation* (15 points) The Secretary reviews each application to determine the quality of the plan of operation for the project, including—

(1) The quality of the project design, especially the establishment of measureable objectives for the project that are based on the project's overall goals;

(2) The extent to which the plan of management is effective and ensures proper and efficient administration of the project over the award period;

(3) How well the objectives of the project relate to the purpose of the program;

(4) The quality of the applicant's plan to use its resources and personnel to achieve each objective; and

(5) How the applicant will ensure that project participants who are otherwise eligible to participate are selected without regard to race, color, national origin, gender, age, or disability.

(d) *Evaluation plan* (15 points) The Secretary reviews each application to determine the quality of the project's evaluation plan, including the extent to which the plan—

(1) Carries out the requirements in 34 CFR 425.30;

(2) Is clearly explained and is appropriate to the project;

(3) To the extent possible, is objective and will produce data that are quantifiable;

(4) Includes quality measures to assess the effectiveness of the curricular developed by the project;

(5) Identifies expected outcomes of the participants and how those outcomes will be measured;

(6) Includes activities during the formative stages of the project to help guide and improve the project, as well as a summative evaluation that includes recommendations for replicating project activities and results;

(7) Will provide a comparison between intended and observed results, and lead to the demonstration of a clear link between the observed results and the specific treatment of project participants; and

(8) Will yield results that can be summarized and submitted to the Secretary for review by the Department's Program Effectiveness Panel, as defined in 34 CFR 400.4(b). NOTE: The Program Effectiveness Panel (PEP) is a mechanism the Department has developed for validating the effectiveness of educational programs developed by schools, universities, and other agencies. The PEP is composed of experts in the evaluation of educational

programs and in other areas of education, at least two-thirds of whom are non-Federal employees who are appointed by the Secretary. Regulations governing the PEP are codified in 34 CFR Parts 785–789. Specific criteria for PEP review are found in 34 CFR 786.12 or 787.121.

(e) *Demonstration and dissemination.* (10 points) The Secretary reviews each application for information to determine the effectiveness and efficiency of the plan for demonstrating and disseminating information about project activities and results throughout the project period, including—

(1) High quality in the design of the dissemination plan and procedures for evaluating the effectiveness of the dissemination plan;

(2) Identification of the audience to which the project activities will be disseminated and provisions for publicizing the project at the local, State, and national levels by conducting, or delivering presentations at, conferences, workshops, and other professional meetings and by preparing materials for journal articles, newsletters, and brochures;

(3) Provisions for demonstrating the methods and techniques used by the project to others interested in replicating these methods and techniques, such as by inviting them to observe project activities;

(4) A description of the types of materials the applicant plans to make available to help others replicate project activities and the methods for making the materials available; and

(5) Provisions for assisting others to adopt and successfully implement the methods, approaches, and techniques developed by the project.

(f) *Key personnel.* (10 points)

(1) The Secretary reviews each application to determine the quality of key personnel the applicant plans to use on the project, including—

(i) The qualifications, in relation to project requirements, of the project director;

(ii) The qualifications, in relation to project requirements, of each of the other key personnel to be used in the project;

(iii) The appropriateness of the time that each person referred to in paragraphs (f)(1) (i) and (ii) will commit to the project; and

(iv) How the applicant, as part of its nondiscriminatory employment practices, will ensure that its personnel are selected for employment without regard to race, color, national origin, gender, age, or disability.

(2) To determine personnel qualifications under paragraphs (f)(1) (i) and (ii), the Secretary considers—

(i) The experience and training of key personnel in project management and in fields related to the objectives of the project; and

(ii) Any other qualifications of key personnel that pertain to the quality of the project.

(g) *Budget and cost effectiveness.* (10 points) The Secretary reviews each application to determine the extent to which the budget—

(1) Is cost effective and adequate to support the project activities;

(2) Contains costs that are reasonable and necessary in relation to the objectives of the project; and

(3) Proposes using non-Federal resources available from appropriate employment, training, and education agencies in the State to provide services and activities and to acquire project equipment and facilities, to ensure that funds awarded under this part are used to provide instructional services.

(h) *Adequacy of resources and commitment.* (5 points)

(1) The Secretary reviews each application to determine the extent to which the applicant plans to devote adequate resources to the project. The Secretary considers the extent to which—

(i) The facilities that the applicant plans to use are adequate; and

(ii) The equipment and supplies that the applicant plans to use are adequate.

(2) The Secretary reviews each application to determine the commitment to the project, including whether the—

(i) Uses of non-Federal resources are adequate to provide project services and activities, especially resources of community organizations and State and local educational agencies; and

(ii) Applicant has the capacity to continue, expand, and build upon the project when Federal assistance under 34 CFR part 425 ends.

Additional Factors ⑦

(a) After evaluating the applications according to the selection criteria, the Secretary determines whether the most highly rated applications—

(1) Are equitably distributed throughout the Nation;

(2) Offer significantly different approaches to integrating vocational and academic curricula; and

(3) Serve—

(i) Individuals who are members of special populations;

(ii) Vocational students in secondary schools;

(iii) Vocational students at postsecondary institutions;

Sᴀᴍᴘʟᴇ ᴏғ ᴛʜᴇ *Fᴇᴅᴇʀᴀʟ Rᴇɢɪsᴛᴇʀ (continued)*

EXHIBIT 9.4

(iv) Individuals enrolled in adult programs; or

(v) Single parents, displaced homemakers, and single pregnant women.

(b) The Secretary may select other applications for funding if doing so would improve the geographical distribution of, diversity of approaches in, or the diversity of populations to be served by projects funded under this program.

⑧ **Intergovernmental Review of Federal Programs**

This program is subject to the requirements of Executive Order 12372 (Intergovernmental Review of Federal Programs) and the regulations in 34 CFR Part 79.

The objective of the Executive order is to foster an intergovernmental partnership and to strengthen federalism by relying on State and local processes for State and local government coordination and review of proposed Federal financial assistance.

Applicants must contact the appropriate State Single Point of Contact to find out about, and to comply with, the State's process under Executive Order 12372. Applicants proposing to perform activities in more than one State should immediately contact the Single Point of Contact for each of those States and follow the procedure established in each State under the Executive order. If you want to know the name and address of any State Single Point of Contact, see the list published in the **Federal Register** on May 3, 1994 (59 FR 22904–22905). In States that have not established a process or chosen a program for review, State, areawide, regional, and local entities may submit comments directly to the Department.

Any State Process Recommendation and other comments submitted by a State Single Point of Contact and any comments from State, areawide, regional, and local entities must be mailed or hand-delivered by the date indicated in this notice to the following address: The Secretary, E.O. 12372–CFDA# 84.248, U.S. Department of Education, Room 4181, 400 Maryland Avenue SW., Washington, DC 20202–0125.

Proof of mailing will be determined on the same basis as applications (see 34 CFR 75.102). Recommendations or comments may be hand-delivered until 4:30 p.m. (Washington, DC time) on the date indicated in this notice.

PLEASE NOTE THAT THE ABOVE ADDRESS IS NOT THE SAME ADDRESS AS THE ONE TO WHICH THE APPLICANT SUBMITS ITS COMPLETED APPLICATION. *DO NOT SEND APPLICATIONS TO THE ABOVE ADDRESS.*

Instructions for Transmittal of Applications ⑨

(a) If an applicant wants to apply for a grant, the applicant shall—

(1) Mail the original and six copies of the application on or before the deadline date to: U.S. Department of Education, Application Control Center, Attention: (CFDA# 84.248), Washington, DC 20202–4725, or

(2) Hand deliver the original and six copies of the application by 4:30 p.m. (Washington, DC time) on the deadline date to: U.S. Department of Education, Application Control Center, Attention: (CFDA# 84.248), Room #3633, Regional Office Building #3, 7th and D Streets SW., Washington, DC.

(b) An applicant must show one of the following as proof of mailing:

(1) A legibly dated U.S. Postal Service postmark.

(2) A legible mail receipt with the date of mailing stamped by the U.S. Postal Service.

(3) A dated shipping label, invoice, or receipt from a commercial carrier.

(4) Any other proof of mailing acceptable to the Secretary.

(c) If an application is mailed through the U.S. Postal Service, the Secretary does not accept either of the following as proof of mailing:

(1) A private metered postmark.

(2) A mail receipt that is not dated by the U.S. Postal Service.

Notes: (1) The U.S. Postal Service does not uniformly provide a dated postmark. Before relying on this method, an applicant should check with its local post office.

(2) The Application Control Center will mail a Grant Application Receipt Acknowledgement to each applicant. If an applicant fails to receive the notification of application receipt within 15 days from the date of mailing the application, the applicant should call the U.S. Department of Education Application Control Center at (202) 708–9494.

(3) The applicant *must* indicate on the envelope and—if not provided by the Department—in Item 10 of the Application for Federal Assistance (Standard Form 424) the CFDA number—and suffix letter, if any—of the competition under which the application is being submitted.

Application Instructions and Forms ⑩

To apply for an award under this program competition, your application must be organized in the following order and include the following five parts:

Application for Federal Assistance (Standard Form 424 (Rev. 4–88)).

Budget Information (ED Form No. 524).

Budget Narrative.

Program Narrative.

Additional Assurances and Certifications:

a. Assurances—Non-Construction Programs (Standard Form 424B).

b. Certification regarding Lobbying; Debarment, Suspension, and Other Responsibility Matters; and Drug-Free Workplace Requirements (ED 80–0013) and Instructions.

c. Certification regarding Debarment, Suspension, Ineligibility and Voluntary Exclusion: Lower Tier Covered Transactions (ED 80–0014, 9/90) and Instructions.

(Note: ED 80–0014 is intended for the use of grantees and should not be transmitted to the Department.)

d. Disclosure of Lobbying Activities (Standard Form LLL) (if applicable) and Instructions, and Disclosure of Lobbying Activities Continuation Sheet (Standard Form LLL–A).

All forms and instructions are included as Appendix A of this notice. Questions and answers pertaining to this program are included, as Appendix B, to assist potential applicants.

An applicant may submit information on a photostatic copy of the forms in Appendix A. However, each of the pertinent documents must include an original ink signature. All applicants must submit ONE *original signed application*, including ink signatures on all forms and assurances and SIX *copies of the application*. Please mark each application as original or copy. Local or State agencies may choose to submit two copies with the original. No grant may be awarded unless a *complete* application form has been received.

Sᴍᴀᴘʟᴇ ᴏғ ᴛʜᴇ *Fᴇᴅᴇʀᴀʟ Rᴇɢɪsᴛᴇʀ (continued)*

EXHIBIT 9.4

Federal Register / Vol. 59, No. 146 / Monday, August 1, 1994 / Notices

⑪ FOR FURTHER INFORMATION CONTACT:
Pariece M. Wilkins, U.S. Department of
Education, 400 Maryland Avenue, S.W.
(Room 4512—MES), Washington, D.C.
20202–7242. Telephone (202) 205–9673.
Individuals who use a
telecommunication device for the deaf
(TDD) may call the Federal Information
Relay Service (FIRS) at 1–800–877–8339
between 8 a.m. and 8 p.m., Eastern time,
Monday through Friday.

Information about the Department's
funding opportunities, including copies
of application notices for discretionary
grant competitions, can be viewed on
the Department's electronic bulletin
board (ED Board), telephone (202) 260–
9950; or on the Internet Gopher Server
at GOPHER.ED.GOV (under
Announcements, Bulletins, and Press
Releases). However, the official
application notice for a discretionary

grant competition is the notice
published in the **Federal Register**.

Program authority: 20 U.S.C. 2420.
Dated: May 18, 1994.
Augusta S. Kappner,
*Assistant Secretary, Office of Vocational and
Adult Education.*
Appendix A
BILLING CODE 4000–01–M

SAMPLE OF THE *FEDERAL REGISTER* (continued)

EXHIBIT 9.4

- Deadline for Transmittal of Applications—While this application is due in six weeks, it is not uncommon for deadlines to be four to six months from the date the information is presented in the *Federal Register.*
- Deadline for Intergovernmental Review—See number 8.
- Available Funds—Total amount to be granted for the first 12 months.
- Estimated Range of Awards—Although this information is useful as a general guide, you really need to know what types of organizations and projects will fall in the high range and what types will fall in the low range.
- Estimated Average Size of Awards—Because the estimate here is not $400,000, it is likely that more awards will fall in the lower end of the range.
- Estimated Number of Awards
- Project Period—Number of possible months of funding.
- Applicable Regulations—Lists applicable regulations from the *Code of Federal Regulations* (CFR). These regulations are available from the Superintendent of Documents and may be included in the application package.

5. Invitational Priorities: Provides more insight into what may be favored and should be incorporated in your application.
6. Selection Criteria: Outlines how the proposals will be evaluated. Also states the number of points to be assigned to certain sections, which can give you a sense of areas of emphasis.
7. Additional Factors: Explains how grants will be distributed geographically and accounts for special needs applications, etc. This section can be useful for determining potential partners for consortia proposals and cooperative agreements.
8. Intergovernmental Review of Federal Programs: Outlines the process for ensuring that your application and proposed project are not

at odds with state and local government programs. Each state has what is known as a Single Point of Contact, and a list of these contacts is published in the *Federal Register* (May 3, 1994, in this exhibit). Applicants should contact the Single Points of Contact for the states in which they are proposing to perform activities and then follow the procedure established in each state. The deadline for this review is listed as November 15, 1994. Because the deadline for transmittal of applications, as stated in number 4, is September 16, grantseekers do not have to get the intergovernmental review done before submitting their application.

9. Instructions for Transmittal of Applications: Whatever process you choose, you must follow the rules exactly.
10. Application Instructions and Forms: Lists the official forms that must be used in your final application. These forms are usually included in the application package when it becomes available, but they are standard forms, so you can take them from another package to get a jump start on the process.
11. For Further Information Contact: Is valuable because the person listed may be different from the one listed in the *CFDA*. This section also includes information on access through any electronic bulletin boards and the Internet Gopher server.

The *Federal Register* is also available in an electronic format for those who want to avoid having to store 10 linear feet of it each year! However, with a resource as voluminous as the *Federal Register*, it could get expensive to use an online system that is accessed by telephone. Therefore, the *Federal Register* is also offered in a CD-ROM format. The user loads the discs and searches for the rules relating to chosen grant programs without having to worry about a per-minute charge. The electronic CD-ROM versions allow for fast and easy searching by agency, title fields, and key words, and provide tables of contents and summaries of the last six months of rules and regulations.

Compact Disc Federal Register (CD/FR)

CD/FR is a CD-ROM version of the *Federal Register* produced by Counterpoint Publishing and has been designed for frequent and heavy users of the *Federal Register*. For an annual fee of $1,950, users are provided with a new disc every week, a user's manual, newsletters, telephone support, and all software upgrades. For more information, contact Counterpoint Publishing, P.O. Box 928, 84 Sherman Street, Wellesley, MA 02181, (617) 547-4515, fax (617) 547-9064.

KR Information OnDisc: Federal Register

Knight-Ridder Information Services also provides a CD-ROM version of the *Federal Register* entitled *KR Information OnDisc: Federal Register*. It is difficult to compare this system to *CD/FR*, and your choice of CD-ROM may be based on whether your organization is currently a subscriber to other Knight-Ridder searching services. The price for this service at publication was $750 annually, plus an additional $750 for a basic Local Area Network (LAN) subscription. For more information contact Knight-Ridder Information Services, 3460 Hillview Avenue, Palo Alto, CA 94304, (800) 334-2564 or (415) 858-3785.

Other Publications

Federal granting agencies may choose to use their own vehicle for disseminating grant-related information instead of the *Federal Register*. For example, the National Institutes of Health (NIH) offer the *NIH Guide*. This is a free newsletter that provides the same basic information as the *Federal Register* but allows the grantseeker to avoid all the nongrant-related information that is in the *Federal Register*. The National Science Foundation (NSF) offers the *National Science Foundation Bulletin* free to prospective grantseekers. This publication, which is similar in function to the *NIH Guide*, includes announcements of NSF grants activities and provides a mechanism for feedback. The proactive grantseeker can use these tools to develop insight into the hidden agendas of federal grantors and to maintain a critical lead time for developing proposal ideas.

The *United States Government Manual* is one particularly good source of information on the activities, functions, organization, and principal officials of the agencies of the legislative, judicial, and executive branches. Published by the Office of the Federal Register, National Archives and Records Administration, the manual's "Sources of Information" section provides addresses and telephone numbers for obtaining specifics on grants and is helpful for those interested in determining where to go and whom to see (see list of resources).

In addition to government publications such as these, several for-profit companies provide a variety of grant aids to help grantseekers understand where government granting programs fit in the federal bureaucracy and to provide them with names and telephone numbers.

If your requests are not met by program officials for items such as lists of grantees and reviewers, refer to the *Federal Yellow Book*, published by Monitor Publishing Company (call (202) 347-7757). This resource provides you with several offices, names, and telephone numbers to access program information under the Freedom of Information Act.

Commerce Business Daily (CBD)

Exhibit 9.5 shows sample pages of *Commerce Business Daily*. This publication provides information regarding government procurement through contracts. Published daily Monday through Friday, CBD lists all available contracts in excess of $25,000. Approximately 4,000 to 5,000 separate contracting offices and countless grant programs advertise over $200 billion in government contracts each year. The 60,000 successful bidders are listed in the back section of each issue.

Many successful nonprofit organizations have used the list of successful bidders to develop subcontracts and form consortia. Through subcontracts and consortia, these organizations are able to build a track record and gain familiarity with both the contracts process and federal contract offices. The CBD also advertises notices of meetings that assist bidders in developing insight into upcoming contracts.

For more information on the CBD, contact Norman Meltzer, *Commerce Business Daily*, Commerce Department, Washington, DC 20230, (202) 482-0732. To purchase the CBD, contact Superintendent of Documents, Washington, DC 20402-9238, (202) 783-3238. Each congressional district has at least two libraries designated as federal depositories that receive the CBD daily at no charge.

Accessing the information you need to locate available government funding is not difficult or expensive. While this chapter provides sufficient detail to satisfy the computer-literate grantseeker, such skills and equipment are not prerequisites for accessing information.

Whether you use the Internet, a commercial database, or a hard copy of the *Catalog of Federal Domestic Assistance*, the key to locating federal grant funds and to commanding the respect of the bureaucrats you will interact with in your quest for grants is to do your homework and learn all you can about each program you are thinking about approaching.

TUESDAY
August 2, 1994

COMMERCE

Issue No. PSA-1150

A daily list of U.S. Government procurement invitations, contract awards, subcontracting leads, sales of surplus property and foreign business opportunities

BUSINESS DAILY

U.S. GOVERNMENT PROCUREMENTS

The Commerce Business Daily publishes, for Federal agencies, synopses of proposed contract actions that exceed $25,000 in value.

Services

A Research and Development

US Army Research Laboratory, Operations Directorate, ATTN: AMSRL-OP-PR-FM(BON), Fort Monmouth, New Jersey 07703-5601
A -- A--ARL BROAD AGENCY ANNOUNCEMENT PART I OF II USARL, ELECTRONICS AND POWER SOURCES DIRECTORATE FY 94 SINGLE TOPIC BROAD AGENCY ANNOUNCEMENT, ENTITLED "COMPACT HIGH-VOLGATE STACKED-BLUMLEIN MODULATOR" This Single Topic Broad Agency Announcement is issued under the Provisions of paragraph 6.102(d)(2) of the Federal Acquisition Regulation (FAR) which provides for the competitive selection of basic research proposals. Proposals submitted in response to this BAA that are selected for award are considered to be the result of Full and Open competition and are in full compliance with the Provisions of Public Law 98-369, "The Competition in Contracting Act of 1984". Questions concerning contractual, cost or pricing proposal format matters may be directed to Karen A. Bonafide, Contract Specialist at (908)544-3914. Individuals with questions on technical matters may contact the technical representative Lawrence E. Kingsley at (908)544-2895. CLOSING DATE: PROPOSALS ARE DUE BY 26 AUG 94. The U.S. Army Research Laboratory, Electronics and Power Sources Directorate is interested in receiving proposals in support of the research and development of high-power, high-voltage modulators for high-power microwave applications. Existing sources of multi-MW electrical pulses either do not have sufficient switching speed or repetition rate, or are of cumbersome construction difficult to imagine in a tactical environment, so new concepts and techniques are sought leading to more practical high-voltage modulators. The studies and all hardware produced through this effort are intended to demonstrate the feasibility in terms of cost, size, and performance of stacked-Blumein-based modulators. What is envisioned is a modulator utilizing a stacked-Blumlein design producing 150 kV pulses of 1-2 kA at 1-5 kHz (burst mode) with an input charge voltage no greater than 20 kV. The output impedance of the modulator is to be 70-100 Ohms. Solid-state, semiconductor switching and scalability to higher voltages is highly desirable. A modulator utilizing a single switching assembly would be of particular interest. Three ranges of pulse width and pulse rise time are of interest, a long-pulse (600 ns width, 10-100 ns rise time) regime; and intermediate-pulse (10 nsec width; 300 ps rise time) regime; and a short-pulse (1 ns width, 200 ps rise time) regime. The Basic Task of this effort is a feasibility study to research and identify stacked-Blumlein configurations and switch technologies which show likelihood of successful application to compact modulators with the aforementioned operating parameters. Based on the results of the Basic Task, further tasks (Options) may be

Reader's Guide

The **Reader's Guide** is published in every Monday edition of the Commerce Business Daily (CBD). The Reader's Guide includes the CBD's Numbered Notes, an index of the Classification Codes and other information. If the Monday edition of the CBD is not printed because of a holiday, the Reader's Guide will appear in the next day's issue.

exercised at the discretion of the Government. The first Option would be to produce conceptual designs for each of a long-pulse, intermediate-pulse, and short-pulse modulator. At least one of these designs must utilize a single switching assembly. The second Option would be for the fabrication of laboratory prototypes based on the conceptual designs. The third Option would be for fabrication of a compact, self-contained modulator for delivery to the Government for evaluation. The operating parameters of the laboratory-scale and deliverable modulator will be determined by mutual agreement between the Government and the contractor. For the purposes of estimating, the Government anticipates a program consisting of a six-month Basic Task, the feasibility study, which would be followed by several Options for the preparation of detailed modulator designs and fabrication of the laboratory and deliverable modulators. Period of performance is expected to range from 6 to 36 months including all Options. TYPE OF CONTRACT: COST PLUS FIXED FEE General Information: This announcement is an expression of interest only and does not commit the Government to make any award or to pay for any response preparation costs. Pursuant to the requirements of FAR 52.219-9, if the total amount of the proposal exceeds $500,000, offeror(s) selected for award will be required at that time to submit a Subcontracting Plan for Small Business and Small Socially and Economically Disadvantaged Business Concerns. PROPOSAL INSTRUCTIONS: Because both the technical and cost aspects of an offeror's submission will be evaluated at the same time. It is desirable that one volume containing all information be submitted. One original and four copies of the proposal are to be submitted directly to USARL, Operations Directorate, ATTN: AMSRL-OP-PR-FM(BON), Ft. Monmouth, NJ, 07703-5601. TECHNICAL PROPOSAL: The technical proposal shall include: 1)Table of Contents; 2) A description of the technical and or design approach to meet the topic requirements; 3) A Statement of Work (SOW) detailing the technical tasks proposed to be accomplished under the effort and the schedule for performance of those tasks; 4) description of available equipment, data, and facilities; 5) methodology, techniques, and approach to technology transfer for developments under this program; 6) identify any technical data proposed to be delivered with less than unlimited rights in the technical proposal. Unless otherwise stated in the proposal, all data delivered to the Government shall be with unlimited rights. 7) the organization structure and roles/qualifications of each team member and brief resumes of personnel; 8) breakout of materials including the types and quantities. If subcontracting is anticipated, provide name, qualifications, and level of effort to be subcontracted. COST PROPOSAL: The cost proposal shall be prepared in general in accordance with FAR 15.804-6 and shall include a Standard Form 1411, Contracting Pricing Proposal Cover Sheet with all supporting data in order to allow for a complete review by the Government. When cost of money is being proposed, the offeror is required to complete a DD Form 1861. The breakdown of cost data shall include all costs expected to be incurred under the contract. All details, broken down by cost element, are to be prepared for each major task along with supporting rationale. All cost details shall be broken down to coincide with the offeror's accounting periods as related to the specific period of performance as indicated in the milestone chart. The cost proposal shall include all supporting information including, but not limited to: breakdown of labor hours by category, materials (vendor quotes or method of establishing cost), travel, direct and indirect costs. Prime contractors are responsible for insuring that all proposed contractors are responsible for insuring that all proposed subcontracts are in excess of $100,000 are supported by an executed SF 1411. (0210)

US Army Research Laboratory, Operations Directorate, ATTN: AMSRL-OP-PR-FM(BON), Fort Monmouth, New Jersey 07703-5601
A -- A--ARL BROAD AGENCY ANNOUNCEMENT PART II OF II USARL, ELECTRONICS AND POWER SOURCES DIRECTORATE FY 94 SINGLE TOPIC BROAD AGENCY ANNOUNCEMENT, ENTITLED "COMPACT HIGH-VOLTAGE STACKED-BLUMLEIN MODULATOR" EVALUATION CRITERIA: All proposals received will be evaluated in accordance with the following criteria listed in order of importance: A) New and Creative Solutions to the technical issues presented in the BAA; B) the feasibility of the approach and technical objectives; C) understanding of the technical matters being presented for consideration; D) ability to implement the proposed approach as demonstrated by adequate detailed analysis and supported by

specific accomplishments in the technical field to be studied; E) the availability of qualified personnel with the requisite expertise to accomplish the tasks as proposed; F) record of past performance; G) cost and cost realism and, H) the availability of unlimited rights in technical data and/or computer software. The purpose of the evaluation will be to determine the relative merit of the technical approach proposed in response to this BAA. Evaluation and selection of proposal(s) for award will be made to those offerors whose proposal is considered most advantageous to the Government, price and other factors considered; (i.e.; an independent Government assessment of the probability of success of the proposed approach and the availability of funding). Responses must provide new or unique concepts, ideas or approaches in order to qualify for evaluation and consideration for award. The Government reserves the right to select for award any, all, part or none of the responses received. OTHER TERMS AND CONDITIONS: Proposals are to address the following business aspects of the program. 1) Plan for how the results of the program will be made available to all DoD contractors involved in the development of the applicable military systems; 2) Plan for establishment of a technology base that will ensure affordable, economically secure sourcing of the technology for military applications; 3) Plan for ensuring that future applications of the R&D results achieved under the program will allow for a globally competitive capability without undue dependency on foreign sources; 4) Plan for technology insertion into military systems and describe the mechanism that will provide for the insertion. Upon completion of negotiations and agreement on contract price, a Certificate of Current Cost or Pricing Data pursuant to FAR 15.804-4 shall be submitted by the offeror if required

Content

SUBSCRIPTION INFORMATION

$324.00 a year (First Class mailing), $275.00 a year (Second Class mailing). 6 Month Trial Subscription: $162.00 (First Class), $137.50 (Second Class). Foreign Rate: $343.75 a year - $171.90 six months, plus Air Mail rates. Two year subscription available at above yearly rates

To Order. Send remittance with full mailing address to the Superintendent of Documents, Government Printing Office, Washington, DC 20402-9371, Tel. 202/783-3238 or fax 202/512-2233. Purchase order must be accompanied by payment. Make check payable to Superintendent of Documents. Visa or Master Card are acceptable. Allow approximately 6 weeks for delivery of first issue.

Service problems. Call Superintendent of Documents, Government Printing Office, Washington, DC, Tel. 202/512-2303 or fax 202/512-2168.

Expiration. Subscriptions expire one year from the date of the first issue. One expiration notice is mailed about 90 days before expiration date.

Address Changes. Send to Superintendent of Documents, Government Printing Office, Washington, DC 20402-9373, with entire mailing label from last issue received.

SAMPLE OF THE COMMERCE BUSINESS DAILY

EXHIBIT 9.5

Page 2 COMMERCE BUSINESS DAILY Issue No. PSA-1150; Tuesday, August 2, 1994

by FAR 15.804-2. If exemption from the cost or pricing data requirements is claimed; an SF 1412 is required to be submitted. In addition, any offeror who is required to submit and certify cost or pricing data shall submit or procure the submission of accurate, current and complete cost or pricing data from his prospective subcontractors in accordance with the requirements of FAR 15.806. The Government anticipates that any contract resulting from this BAA will be funded on an incremental basis as provided for under FAR 52.232-22 "Limitation of Funds." In view of this and to allow the Government adequate time for budgetary planning, offerors shall submit a monthly funding Expenditure and Termination Liability Profile covering the total period of performance. The Expenditure and Termination Liability Profile should contain a breakout of projected funding requirements which are commensurate with the proposed level of effort, technical approach and milestones chart. The contractor will be required to submit a revised expenditure profile upon completion of negotiations. RESTRICTIVE MARKINGS ON PROPOSALS: Notwithstanding Army policy, if information contained in the proposal is in the public domain or can not be protected under law as a trade secret (e.g., a patent application), the Army will not accept liability for failure to safeguard against open disclosure. If a responder wishes to restrict the proposal, the responder offeror should mark the title page with the following legend: This data shall not be disclosed outside the Government and shall not be duplicated, used or disclosed in whole or in part for any purpose other than to evaluate the proposal; provided that if a contract is awarded to this BAA responder as a result of or in connection with the submission of this data, the Government shall have the right to duplicate, use or disclose the data to the extent provided in the contract. This restriction does not limit the Government's right to use information contained in the data if it is obtained from another source without restriction. The data subject to this restriction is contained on page---------." REPORTS AND OTHER REQUIREMENTS: As a minimum, all offerors will be required to submit a quarterly technical status report,a monthly financial report, a final report, and other deliverables as appropriate. The offeror will be required to arrange and hold quarterly meetings at the offerors site with Government personnel to review technical progress. It is anticipated that the offeror will report technical results in at least one archival publication during the contract performance period. In addition to travel mandated solely by the proposed work, it is anticipated that travel to attend either the Power Modulator Symposium or the IEEE Pulsed Power Conference will be required. It is anticipated that the offeror will present a technical paper annually at one of the aforementioned conferences. For the purpose of estimating, proposers should include: pricing for at least (1) trip each year for conference presentations; and pricing for archival paper preparation and publication charges . REPRESENTATIONS AND CERTIFICATIONS: Offerors to complete the following required representations and certifications, and submit them as part of the proposal: 52.204-3 Taxpayer Identification (SEP 89); 52.204-4 Contractor Establishment Code (AUG 89); 52.209-5 Certification Regarding Debarment, Suspension, Proposed Debarment, and Other Responsibility Matters (MAY 89); 52.215-6 Type of Business Organization (JUL 87); 52.215-11 Authorized Negotiators (APR 84); 52.215-20 Place of Performance (APR 84); 52.219-1 Small Business Concern Representation (JAN 91); 52.219-2 Small Disadvantaged Business Concern Representation (FEB 90); and 52.219-3 Women-Owned Small Business Representation (APR 84). Short Form Research Contract Forms DD 2222, 2222-1 and 2222-2 (MAY 89) - Offerors eligible to utilize these forms are to submit all information necessary to process an award pursuant to the terms and conditions set forth in Subpart 35.70 of the Defense FAR Supplement. Other additional certifications will be required at time of award. (0210)

Bureau of the Census, Procurement Office, Room 1541, FB#3, Washington, (Suitland, MD) DC 20233

A -- ELECTRONIC IMAGE FORMS PROCESSING SOFTWARE POC Frances I. Toole, 301-763-4560 The Bureau of the Census (BOC) is performing research and development (R&D) to investigate alternative data capture technologies for use in the Year 2000 Decennial Census. Requested is information from vendors who have electronic image forms processing software capable of performing highly accurate and efficient management and manipulation of forms images in a large volume production environment. Specifically, the BOC is interested in commercial products that can perform the following functions on images from respondent-friendly questionnaires. Respondent-friendly questionnaires are forms that are designed to maximize responses from the public rather than forms designed to facilitate data capture through image processing: 1) index and store images sent from a digital scanner; retrieve and serve images from a data base to other image processing tasks; 2) preprocess images into "clips" or "snippets" to serve to Optical Mark Recognition (OMR), Optical Character Recognition (OCR), and keying functions; 3) serve batches of images to keying workstations for key entry operations maintaining a steady state workflow to available key operators; 4) serve image files to an archival storage medium with full retrieval capability into an image database server; 5) indexed searches and retrieval of full form images, or batches of images, to a workstation and print on demand; 6) Optical Character Recognition (OCR) of numeric handwritten fields, such as date of birth and age; and handwritten (printed or script) alphabetic fields such as full name, race, household relationship, and so forth; 7) scoring systems to measure recognition confidence levels and rejection rates. As part of the R&D program mentioned above, the information gathered from this RFI will be used to determine the extent to which commercially-available technology can be used in a Census environment. Interested vendors should submit their capabilities and any relative information within thirty (30) days from publish date of this notice to the above address and reference RFI-94-005. (0210)

The **Commerce Business Daily** (USPS 966-360) is published daily, except Saturdays, Sundays and holidays, for $324.00 a year (1st Class mailing) or $275.00 a year (2nd Class mailing) by the U.S. Government Printing Office, Washington, DC 20402. Second Class postage paid at Washington, DC and additional mailing offices. POSTMASTER: Send address changes to Superintendent of Documents, U.S. Government Printing Office, Washington, DC 20402-9373, with entire mailing label from last issue received.

AFDTC/PKZA, 205 West D Avenue, Suite 428, Eglin AFB FL 32542-6864

A -- CAPTIVE FLIGHT TEST OF BOEING SEEKER SENSOR SYSTEM POC Lafayette Turner, Contract Specialist, (904) 882-3377. The Air Force Development Test Center, Joint Munitions Test and Evaluation Program Office (also known as CHICKEN LITTLE), intends to let a contract for the captive flight test of a unique seeker/sensor system in support of the Signature Measurement Program (SMP). It is contemplated that the sole source contract will be awarded to The Boeing Co. The CHICKEN LITTLE (CL) program office will be functioning as the executive test agent for the Program manager for Survivability Systems to conduct test and evaluation activities related to their SMP. For this activity, CL will require access to a 35 Ghz, circular polarized, real-beam millimeter wave radar seeker which can function as a surrogate for a number of near-term and perceived threat seekers. The seeker system must be capable of executing multiple detection algorithms in real-time, ranging from simple to highly sophisticated polarimatic algorithms. These capabilities are required to properly emulate the required level of sophistication of the various threat seekers. Due to the nature of the desired target set, the seeker must also be capable of providing highly accurate beam-pointing information to allow for determination of target-to-clutter ratio in the cases of non-target detection. This capability must be available to CL in the March-June 1995 timeframe. The Boeing seeker system is the only known source which can satisfy all of these requirements, in the required timeframe. A SECRET security restriction applies and must be satisfied at the time of award. Responses to this notice of contract action must fully document their ability to satisfy all contractual requirements and provide the entire range of services anticipated under this contract. (0210)

Department of the Navy, Carderock Division Headquarters, Naval Surface Warfare Center, Code 3322: Lisa A. Holland, Bethesda, MD 20084-5000

A -- ENGINEERING SERVICES TO PROVIDE ANALYTICAL AND ENGINEERING SUPPORT IN HYDRODYNAMIC MODEL/INSTRUMENTATION DESIGN, CONSTRUCTION, TESTING, AND MAINTENANCE AND REPAIR OF EQUIPMENT SOL N00167-94-R-0097 DUE 091294 POC Lisa Holland (301)227-1100 or Catherine Rowe, Contracting Officer. The Carderock Division, Naval Surface Warfare Center intends to award a sole source contract to Chicago Bridge and Iron Technical Services Company, Plainfield, IL, to obtain engineering services for the design and fabrication of captive and radio controlled models with specialized instrumentation to measure highly nonlinear hydrodynamic forces and moments during submarine maneuvers. It is anticipated that the contract for the services described shall be an indefinite delivery indefinite quantity type contract, effective for a period of three years from the date of award. The basis for a sole source is by the authouity of 10 U.S.C. 2304(c)(1), only one responsible source, and FAR 6.302-1, no other supplies or services will satisfy agency requirements. The need to procure these services from Chicago Bridge and Iron Technical Services Company is based on their expertise in Radio Controlled Model (RCM) construction and operations that no other contractor possesses. It is expected that a solicitation shall be issued on or about 12 September 1994, with the closing date thirty (30) days thereafter. See note 22. (0210)

Defense Nuclear Agency, 6801 Telegraph Road, Alexandria, VA 22310- 3398

A -- MASTER AGREEMENT FOR OPERATIONAL ASSESMENTS SOL DNA001-94-R-0100 DUE 090694 POC Michael Jackson, Negotiator, (703) 325-9211, Edward Archer, Contracting Officer, (703) 325-5028. The Defense Nuclear Agency (DNA) intends to issue an unrestricted solicitation for a Master Agreement for Operational Assessments. Evaluation of proposals will be based on technical merit. It is anticipated that 3 Master Agreements will be issued. Individual tasks, deliverables, period of performance, and specific evaluation factors will be identified by Delivery Order (DO). Each DO will be competed among all contractors holding a Master Agreement. Contractor personnel will require a DoD security clearance of TOP SECRET. Contemplated term of the Master Agreement is 24 months. Requests for copies of the solicitation must be in writing, no telephone requests will be accepted. Faxed requests are acceptable and should be addressed to the attention of Michael Jackson/AM-1 and faxed to (703) 325-2955. Information on DNA solicitations, already released, can be obtained by calling the DNA Hotline at (703) 325-1173. Reference Synopsis No. 94-115 (0210)

Defense Nuclear Agency, 6801 Telegraph Road, Alexandria, VA 22310- 3398

A -- MASTER AGREEMENT FOR NUCLEAR SURVIVABILITY SOL DNA001-94-R-0101 DUE 090694 POC Michael Jackson, Negotiator, (703) 325-9211, Edward Archer, Contracting Officer, (703) 325-5028. The Defense Nuclear Agency (DNA) intends to issue an unrestricted solicitation for a Master Agreement for Nuclear Survivability. Evaluation of proposals will be based on technical merit. It is anticipated that 3 Master Agreements will be issued. Individual tasks, deliverables, period of performance and specific evaluation factors will be identified by Delivery Order (DO). Each DO will be competed among all contractors holding a Master Agreement. Contractor personnel will require a DOD security clearance of TOP SECRET. Contemplated term of the Master Agreement is 24 months. Requests for copies of the solicitation must be in writing, no telephone requests will be accepted. Faxed requests are acceptable and should be addressed to the attention of Michael Jackson/AM-1 and faxed to (703) 325-2955. Information on DNA solicitations, already released, can be obtained by calling the DNA Hotline at (703) 325-1173. Reference Synopsis No. 94-116 (0210)

U.S. Army Missile Command, Research, Development, and Engineering Center, RDEC Procurement Office, R&D Contracts Division, Redstone Arsenal, AL 35898-5275

A -- ADVANCED MISSILE MATERIAL SCIENCE AND ENGINEERING SOL DAAH01-94-R-R022 DUE 091594 POC (RDPC) Gale Uselton, Contract Specialist, AMSMI-RD-PC-HB, (205) 876-1647, Barbara K. Dobbins, Contracting Officer. Synopsis No. 167-94. This acquisition is sole source to Alabama A&M University for a cost-reimbursement-no-fee type contract with a nonprofit educational institution. The authority for other than full and open competition is 10 U.S.C. 2304(c)(3) as implemented by FAR 6.302-3. Description of supplies and services: This effort is to conduct research and development activities both in advanced materials engineering and processing and in manufacturing science and technology. The purpose is to develop and implement new design and manufacturing technologies required to assure availability and affordability of new or improved missile systems, subsystems, and/or components. See Numbered Note(s): 22. (0210)

A Research and Development - Potential Sources Sought

U.S. Army Space And Strategic Defense Command, ATTN: CSSD-CM-TS, P.O. Box 1500, Huntsville, AL 35807-3801

A -- KINETIC ENERGY WEAPONS (KEW) DIGITAL EMULATION CENTER (KDEC) POC Robbie Phifer, Contract Specialist/Beverly L. Fulton, Contracting Officer, (205) 955-1187. Sources are sought for this effort which will involve performing software maintenance and development for a collection of Ada-based missile interceptor models and simulations. As part of the maintenance effort, the contractor shall migrate the various character-based user interfaces into a single Motif user interface, consisting of one or two computer software configuration items (CSCI). The current software design contains multiple CSCIs hosted separately on OpenVMS (Alpha) and SunOS (SPARC) platforms. Development activities are anticipated to be task assignment driven. The use of GNU Ada 9x and other GNU tools shall be preferred for development and maintenance activities. Continued adherence with the Software Engineering Institute's (SEI) Object Connection Architecture, currently implemented in one of the system's CSCIs, during maintenance and development activities shall be a part of this effort. Through technical directives, the contractor shall coordinate and assist other government programs and projects with analysis activities derived from the use of this simulation tool. The contractor shall provide training and user support. The contractor shall propose and manage the program using system engineering management planning techniques. Optional yearly contract monitoring using the SEI software maturity model, level 2, shall be a part of this effort. Formal use of the SEI software maturity model for the purposes of source selection is not part of this effort. Source code will be released with the request for proposal on CDROM or magnetic tape. A cost plus fixed fee level of effort, five-year contract is anticipated. This acquisition is being considered for a competitive 8(a) effort. Interested firms should submit written qualifications/capabilities to CSSD-CM-TS/Robbie Phifer within fifteen days from the publication date of this notice. It is anticipated that SIC Code 8731 with a size standard of 1000 employees will apply. It is anticipated that allied participation will be allowed at the subcontractor level. This synopsis is an advance notice for information and planning purposes only and is not a formal solicitation for proposals. Responsibility lies with prime contract offerors to ensure that both they and their subcontractors are not restricted from participating in this proposed acquisition due to either (i) an OCI clause in any U.S. Army Space and Strategic Defense Command (USASSDC) contract or (ii) work performed under any Government contract that would result in a potential conflict as set forth in FAR 9.5. Any offeror who has signed or any of whose proposed subcontractors have signed a contract with an OCI agreement as either a prime contractor or subcontractor under any government contract shall submit a written request to this office to obtain approval to participate in this acquisition (if the the technology area is the same as or is closely related to the subject of this effort). This request from offerors with an OCI restricton under a USASSDC prime contract or under a subcontract to a USASSDC prime contract shall provide (i) a copy of the prime contract or subcontract OCI clause and (ii) a copy of each scope of work (SOW) or task asssignment of the effort the offeror is performing or has performed. Four copies plus a copy for each office that has a SOW/task assignment of the above data shall be provided for review. A technical government point of contact, including name and office symbol, shall be provided for each SOW/tasks assignment submitted for review. Any request pursuant to this shall be submitted to arrive at this office not later than ten (10) calendar days from the date of issuance of the solicitation. See Numbered Note(s): 25. (0210)

Aeronautical Systems Center (ASC/YHS), 102 West D Aveune Suite 168, Eglin AFB FL 32542-6807

A -- RADIO FREQUENCY (RF) PAYLOAD FOR AERIAL DECOY APPLICATION DUE 100594 POC For contracting information, contact Ms Charlotte Puthoff, (904) 882- 5745. For technical matters, contact Rick Phillips, (ASC/YHSE), (904) 882-4808/4809. The Lethal SEAD Division, Conventional Munitions System Program Office, as the lead for the Decoy Integrated Product Team (IPT), plans to contract for a Radio Frequency (RF) package which is capable of being integrated as a payload into a Miniature Air-Launched Decoy (MALD) air vehicle. The RF package should be suitable for use as an Air Defense Unit (ADU) threat environment stimulant. When integrated into the air vehicle, the RF payload should be capable of stimulating the threat environment for targeting by manned destructive SEAD (MDS) forces. At this time, the detailed performance requirements for the RF package are not known. In anticipation of an FY 96 contract to integrate the RF package into 24 flight-worthy vehicles, the Decoy IPT is requesting information from industry concerning existing or near term capability in this technology arena. Respondents will be provided the results of on-going studies which are intended to determine the system level performance requirements for the RF package. (0210)

SAMPLE OF THE *COMMERCE BUSINESS DAILY (continued)*

EXHIBIT 9.5

CHAPTER

● ● ● ● ● ● ● ● ●

How to Contact Government Funding Sources

The importance of pre-proposal contact with government funding sources cannot be overemphasized. In a study of 10,000 federal proposals, the only variable that was statistically significant in separating the funded and rejected proposals was pre-proposal contact with the funding source.

Chances for success increase an estimated threefold when contact with the funding source takes place before the proposal is written. Up to this point in the book, we have not discussed the writing of the proposal; instead, we have focused on efforts to get ready to seek support for your project. To write a winning proposal, you must know more about the funding source and its hidden agenda. Who will read your application? What will appeal to them? What should you avoid saying? To find the answers to these questions, contact the funding source by letter, by phone, and, when possible, in person.

WHEN TO MAKE PRE-PROPOSAL CONTACT

The timing of contact is critical. Each of the 1,000-plus federal programs has its own time frame and sequence of events. Review the diagram of the federal grants clock whenever you need to determine where a particular federal agency or program is in the grants process (see figure 10.1).

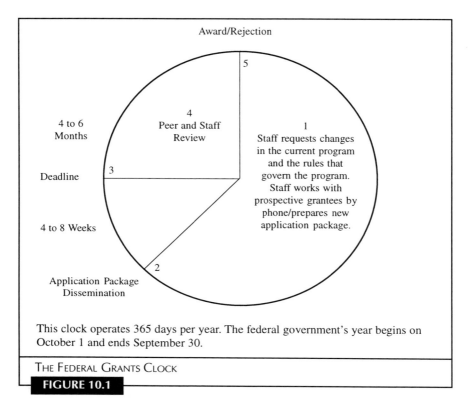

Award/Rejection

4

5

4 to 6
Months

Peer and Staff
Review

1
Staff requests changes
in the current program
and the rules that
govern the program.
Staff works with
prospective grantees by
phone/prepares new
application package.

Deadline   3

4 to 8 Weeks

2

Application Package
Dissemination

This clock operates 365 days per year. The federal government's year begins on
October 1 and ends September 30.

THE FEDERAL GRANTS CLOCK

FIGURE 10.1

The federal grants clock can be thought of as a five-step cycle or process.

1. The first step involves the dissemination of and comment on the rules
   and regulations governing the program. Federal regulations man-
   date that the rules governing each program be reviewed, and comments are encouraged from any interested party. The comments are
   published, the final rules are printed, and the announcements of deadlines are made in such publications as the *Federal Register, NIH
   Guide,* and *National Science Foundation Bulletin.*
2. The federal program officer then develops the actual application package and mails it to prospective grantees who have requested it. This
   package is referred to as the Request for Proposal (RFP) or the Request for Application (RFA).
3. The deadline for submission occurs.
4. Once proposals are submitted, they are sent to selected peer reviewers for evaluation. The reviewers must follow the agency's evaluation system and distribute points to each proposal according to the
   published guidelines.

5. The notices of award and rejection are made and the cycle starts again.

Establishing pre-proposal contact for the next funding cycle is most productive when initiated after the notices of award or rejection have been given (step 5) for the previous cycle and before the application packages are sent out (step 2) in the new cycle. Use the techniques outlined in this chapter to maximize the benefits of pre-proposal contact and gain the insight you will need to prepare a grant-winning proposal.

GETTING THE MOST FROM PAST GRANTEES

Use the sample letter in exhibit 10.1 to request a list of past grantees, guidelines, and an application package when it becomes available. Enclose a return label or self-addressed stamped envelope with your letter for the funding source's convenience.

You may have to request the list of past grantees again by phoning the funding source. Access to this list and the valuable information it provides is

---

Date

Name
Title
Address

Dear [Contact Person]:

I am interested in receiving information on [CFDA # Program Title]. I am particularly interested in receiving application forms, program guidelines, and any materials you think would be helpful.

In order to increase my understanding of your program, I am also requesting a list of last year's grant recipients. I have enclosed a label to assist you in forwarding the requested items. Thank you.

Sincerely,

Name/Title
Phone Number

SAMPLE LETTER TO A FEDERAL AGENCY REQUESTING INFORMATION AND GUIDELINES

EXHIBIT 10.1

your right. Let the funding source know you are aware that you are entitled to this list under the Freedom of Information Act. If all else fails, you may be able to get this information from the public information office of the appropriate branch of government, or you can ask your congressperson to get the list for you. By law, federal bureaucrats have to respond to a congressperson's request. He or she *will* get the list. Be aware, though, that bureaucrats may react negatively to the intervention of elected officials.

Due to federal paperwork reduction guidelines, some agencies now require that grantseekers who desire both information on past grantees and an application send two separate request letters. Check with your selected grantor to determine whether you will automatically be placed on the mailing list to receive guidelines and an application or whether you need to make separate and continual requests.

With your list in hand, you are now ready to analyze your chances for success. Complete the federal funding source evaluation worksheet (exhibit 10.2) and analyze the information contained in the list of grantees. When this worksheet is completed, you will be able to approach the grantor with knowledge and insight into its granting program.

Contacting a Past Grantee

Successful grant recipients can be approached and will generally share helpful information with you. Grantees will generally feel flattered you called. They are usually not competing with you for funds because you will be seeking a first year of funding and they will be seeking a second year. Select a grantee to call. Tell the grantee how you got his or her name, congratulate him or her on the award, and then ask to speak to the director or person who worked on the proposal.

Select questions from the following list to ask the person who worked on the proposal, or ask any other questions that will help you learn about the funding source.

- Did you call or go to see the funding source before writing the proposal?
- Whom did you find most helpful on the funding source's staff?
- How did you use your advocates or congresspeople?
- Did the funding source review your idea or proposal before submission?
- Did you use consultants to help you on the proposal?
- Was there a hidden agenda to the program's guidelines?
- When did you begin the process of developing your application? When did you first contact the funding source?
- What materials did you find most helpful in developing your proposal?
- Did the funding source come to see you (site visit) before or after the proposal was awarded? Who came? What did they wear? How old were

1. Award Size

    •   What was the largest award granted? _____
        For what type of project? _____

    •   What was the smallest award granted? $ _____
        For what type of project? _____

    •   Based on last year's grantees, what would be your project's likely award size? $ ____

2. Grantor Type

    • What characteristics or similarities can be drawn from last year's list of grant
      recipients?

    •   What is the size or type of grantee organization?

    •   What are the geographic preferences or concentrations?

3. Project Director/Principle Investigator

    •   What title or degrees appear most frequently on the list of last year's recipients?

    •   Does there seem to be a relationship between award size and project director degree?

4. From the list of last year's grantees, select two to contact for more information. Select
    grantees that you may have a link with and/or organizations that you are familiar with.

5. Based on the information gathered in questions one through four, rate how well your
    proposal idea matches the prospective grantor's profile.

    _____ very well   _____ good   _____ fair   _____ not well

FEDERAL FUNDING SOURCE EVALUATION WORKSHEET

EXHIBIT 10.2

they? Would you characterize them as conservative, moderate, or lib-
eral? Did anything surprise you during their visit?
•   How close was your initial budget to the awarded amount? (You can
    check for honesty here by taking a look at the proposal when you visit
    the funding source. The Freedom of Information Act allows you to see
    any proposal funded by government money.)
•   Who on the funding source's staff negotiated the budget?
•   What would you do differently next time?

UNDERSTANDING THE PROPOSAL REVIEW PROCESS

To prepare the best possible proposal, you must know who will be reading it
and how it will be reviewed. Request a list of last year's reviewers in writing,
by phone, or in person. I suggest making a written request and then following
up with the other methods if necessary. Exhibit 10.3 provides a sample letter
you may use.

Date

Name
Title
Address

Dear _____:

I am presently developing a proposal under your _____ program. I would find it
very helpful if you could send me a list of last year's reviewers and information on the
makeup of this year's review committee.

The list of last year's reviewers and information on the composition of this year's
committee will help me prepare a quality proposal based upon the level, expertise, and
diversity of the reviewers.

I have enclosed a self-addressed stamped envelope for your convenience in responding
to this request. I will use the materials you send, and I thank you for your consideration in
providing them.

Sincerely,

Name
Title
Phone Number

SAMPLE LETTER TO A FEDERAL AGENCY FOR A LIST OF REVIEWERS

EXHIBIT 10.3

You want a list of last year's reviewers so you can write a proposal based
on their expertise, reading level, biases, etc. Once you have the list, you
can contact the reviewers to discuss the points they look for when reviewing
proposals.

Some federal programs use the same reviewers each year and may be reluctant to give you their names. If this is the case, tell the federal bureaucrat that
you would like to know at least the general background and credentials of the
reviewers so that you can prepare the best possible proposal by writing toward
their level. You would ultimately like to know the types of organizations the
reviewers come from, their titles and degrees, and, if possible, the selection
criteria for choosing them. This may be a good opportunity to make your
interest in becoming a reviewer known to the program officer. Whether the
reviewers meet in Washington, DC, or review proposals at home, you would
learn a great deal about the evaluation process and the grantor by being a
member of a peer review committee.

If the system that the reviewers must adhere to has been published in the
Federal Register or an agency publication, request a copy or the date of publi-

cation. Let the funding source know that you will be using a quality circle to perform a mock review of your proposal before submission and that you would like to mirror the actual review process as closely as possible.

Contacting a Past Reviewer

As you examine the list of reviewers, look for any links you could use in contacting them. If none is apparent, select any reviewer to call. When calling a past reviewer, explain that you understand he or she was a reviewer for the program you are interested in and that you would like to ask a few questions about his or her experience as a reviewer for that program. Select a few questions to ask from the following list, or make up your own.

- How did you get to be a reviewer?
- Did you review proposals at a funding source location or at home?
- What training or instruction did the funding source give you?
- Did you follow a point system? What system? How did you follow it?
- What were you told to look for?
- How would you write a proposal differently now that you have been a reviewer?
- What were the most common mistakes you saw?
- Did you meet other reviewers?
- How many proposals were you given to read?
- How much time did you have to read them?
- How did the funding source handle discrepancies in point assignments?
- What did the staff members of the funding source wear, say, and do during the review process?
- Did a staff review follow your review?

CALLING FEDERAL AND STATE FUNDING SOURCES

Calling public funding sources is an experience in itself. Initial research seldom yields the correct name and phone number of the best individual to handle your request, but at least it gives you a place to start. Once you have found a contact name and telephone number, call and ask who would be the best individual to help you. After several referrals, you should locate the office that administers the funds for the program you have uncovered in your research and the program officer. You could use the *United States Government Manual* or the *Federal Yellow Book* to track down the phone number of the office likely to handle the funds you are seeking.

After you have identified the program officer, the best approach is to go see him or her in person. If this is the approach you choose, use the techniques outlined in the following section on making an appointment with a public funding source official.

If you cannot visit the funding source, you should gather the same information over the phone that you would face-to-face. Since it may be difficult for the funding official to discuss your idea and approaches without seeing a written description of your project, ask whether you could mail or fax a one-page concept paper. Set up a time for a return call and ask the same types of questions you would ask if you were meeting in person.

Although it may be difficult for you to "read" what the funding source is really saying through voice inflection, you must at least try to uncover any hidden agenda so that you can meet the grantor's needs and increase your chances of success. Review the list of questions in the "Questions to Ask a Program Officer" section of this chapter.

Making an Appointment with a Public Funding Source Official

The objective of seeking an appointment is to get an interview with an administrator of the program. Start by sending a letter requesting an appointment. Exhibit 10.4 provides a sample letter you may use. You will not get a response to this letter. Its intent is to show that you mean business. Then follow the next few steps.

1. Call and ask for the program officer or information contact.
2. Get the secretary's name and ask when his or her boss can be reached. (Some federal employees are on flextime or come in and leave at odd hours to cope with the DC traffic.)
3. Call back. Try person-to-person, and, if that fails, ask the secretary whether anyone else can answer technical questions about the program. You may get an appointment with an individual whose job is to screen you from the boss, but this is still better than talking to yourself. As an alternative, try to get an advocate to help you set up an appointment, or try going in "cold" early in the week to set an appointment for later in the week. Do not be surprised if this results in an immediate appointment. Staff members may decide they would prefer to deal with you on the spot rather than later. Be careful using elected officials to make appointments for you or to accompany you on an appointment. Bureaucrats and politicians often do not get along well.
4. When you get the program person on the phone, introduce yourself and give a brief (10-word) description of your organization. Explain that
   - the need to deal with the specific problem your project addresses is extreme
   - your organization is uniquely suited to deal with this problem
   - you understand that the grantor's program deals with this need

---

Date

Name
Title
Address

Dear _____:

My research on your funding program indicates that a project we have developed would be appropriate for consideration by your agency for funding under _____.

I would appreciate 5 to 10 minutes of your time to discuss my project. Your insights, knowledge, and information on any grants that have been funded using a similar approach would be invaluable.

My travel plans call for me to be in your area on _____. I will phone to confirm the possibility of a brief meeting during that time to discuss this important proposal.

Sincerely,

Name
Title
Phone Number

SAMPLE LETTER TO A FEDERAL AGENCY REQUESTING AN APPOINTMENT

EXHIBIT 10.4

- you would like to make an appointment to talk about program priorities and your approach

When you get an appointment, stop and hang up. If an appointment is not possible, tell the program representative that you have some questions and ask about the possibility of arranging a 10-minute phone call for the future. If a callback is not possible, ask whether he or she could take the time to answer your questions now. Fill in any information you get (names, phone numbers, and so on) on the federal grants research form (see chapter 9, exhibit 9.1).

VISITING PUBLIC FUNDING SOURCES

The initial meeting is vital to getting the input you need to prepare a proposal that is tailored to the funding source. A visit also will provide you with the opportunity to update any information you have gathered on the funding source through your research.

The objective of this pre-proposal visit is to find out as much as possible about the funding source and how it perceives its role in the awarding of grants. Then you can use the newly acquired information to produce a proposal that reflects a sensitivity to the funding source's needs and perception of its mission. According to the theory of cognitive dissonance, the more the funding source perceives a grantseeker as different from what the funding source expects, the greater the problems with communication, agreement, and acceptance. We want the funder to love us, so we need to produce as little dissonance as possible by looking and talking as the funder "thinks" we should. If you do not know the funding source's expectations on dress, play it safe and read the *New Dress for Success* by John T. Molloy (New York: Warner Books, 1988).

Plan for Your Visit

When planning for a personal visit, remember that it is better to send two people than one, and that an advocate, advisory committee member, or graduate of your program has more credibility than a paid staff member. In deciding whom to send, try to match the age, interests, and other characteristics of your people with any information you have on the funding official. Before the visit, role-play your presentation with your team members and decide who will take responsibility for various parts of the presentation.

What to Take

It may be helpful to bring the following items with you on the visit:

1. Materials that help demonstrate the need for your project.
2. Your proposal development workbook (Swiss cheese book).
3. Audiovisual aids that document the need, such as pictures or a brief (three to five minutes long) filmstrip, videotape, slide presentation, or cassette tape. Be sure you can operate all equipment with ease, and know how to replace bulbs. Bring extension cords, three-prong—to–two-prong plug adapters, and whatever other peripheral equipment you may need.
4. Information on your organization that you can leave with the funding official (but never leave a proposal).

Questions to Ask a Program Officer

Review the following list of possible questions to ask a program officer:

- Do you agree that the need addressed by our project is important?
- Your average award in this area last year to an organization like ours was $_____. Do you expect that to change?
- How will successful grantees from last year affect the chances for new or first applicants? Will last year's grantees compete with new grant-

ees, or have their funds been set aside? If their funds have been set aside, how much is left for new awards?

- Are there any unannounced program or unsolicited proposal funds in your agency to support an important project like ours?
- The required matching portion is ___ percent. Would it improve our chances for funding if we provided a greater portion than this?
- If no match is required, would it help our proposal if we volunteered to cost share?
- What is the most common mistake or flaw in the proposals you receive?
- Are there any areas you would like to see addressed in a proposal that may have been overlooked by other grantees or applicants?
- We have developed several approaches to this needs area. You may know whether one of our approaches has already been tried. Could you review our concept paper and give us any guidance?
- Would you review or critique our proposal if we got it to you early?
- Would you recommend a previously funded proposal for us to read for format and style? (Remember, you are entitled to see funded proposals, but be cool.)
- What changes do you expect in type or number of awards this year (for example, fewer new awards versus continuing awards)?
- Is there a relationship between the type of project or proposal and the amount awarded? Is there a sequence or progression in the type of grant awarded? For example, do you have to get a consultant grant before you can receive a demonstration grant or an evaluation grant? Is there a hidden agenda?
- Is it okay to use tabs or dividers in my proposal?
- The guidelines call for ___ copies of the proposal. Could you use more? (New guidelines on paperwork reduction sometimes restrict the number of proposal copies an agency can require, but the agency may really need more copies and will be pleased if you volunteer to send extras.)

Immediately after your visit, record any information you have gathered about the funder on the funding source staff profile (exhibit 10.5). Record the results of your visit on the public funding source contact summary sheet (exhibit 10.6).

MAKING YOUR DECISION TO DEVELOP A PROPOSAL

So far you have not invested a tremendous amount of time in writing your proposal. You have taken time to gather data and contact potential grantors. Now you must decide which federal grant program you will apply to.

Your best prospect is the grant program that provides the closest match between the program you want to implement, your nonprofit organization, and the profile you have developed of the grantor. Seldom is there a perfect fit between your project and the grantor's program, and some tailoring and changes in your program will likely add to your chances of success. Use the tailoring worksheet (exhibit 10.7) to analyze each grant program you are interested in and to select your first choice.

Before each visit to a funding source, review this sheet to be sure you are taking the correct materials, advocates, and staff.

Agency Director: _____

Program Director: _____

Contact Person: _____

Profile: Birthdate: _____   Birthplace: _____

Education: College: _____

                Postgraduate: _____

Work Experience: _____

Military Service: _____

Service Clubs: _____

Religious Affiliations: _____

Interests/Hobbies: _____

Publications: _____

Comments: _____

_____

_____

_____

Note: Do not ask the staff person direct questions related to these areas. Instead, record information that has been volunteered or gathered from comments or observations made in the office.

FUNDING SOURCE STAFF PROFILE

EXHIBIT 10.5

Project Title: _____

Add to this sheet each time you contact a public funding source.

Agency Name: _____
Program Officer: _____
Contacted On (Date): _____
By Whom: _____
Contacted By: Letter _____ Phone _____
            Personal Visit _____
Staff or Advocate Present: _____
Discussed: _____
_____
_____

Results: _____
_____
_____

PUBLIC FUNDING SOURCE CONTACT SUMMARY SHEET

EXHIBIT 10.6

Federal Program: _____ 　　Prospect Rating: _____
　　　　　　　　　　　　　　　　　Amount Requested: _____
　　　　　　　　　　　　　　　　___ Percent Match/In-kind: _____

1. How does your grant request match with the average award size to your:
   • type of organization _____
   • size of organization _____
   • location of organization _____
   • proposal focus _____
2. What was the number of applications received versus the number of grants awarded in your area of interest?
   • applications received _____
   • grants awarded _____
3. How would you rate the funding staff's interest in your concept?
   • very interested _____
   • interested _____
   • not interested _____
   • unknown _____
4. From the information you obtained on the reviewers and the review process, what should your writing strategy include? _____
   _____
   _____
5. Based on the information you obtained on the review process, how will points be distributed in the funding source's evaluation process?

Area	*Point Value*
_____	____
_____	____
_____	____

TAILORING WORKSHEET

EXHIBIT 10.7

CHAPTER 11

· · · · · · · · ·

Planning the Successful Federal Proposal

Each federal agency has its own proposal format to which applicants must adhere. If you have been successful in obtaining a copy of a previously funded proposal, you have a quality example of what the funding source expects. After reading exemplary proposals for 25 years, I have learned that really excellent proposals do stand out. One does not have to be an expert in a proposal's particular area of interest to determine whether the proposal is good. The required components or sections of each type of proposal—a research proposal or a proposal for a demonstration or model project—are remarkably similar. In general, federal applications include sections on

- Documentation of need: To demonstrate that you have a command of the relevant literature in the field.
- What you propose to study, change, or test: For a research project, the hypothesis and specific aims; for a model project, the measurable objectives.
- Proposed intervention: What you will do and why you have selected these methods or activities.
- Budget: The cost of the project broken down by category of expenditure.
- Evaluation: How you will establish the levels of change that constitute success and demonstrate that your intervention worked.
- Grantee credibility: Unique qualities and capabilities that you possess and believe are relevant to support and complete the project.

Most federal grantors will also require or expect a summary or abstract, a title, an agreement to comply with federal assurances, and attachments of pertinent materials that the reviewer may want to refer to while evaluating the proposal. Sections on future funding and dissemination of the research findings or model may also be included.

While the inclusion of these general components seems logical, the differences in terminology, space restrictions, and order or sequence from one federal application to another can be very perplexing. The novice grantseeker frequently asks why there is not a standard federal grant application form for all programs. It seems that this would make sense. Due to the variety of federal programs and the deep-seated conviction that each area of interest is distinct, however, this type of standardization will probably never happen. The point is that you must follow each agency's format exactly, make no changes and no omissions, and give each agency what it calls for, not just what you want to give.

DOCUMENTATION OF NEED

Most grantseekers begin their proposal with *what* they propose or want to do. It is much better to begin by focusing on *why* there is a need to do anything at all, including your proposed intervention. To gain the reviewer's respect, you must show that you are knowledgeable about the need in a particular area. Your goal in this section of the proposal is to use articles, studies, and statistics to demonstrate a compelling reason or motivation to deal with the problem now.

The grantor invariably must choose which proposals to fund this year and which to reject or put on hold; therefore, you must demonstrate the urgency to close the gap between what exists now and what ought to be in your special field (see figure 11.1). Your proposed project will seek to close or reduce this gap.

THE GAP	
What exists now. What is real. What the present situation is.	What could be. The goal. The desired state of affairs, level of achievement.

The Gap Diagram

FIGURE 11.1

In a research proposal, need documentation involves a search of relevant literature in the field. The point of the literature search is to document that there is a gap in knowledge in a particular area. Currently in the scientific community it is necessary to enhance the motivation of the reviewer to fund your research project by suggesting the value of closing the gap, in monetary terms or in terms of increased knowledge.

In proposals for model projects and demonstration grants, this section is referred to as the needs statement or need documentation. To be successful in grantseeking, you must produce a clear, compelling picture of the current situation and the desired state. Grantors are "buying" a changed or better state of affairs.

Creating a sense of urgency depends on how well you document the need. Since not all proposals can be funded, you must make the funding source believe that movement toward the desired state cannot wait any longer. Those proposals that do not get funded did not do as good a job of

- documenting a real need (perceived as important)
- demonstrating what ought to be (for clients)
- creating the urgent need to close the gap by demonstrating that each day the need is not addressed the problem grows worse

Documenting What Is

Use the following steps to document a need:

1. Review the section on performing a needs survey (chapter 2) to assess whether any of the methods described could help document the need.
2. Use statistics from articles and research (e.g., "Approximately ___ women in the United States were murdered by their husbands or boyfriends in 1993.").
3. Use quotes from leaders or experts in the field (e.g., "Dr. Flockmeister said children who are raised in a family with spouse abuse have a ___ percent chance of being abused or of abusing their partners.").
4. Use case statements (e.g., "John Quek, a typical client of the Family Outreach Center, was abused as a child and witnessed his mother and aunt being abused.").
5. Describe a national need and reduce it to a local number that is more understandable (e.g., "It is estimated that ___ percent of teenagers are abused by their boyfriend or girlfriend by the time they reach age 17; this means that at the West Side High School ___ seniors in the graduating class may have already experienced abuse.").
6. State the need in terms of one person (e.g., "The abused spouse generally has . . .").
7. Use statements from community people such as police, politicians, and clergy.

Demonstrating What Ought to Be

To establish what ought to be, proven statistics may be difficult or impossible to find. Using experts' statements and quotes to document what ought to be is much more credible than using your opinion. Do not put your opinion in the needs statement. In this section you are demonstrating your knowledge of the field and showing that you have surveyed the literature.

Stay away from terms that point to a poorly documented needs statement. They include the words *many* and *most* and expressions like *a great number* and *everyone knows the need for*. Make sure your needs statement does not include any of these types of words or expressions.

Creating a Sense of Urgency

The needs section should motivate the prospective funding source. One way to do this is to use the funding source's own studies, surveys, or statistics. The same basic proposal can be tailored to two different funding sources by quoting different studies that appeal to each source's own view of the need. By appealing to the views of individual sources, you will appear to be the logical choice to close the gap and move toward reducing the problem.

If the proposal format required by the funding source does not have a section that deals with your capabilities, the end of the needs statement is the best place to put your credentials. To make a smooth transition from the need to your capabilities:

- State that it is the mission of your organization to deal with this problem.
- Summarize the unique qualities of your organization that make it best suited for the job. For example, your organization has the staff or facilities to make the project work.
- Capitalize on the similarities you share with other organizations. For instance, "Our project will serve as a model to the other agencies that face this dilemma each day." Such statements will help the prospective grantor realize that the results of your project could affect many.
- Emphasize that the needs are urgent and that each day they go unmet the problem grows. For example, "Each year that teacher education colleges put off comprehensive computer education, a new group of teachers with limited computer skills enters our schools and the problem grows."

WHAT YOU PROPOSE TO STUDY OR CHANGE

Objectives outline the steps you propose to take to narrow or close the gap created in the needs statement. Objectives follow the needs statement because they cannot be written until the need has been documented.

Since the accomplishment or attainment of each objective will help to close the gap, you must write objectives that are measurable and can be evaluated. It is critical to be able to determine the degree to which the objectives have been attained and, thus, demonstrate the amount of the gap that has been closed. Grantseekers preparing research proposals should note that the objective of a research proposal is to close the gap of ignorance.

Government grantors have been putting increasing pressure on researchers to explain how their research can be used on a very practical level. Philosophical (and the author's) arguments aside, there are conservative elements that want a component of even basic research grants to deal with such issues as dissemination of results and how findings can be applied to benefit the general public.

Objectives versus Methods

Objectives tell the grantseeker and funding source what will be accomplished by this expenditure of funds and how the change will be measured. *Methods* state the means to the end or change. They tell how you will accomplish the desired change. Naturally, the ability to accomplish an objective depends on the methods or activities chosen.

When in doubt as to whether you have written an objective or a method, ask yourself whether there is only one way to accomplish what you have written. If your answer is yes, you have probably written a method. For example, once a participant at one of my seminars told me that his objective was to build a visitors' center for his organization's museum. When asked why he wanted to build a visitors' center, he responded, "To help visitors understand the relationship between the museum buildings so that they can more effectively use the museum." Once he stated this out loud, he realized that his objective was really the effective utilization of the museum and that building a visitors' center was just one method for accomplishing this objective. In other words, building the visitors' center was a means to an end, just one way that my seminar participant could attempt to accomplish his objective. In fact, the reason a funding source might give money to support his project would be to help people use and appreciate the museum, not to build the visitors' center. The bricks and mortar that make up the visitors' center simply do not lend themselves to the kind of measurement that the issue of effective utilization does.

The following is a technique for writing objectives:

1. Determine result areas. Result areas are the key places you will look for improvement or change in the client population. Examples include the health of people over 65 years of age in St. Louis, better-educated minority students, and more efficient use of a museum.
2. Determine measurement indicators. Measurement indicators are the quantifiable parts of your result areas. By measuring your performance with these indicators, you will be able to determine how well you are doing. Examples include the number of hospital readmissions of people over 65 years old, scores on standardized tests, and

the number of people who understand the relationship between museum buildings. Brainstorm a number of measurement indicators for each of your result areas, and then select the ones that reflect your intent and are the least difficult to use.

3. Determine performance standards. Performance standards answer the question "How much (or how little) of a change do we need to consider ourselves successful?" Using our above examples, we might determine the following performance standards: a 10 percent drop in hospital readmissions, scores rising from the 80th to the 90th percentile on the Flockmann reading scale, or a 50 percent reduction in direction giving by museum staff.

4. Determine the time frame. The time frame is the amount of time in which you want to reach your performance standards. It is *your* deadline. You might decide you want to see a 10 percent drop in hospital readmissions within 6 or 18 months. Usually, this time frame is determined for you by the funding source. Most grants are for 12 months. In setting your deadlines, use months 1 through 12 instead of January, February, and so on because you seldom will start the grant when you expect to.

5. Determine cost frame. This is the cost of the methods or activities you have selected to meet your objective. (This cost estimate can be obtained retrospectively from the project planner, the document you will fill out next.)

6. Write the objective. This step combines the data you have generated in the previous five steps. The standard format for an objective is: "To [action verb and statement reflecting your measurement indicator] by [performance standard] by [deadline] at a cost of no more than [cost frame]." The example concerning reading scores might look like this: "To increase the reading scores of freshmen in Flockmann University's Minority Skills Program from the 80th to the 90th percentile on the Flockmann reading scale in 12 months at a cost of $50,000."

7. Evaluate the objective. Review your objective and answer the question "Does this objective reflect the amount of change we want in the result area?" If your answer is yes, you probably have a workable objective. If your answer is no, chances are that your measurement indicator is wrong or your performance standards are too low. Go back to steps two and three and repeat the process.

When writing program objectives, you should follow the same seven steps. Again, remember to emphasize end results, not tasks or methods. Do not describe how you are going to do something; instead, emphasize what you will accomplish and the ultimate benefit of your program's work.

In a research proposal, the section on what the researcher proposes to study or change is referred to as the research question and hypothesis to be tested. The development of research proposals follows an analogous route to model and demonstration grants. There must be a clearly defined problem, question, or gap to be addressed.

Researchers are inoculated with the same virus that all grantseekers share—the "why virus." (Why does this happen? What can we do to change it?) The researcher asks a question and then must search the literature in the field to determine what is already known and who would care if the question were answered. (What is the value or benefit? Who would value the closing of the gap?) For example, the question of whether treatment X or Y influences the healing time of a pressure sore (bedsore) is subject to a search of the literature to see what work has already been done in this area and to determine the importance of the question. (What exists now? What is the incidence or extent of the problem, and the future impact of not addressing the question?) If there is no compelling or motivating reason to use grant monies to answer the question, the researcher is not likely to be successful.

The research question must be specific and focused. Many researchers are overly optimistic and select too broad a question or too many questions to investigate. This sets them up for failure because they cannot control the situation. In other words, they have too many forces or variables to deal with that can influence the outcome.

Researchers must develop their questions into either a null hypothesis or an alternative hypothesis. The null hypothesis predicts that there is no basic difference between the two selected areas. For example, "There is no difference between pressure sores treated with X or Y." The researcher sets up the study to measure the outcome, or the *dependent* variable (increased healing of pressure sores). The researcher manipulates or changes the intervention, or the *independent* variable (use of treatment X or Y), to observe the effect of the two treatments on the dependent variable. Just as behavioral objectives contain a measurement indicator for success (increasing reading scores from the 80th to the 90th percentile as measured by the Flockmann reading scale), the researcher must select a statistical evaluation model, before data are collected, that will be used to evaluate the differences in the intervention. When there are significant differences between the two treatments, the null hypothesis is disproved and the results are based on differences in treatment rather than on chance.

The alternative hypothesis predicts that there is indeed a difference between the two treatments and suggests the direction of that difference. For example, "Treatment X will result in a healing rate that is 50 percent faster than treatment Y."

PROPOSED INTERVENTION

The methods, activities, or protocol section is the detailed description of the steps you will take to meet the objectives. Methods identify:

- what will be done
- who will do it
- how long it will take
- the materials and equipment needed

The protocol of a research proposal details how each experiment or trial will be carried out.

The methods or protocols are all a function of what you set out to accomplish. The best order to follow is to write your objectives first and then develop your methods to meet them. In making up a realistic estimate of your project costs, avoid inflating your budget. Instead, consider adding several more methods to this section than absolutely necessary to ensure that your objectives are met. When you negotiate the final award, you will gain much more credibility with the funding source by eliminating methods instead of lowering the price for the same amount of work.

Historically, final awards for research proposals were arrived at in a manner much different from that for model project proposals. Notification of a research award was frequently followed by a letter that included a dollar amount significantly less than what was applied for, and there was little or no opportunity for negotiation. Criticism of this practice led many major grantors to announce that the methods for both types of proposals should be cost analyzed and negotiated. Now both demonstration and research proposals must include an estimate of the cost of each method or activity and must show each activity's effect on the outcome.

Your methods section should:

- describe your program activities in detail and demonstrate how they will fulfill your objectives or research study
- describe the sequence, flow, and interrelationship of the activities
- describe the planned staffing for your program and designate who is responsible for which activities
- describe your client population and method for determining client selection
- state a specific time frame
- present a reasonable scope of activities that can be accomplished within the stated time frame with your organization's resources
- refer to the cost-benefit ratio of your project
- include a discussion of risk (why success is probable)
- describe the uniqueness of your methods and overall project design

The project planner (see exhibit 11.1) provides you with a format to ensure that your methods section reflects a well-conceived and well-designed plan for the accomplishment of your objectives.

The Project Planner

An outcome of my 25 years of work in grant and contract preparation, the project planner is a spreadsheet-based planning tool designed to assist you in several important ways. It will help you:

1. Develop your budget by having you clearly define which project personnel will perform each activity for a given time frame, with the corresponding consultant services, supplies, materials, and equipment.
2. Defend your budget on an activity-by-activity basis so that you can successfully negotiate your final award.
3. Project a monthly and quarterly cash forecast for year one, year two, and year three of your proposed project.
4. Identify matching or in-kind contributions.

The project planner will also help you develop job descriptions for each individual involved in the project and a budget narrative or written explanation documenting your planned expenses. Several federal granting agencies have been criticized for not negotiating final awards with grantees. Their practice has been to provide grantees with a statement of the final award with no reference or discussion of how the award differs from the amount budgeted in the application or how the reduction will affect the methods and outcome. As more importance is placed on budget negotiation and the planning of project years, the more valuable the project planner will become.

You will find the following explanations of each project planner column helpful as you review the blank project planner in exhibit 11.1 and the sample project planner in exhibit 11.2.

1. Project objectives or outcomes (column A/B): List your objectives or outcomes as A, B, C, and so on. Use the terms the prospective grantor wants. For example, grantors may refer to objectives as major tasks, enabling objectives, or specific aims.
2. Methods (column A/B): Also in the first column, list the methods or protocol necessary to meet the objectives as A-1, A-2, B-1, B-2, C-1, C-2, and so on. These are the tasks you have decided upon as your approach to meeting the need.
3. Month (column C/D): Record the dates you will begin and end each activity in this column.
4. Time (column E): Designate the number of person-weeks (you can use hours or months) needed to accomplish each task.

PROJECT PLANNER™

PROJECT TITLE: _____

A. List Project objectives or outcomes A. B. B. List Methods to accomplish each objective as A-1, A-2, A-3 . . . B-1, B-2 . . .	MONTH		TIME	PROJECT PERSONNEL	PERSONNEL COSTS		
	BEGIN	END			SALARIES & WAGES	FRINGE BENEFITS	TOTAL
	C / D		E	F	G	H	I

TOTAL DIRECT COSTS OR COSTS REQUESTED FROM FUNDER ▶

MATCHING FUNDS, IN-KIND CONTRIBUTIONS, OR DONATED COSTS ▶

TOTAL COSTS ▶

THE PROJECT PLANNER

EXHIBIT 11.1

Sheet _____ of _____

Proposal Developed for _____

PROJECT DIRECTOR: _____ Proposed starting date _____ Proposal Year _____

CONSULTANTS • CONTRACT SERVICES			NON-PERSONNEL RESOURCES NEEDED SUPPLIES • EQUIPMENT • MATERIALS				SUB-TOTAL COST FOR ACTIVITY	MILESTONES PROGRESS INDICATORS	
TIME	COST/WEEK	TOTAL	ITEM	COST/ITEM	QUANTITY	TOT. COST	TOTAL I. L. P	ITEM	DATE
J	K	L	M	N	O	P	Q	R	S
								T	◄ % OF TOTAL
									◄
								100%	◄

THE PROJECT PLANNER *(continued)*

EXHIBIT 11.1

114

PROJECT PLANNER™

PROJECT TITLE: A Contract for Educational Cooperation – Parents, Teachers & Students Charting A Course for Involvement

A. List Project objectives or outcomes A. B. B. List Methods to accomplish each objective as A-1, A-2, A-3 . . . B-1, B-2 . . .	MONTH		TIME	PROJECT PERSONNEL	PERSONNEL COSTS		
	BEGIN	END			SALARIES & WAGES	FRINGE BENEFITS	TOTAL
	C / D		E	F	G	H	I
Objective A: Increase Educational Cooperation of Teachers, Parents & Students 25% as Measured on the Educational Practices Survey in 12 Months at a Cost of $							
A-1 Develop the Responsible Educational Practices Survey with the Advisory Committee	1/2		4	Proj. Dir/PD Smith	West State Univ.		
a. Write questions and develop a scale of responsibility for				2 Grad students	"	"	"
parents, teachers & students				(GS)			
A-2 Administer the Survey to the Target Population	2/3		4	2 GS	"	"	"
a. Develop procedure							
b. Get human subjects approval thru			4	PD	"	"	"
West State University							
c. Graduate students to administer survey			4	2 GS	"	"	"
d. Input survey data			*4	Sec'y	800	160	*960
e. Develop results			1	PD	West State Univ.		
A-3 Develop Curriculum	3/6						
a. Review results of pre-test given to parents, students & teachers			1	PD	"	"	"
b. Develop a curriculum on			5	PD	"	"	"
responsibility concepts in education for each group			*8	Sec'y	1600	320	*1920
(includes workbook & video on each area of curriculum)			8	Senior High Video Club – Using Jones Corp. Video Facility			
• responsible use of time							
• homework responsibility							
• communication skills							
• developing contract for change							
A-4 Promote and Carry Out Program	6/12		24	PD	West State Univ.		
a. Use advisory group to announce program			24	Sec'y	4800	960	*5760
b. Public service spots on radio and television							
c. Develop & send home a program							
d. Schedule meetings with parents							
e. Develop a student video							

TOTAL DIRECT COSTS OR COSTS REQUESTED FROM FUNDER ▶	0
MATCHING FUNDS, IN-KIND CONTRIBUTIONS, OR DONATED COSTS ▶	8640
TOTAL COSTS ▶	8640

SAMPLE PROJECT PLANNER

EXHIBIT 11.2

Proposal Developed for _____

PROJECT DIRECTOR: __D. Smith_____ Proposed starting date _____ Proposal Year _____

CONSULTANTS • CONTRACT SERVICES			NON-PERSONNEL RESOURCES NEEDED SUPPLIES • EQUIPMENT • MATERIALS				SUB-TOTAL COST FOR ACTIVITY	MILESTONES PROGRESS INDICATORS	
TIME	COST/WEEK	TOTAL	ITEM	COST/ITEM	QUANTITY	TOT. COST	TOTAL I. L. P	ITEM	DATE
J	K	L	M	N	O	P	Q	R	S
2	1000	2000	micro/word perfect			2500			
2	500	1000	printer/modem			175			
			phone expense			150			
4	500	2000							
4	1000	4000							
4	500	2000	travel allowance			800			
			modem/phone expense			150			
1	1000	1000	micro processor			---			
1	1000	1000							
5	1000	5000	layout & print			1250			
			workbooks	10	200	2000*			
			blank tapes	2	20	40			
			video studio	5000	5 hrs	25000	*		
			camera edit						
			character generation						
			video camera	1000	6	6000*			
		42000				5065	47065 T	53%	◄ % OF TOTAL
		0				33000	41640	47%	◄
		42000				38065	88705	100%	◄

SAMPLE PROJECT PLANNER *(continued)*

EXHIBIT 11.2

5. Project personnel (column F): List the key personnel who will spend measurable or significant amounts of time on this activity. The designation of key personnel is critical for developing a job description for each individual. If you list the activities for which the key personnel are responsible, and the minimum qualifications or background required, you will have a rough job description. Call a placement agency to get an estimate of the salary needed to fill the position. The number of weeks or months will determine full-time or part-time classification.

    This column gives you the opportunity to look at how many hours of work you are providing in a given time span. If you have key personnel working more than 160 hours per month, it may be necessary to adjust the number of weeks in Column E to fit a more reasonable time frame. For example, you may have to reschedule activities or shift responsibility to another staff member.

6. Personnel costs (columns G, H, I): List the salaries, wages, and fringe benefits for all personnel. Special care should be taken in analyzing staff donated from your organization. The donation of personnel may be a requirement for your grant or a gesture you make to show your good faith and appear as a better investment to the funding source. If you do make matching or in-kind contributions, place an asterisk by the name of each person you donate to the project. Be sure to include your donation of fringe benefits as well as wages. As you complete the remaining columns, put an asterisk by anything else that will be donated to the project.

7. Consultants and contract services (columns J, K, L): These three columns are for the services that are most cost-efficiently supplied by individuals who are not in your normal employ. These individuals may be experts at a skill you need that does not warrant your training a staff member or hiring an additional staff person (evaluation, computers, commercial art, etc.). No fringe benefits are paid to consultants or contract service providers.

8. Nonpersonnel resources needed (columns M, N, O, P): List the components that are necessary to complete each activity and achieve your objective, including supplies, equipment, and materials. Many a grantseeker has gone wrong by underestimating the nonpersonnel resources needed to successfully complete a project. Most grantseekers lose out on many donated or matching items because they do not ask themselves what they really need to complete each activity. Travel, supplies, and telephone communications are some of the more commonly donated items.

    Equipment requests can be handled in many ways. One approach is to place total equipment items as they are called for in your plan under column M (item) and to complete the corresponding columns appropriately—cost per item (column N), quantity (column O), and total cost (column P). However, this approach may cause problems in the negotiation of your final award. The grantor may suggest lowering the grant amount by the elimination of an equipment item that appears as though it is related to the accomplishment of only one activity, when in actuality you plan to use it in several subsequent activities. Therefore, I suggest that if you plan to list the total cost of equipment needed in your work plan next to one particular activity, designate a percentage of usage to that activity and reference the other activities that will require the equipment. This way you will show 100-percent usage and be able to defend the inclusion of the equipment in your budget request.

In some cases, you may choose to allocate the percentage of the cost of the equipment with the percentage of use for each activity. If you allocate cost of equipment to each activity, remember that if you drop an activity in negotiation you may not have all the funds you need to purchase the equipment.

9. Subtotal cost for activity (column Q): This column can be completed in two ways. Each activity can be subtotaled, or you can subtotal several activities under each objective or specific aim.
10. Milestones or progress indicators (columns R, S): Column R should be used to record what the funding source will receive as indicators that you are working toward the accomplishment of your objectives. Use column S to list the date on which the funding source will receive the milestone or progress indicator.

Please note that you might want to develop a computer-generated spreadsheet version of the project planner so that objectives or other information could be easily added, deleted, or changed. This would be especially useful when the grant amount awarded is less than the amount requested, because you could experiment with possible changes without too much trouble.

Indirect Costs

An aspect of federal grants that is critically important yet poorly understood by many grantseekers and other individuals connected with grants is the concept of indirect costs. Indirect costs involve repaying the recipient of a federal grant for costs that are difficult to break down individually but are indirectly attributable to performing the federal grant. These costs include such things as

- heat and lights
- building upkeep
- maintenance staff
- payroll personnel

Indirect costs are calculated using a formula provided by the Federal Regional Controller's Office and are expressed as a percentage of the total amount requested from the funding source (total from Column Q of your project planner), or as a percentage of the personnel costs (total from Column I of your project planner).

BUDGET

While preparing the budget may be traumatic for unorganized grantseekers, you can see that the project planner contains all the information you need to forecast your financial needs accurately. No matter what budget format you use, the information you need to construct your budget lies in your project planner. The project planner, however, is not the budget; it is the analysis of what will have to be done and the estimated costs and time frame for each activity.

In most government proposal formats, the budget section is not located near the methods section. Government funders do not understand why you want to talk about your methods when you talk about money. As you know, the budget is a result of what you plan to do. If the money you request is reduced, you must cut your project's methods. Draw public funding sources back into your project planner so that they too can see what will be missing as a result of a budget cut. If you must cut so many methods that you can no longer be sure of accomplishing your objectives, consider refusing the funds or reducing the amount of change (reduction of the need) outlined in your objectives when negotiating the amount of your award. The sample budget in exhibit 11.3 is provided for your review.

If you are required to provide a quarterly cash forecast, use the grants office time line in exhibit 11.4. The project methods (A-1, A-2, B-1, B-2) from your project planner should be listed in the first column. The numbered columns across the top of the time line indicate the months of the duration of the project. Use a line bar to indicate when each activity/method begins and ends. Place the estimated cost per method in the far-right column. Use a triangle to indicate where milestones and progress indicators are to occur (taken from Columns R and S of your project planner). By totaling costs by quarter, you can develop a quarterly forecast of expenditures. Complete a separate grants office time line and project planner for each year of a continuation grant or multiyear award.

One of the more common federal budget forms for nonconstruction projects is Standard Form (SF) 424A (see exhibit 11.5). The instructions for completing SF-424A are shown in exhibit 11.6. As with other budget forms, if you have completed a project planner, you already have all the information you need to complete SF-424A.

Many grantors also require that you submit a narrative statement of your budget, explaining the basis for your inclusion of personnel, consultants, supplies, and equipment. This is known as a budget narrative. Again, your completed project planner will help you construct the budget narrative and explain the sequence of steps. The budget narrative gives you the opportunity to present the rationale for each step, piece of equipment, and key person that your proposal calls for.

EVALUATION

Federal and state funding sources generally place a much heavier emphasis on evaluation than most private sources do. While there are many books on evaluation, the best advice is to have an expert handle it. I suggest enlisting the services of a professional at a college or university who has experience in evaluation. Professors will generally enjoy the involvement and the extra pay and can lead you to a storehouse of inexpensive labor—undergraduate and graduate students. A graduate student in statistics can help you quantify your results inexpensively, while he or she gathers valuable insight and experience.

Irrespective of who designs your evaluation, writing your objectives properly will make the process much simpler. Most grantseekers have little problem developing objectives that deal with cognitive areas or areas that provide for results that can be easily quantified. The problems start when they move into the affective domain, because values, feelings, and appreciation can be difficult to measure.

If you use the techniques presented in this chapter for writing objectives and ask yourself what your client population will do differently after the grant, you should be able to keep yourself on track and develop an evaluation design that will pass even the most critical federal and state standards. For example, a grant to increase appreciation for opera could be measured by seeing how many of the subjects attend an inexpensive performance after the free performances are completed.

THE SUMMARY OR ABSTRACT

The summary or abstract is written after the proposal is completed. After the title, the summary is the second most often read part of a proposal. The summary must be succinct and motivational so the reader (reviewer) does not lose interest.

The summary is a much-abbreviated version of your proposal and should contain a concise description of the need for your project, your project's goals or hypotheses, objectives or specific aims, approach or protocol, and evalua-

PROJECT NAME: Nutrition Education for Disadvantaged Mothers through Teleconferencing	Expenditure Total	Donated/ In-Kind	Requested from This Source
	$126,075	$60,470	$65,605
I. PERSONNEL			
A. Salaries, Wages			
Project Director @ $2,200/mo. x 12 mos. x 50% time	13,200	13,200	
Administrative Assistant @ $1,600/mo. x 12 mos. x 100% time	19,200		19,200
Secretary @ $1,200/mo. x 12 mos. x 100% time	14,400		14,400
Volunteer Time @ $5.00 x 10 mos. x 400 hours	20,000	20,000	
B. Fringe Benefits			
Unemployment Insurance (3% of first $10,800 of each salary)	972	320	652
FICA (7.65% of first $60,600 of each employee salary)	3,580	967	2,613
Health Insurance ($150/mo. per employee x 12 mos.)	5,400	1,782	3,618
Workmen's Compensation (1% of salaries paid — $46,800)	468	126	342
C. Consultants/Contracted Services			
Copy Editor ($200/day x 5)	1,000		1,000
PR Advisor ($200/day x 10)	2,000		2,000
Accounting Services ($250/day x 12)	3,000	3,000	
Legal Services ($500/day x 6)	3,000	3,000	
Personnel Subtotal	$86,220	$42,395	$43,825
II. NONPERSONNEL			
A. Space Costs			
Rent ($1.50/sq. ft. x 400 sq. ft. x 12 mos.)	7,200	7,200	
Utilities ($75/mo. x 12 mos.)	900	900	
B. Equipment			
Desk ($275 x 1)	275		275
Computer, Printer, Copy Machine Rental ($300/mo. x 12 mos.)	3,600		3,600
Office Chairs (3 x $50)	150		150
File Cabinets (3 x $125)	375	375	

A Sample Project Budget

EXHIBIT 11.3

PROJECT NAME: Nutrition Education for Disadvantaged Mothers through Teleconferencing	Expenditure Total	Donated/ In-Kind	Requested from This Source
	$126,075	$60,470	$65,605

II. NONPERSONNEL *(continued)*

	Expenditure Total	Donated/ In-Kind	Requested from This Source
B. Equipment *(continued)* Electronic Blackboard & Misc. Equip. for Teleconferencing	7,200		7,200
C. Supplies (Consumables) (3 employees x $200/yr.)	600	600	
D. Travel			
Local			
Project Director (29¢/mile x 500 miles/mo. x 12 mos.)	1,740		1,740
Administrative Assistant (29¢/mile x 750 miles/mo. x 12 mos.)	2,610		2,610
Out-of-Town			
Project Director to Nutrition Conference in St. Louis, MO			
Airfare	450		450
Per Diem ($75/day x 3)	225		225
Hotel ($100/nt. x 3)	300		300
E. Telephone			
Installation ($100/line x 3)	300	300	
Monthly Charges ($25/ line x 3 lines x 12 mos.)	900	900	
Long Distance ($40/ mo. x 12 mos.)	480		480
F. Other Nonpersonnel Costs			
Printing (30¢ x 25,000 brochures)	7,500	7,500	
Postage (19¢ x 25,000)	4,750		4,750
Insurance ($25/mo. x 12 mos.)	300	300	
Nonpersonnel Subtotal	$39,855	$18,075	$21,780
Personnel Subtotal	$86,220	$42,395	$43,825
Project Total	$126,075	$60,470	$65,605
Percentage	100%	48%	52%

A SAMPLE PROJECT BUDGET *(continued)*

EXHIBIT 11.3

GRANTS OFFICE TIME LINE

ACTIV-ITY NO.	1	2	3	4	5	6	7	8	9	10	11	12	TOTAL COST FOR ACTIVITY

1st QUARTER	2nd QUARTER	3rd QUARTER	4th QUARTER	TOTAL

QUARTERLY FORECAST OF EXPENDITURES ▲

GRANTS OFFICE TIME LINE

EXHIBIT 11.4

BUDGET INFORMATION — Non-Construction Programs

SECTION A - BUDGET SUMMARY

| Grant Program Function or Activity (a) | Catalog of Federal Domestic Assistance Number (b) | Estimated Unobligated Funds | | New or Revised Budget | | |
		Federal (c)	Non-Federal (d)	Federal (e)	Non-Federal (f)	Total (g)
1.		$	$	$	$	$
2.						
3.						
4.						
5. TOTALS		$	$	$	$	$

SECTION B - BUDGET CATEGORIES

| 6. Object Class Categories | GRANT PROGRAM, FUNCTION OR ACTIVITY | | | | Total (5) |
	(1)	(2)	(3)	(4)	
a. Personnel	$	$	$	$	$
b. Fringe Benefits					
c. Travel					
d. Equipment					
e. Supplies					
f. Contractual					
g. Construction					
h. Other					
i. Total Direct Charges (sum of 6a - 6h)					
j. Indirect Charges					
k. TOTALS (sum of 6i and 6j)	$	$	$	$	$
7. Program Income	$	$	$	$	$

Authorized for Local Reproduction

STANDARD FORM 424A

EXHIBIT 11.5

SECTION C - NON-FEDERAL RESOURCES

(a) Grant Program	(b) Applicant	(c) State	(d) Other Sources	(e) TOTALS
8.	$	$	$	$
9.				
10.				
11.				
12. TOTALS (sum of lines 8 and 11)	$	$	$	$

SECTION D - FORECASTED CASH NEEDS

	Total for 1st Year	1st Quarter	2nd Quarter	3rd Quarter	4th Quarter
13. Federal	$	$	$	$	$
14. Nonfederal					
15. TOTAL (sum of lines 13 and 14)	$	$	$	$	$

SECTION E - BUDGET ESTIMATES OF FEDERAL FUNDS NEEDED FOR BALANCE OF THE PROJECT

(a) Grant Program	FUTURE FUNDING PERIODS (Years)			
	(b) First	(c) Second	(d) Third	(e) Fourth
16.	$	$	$	$
17.				
18.				
19.				
20. TOTALS (sum of lines 16-19)	$	$	$	$

SECTION F - OTHER BUDGET INFORMATION
(Attach additional Sheets if Necessary)

21. Direct Charges:	22. Indirect Charges:

23. Remarks

Authorized for Local Reproduction

SF 424A (4-88) Page 2
Prescribed by OMB Circular A-102

Standard Form 424A *(continued)*

EXHIBIT 11.5

125

INSTRUCTIONS FOR THE SF-424A

General Instructions

This form is designed so that application can be made for funds from one or more grant programs. In preparing the budget, adhere to any existing Federal grantor agency guidelines which prescribe how and whether budgeted amounts should be separately shown for different functions or activities within the program. For some programs, grantor agencies may require budgets to be separately shown by function or activity. For other programs, grantor agencies may require a breakdown by function or activity. Sections A,B,C, and D should include budget estimates for the whole project except when applying for assistance which requires Federal authorization in annual or other funding period increments. In the latter case, Sections A,B, C, and D should provide the budget for the first budget period (usually a year) and Section E should present the need for Federal assistance in the subsequent budget periods. All applications should contain a breakdown by the object class categories shown in Lines a-k of Section B.

Section A. Budget Summary
Lines 1-4, Columns (a) and (b)

For applications pertaining to a *single* Federal grant program (Federal Domestic Assistance Catalog number) and *not requiring* a functional or activity breakdown, enter on Line 1 under Column (a) the catalog program title and the catalog number in Column (b).

For applications pertaining to a *single* program *requiring* budget amounts by multiple functions or activities, enter the name of each activity or function on each line in Column (a), and enter the catalog number in Column (b). For applications pertaining to multiple programs where none of the programs require a breakdown by function or activity, enter the catalog program title on each line in Column (a) and the respective catalog program number on each line in Column (b).

For applications pertaining to *multiple* programs where one or more programs *require* a breakdown by function or activity, prepare a separate sheet for each program requiring the breakdown. Additional sheets should be used when one form does not provide adequate space for all breakdown of data required. However, when more than one sheet is used, the first page should provide the summary totals by programs.

Lines 1-4, Columns (c) through (g.)

For new applications, leave Columns (c) and (d) blank. For each line entry in Columns (a) and (b), enter in Columns (e), (f), and (g) the appropriate amounts of funds needed to support the project for the first funding period (usually a year).

Lines 1-4, Columns (c) through (g.) (continued)

For continuing grant program applications, submit these forms before the end of each funding period as required by the grantor agency. Enter in Columns (c) and (d) the estimated amounts of funds which will remain unobligated at the end of the grant funding period only if the Federal grantor agency instructions provide for this. Otherwise, leave these columns blank. Enter in columns (e) and (f) the amounts of funds needed for the upcoming period. The amount(s) in Column (g) should be the sum of amounts in Columns (e) and (f).

For supplemental grants and changes to existing grants, do not use Columns (c) and (d). Enter in Column (e) the amount of the increase or decrease of Federal funds and enter in Column (f) the amount of the increase or decrease of non-Federal funds. In Column (g) enter the new total budgeted amount (Federal and non-Federal) which includes the total previous authorized budgeted amounts plus or minus, as appropriate, the amounts shown in Columns (e) and (f). The amount(s) in Column (g) should not equal the sum of amounts in Columns (e) and (f).

Line 5 — Show the totals for all columns used.

Section B Budget Categories

In the column headings (1) through (4), enter the titles of the same programs, functions, and activities shown on Lines 1-4, Column (a), Section A. When additional sheets are prepared for Section A, provide similar column headings on each sheet. For each program, function or activity, fill in the total requirements for funds (both Federal and non-Federal) by object class categories.

Lines 6a-i — Show the totals of Lines 6a to 6h in each column.

Line 6j – Show the amount of indirect cost.

Line 6k – Enter the total of amounts on Lines 6i and 6j. For all applications for new grants and continuation grants the total amount in column (5), Line 6k, should be the same as the total amount shown in Section A, Column (g), Line 5. For supplemental grants and changes to grants, the total amount of the increase or decrease as shown in Columns (1)-(4), Line 6k should be the same as the sum of the amounts in Section A, Columns (e) and (f) on Line 5.

Instructions for Standard Form 424A

INSTRUCTIONS FOR THE SF-424A *(continued)*

Line 7 – Enter the estimated amount of income, if any, expected to be generated from this project. Do not add or subtract this amount from the total project amount. Show under the program narrative statement the nature and source of income. The estimated amount of program income may be considered by the federal grantor agency in determining the total amount of the grant.

Section C. Non-Federal-Resources

Lines 8-11 – Enter amounts of non-Federal resources that will be used on the grant. If in-kind contributions are included, provide a brief explanation on a separate sheet.

    Column (a) – Enter the program titles identical to Column (a), Section A. A breakdown by function or activity is not necessary.

    Column (b) – Enter the contribution to be made by the applicant.

    Column (c) – Enter the amount of the State's cash and in-kind contribution if the applicant is not a State or State agency. Applicants which are a State or State agencies should leave this column blank.

    Column (d) – Enter the amount of cash and in-kind contributions to be made from all other sources.

    Column (e) – Enter totals of Columns (b), (c), and (d).

Line 12 — Enter the total for each of Columns (b)-(e). The amount in Column (e) should be equal to the amount on Line 5, Column (f), Section A.

Section D. Forecasted Cash Needs

Line 13 – Enter the amount of cash needed by quarter from the grantor agency during the first year.

Line 14 – Enter the amount of cash from all other sources needed by quarter during the first year.

Line 15 – Enter the totals of amounts on Lines 13 and 14.

Section E. Budget Estimates of Federal Funds Needed for Balance of the Project

Lines 16 - 19 – Enter in Column (a) the same grant program titles shown in Column (a), Section A. A breakdown by function or activity is not necessary. For new applications and continuation grant applications, enter in the proper columns amounts of Federal funds which will be needed to complete the program or project over the succeeding funding periods (usually in years). This section need not be completed for revisions (amendments, changes, or supplements) to funds for the current year of existing grants.

If more than four lines are needed to list the program titles, submit additional schedules as necessary.

Line 20 – Enter the total for each of the Columns (b)-(e). When additional schedules are prepared for this Section, annotate accordingly and show the overall totals on this line.

Section F. Other Budget Information

Line 21 – Use this space to explain amounts for individual direct object-class cost categories that may appear to be out of the ordinary or to explain the details as required by the Federal grantor agency.

Line 22 – Enter the type of indirect rate (provisional, predetermined, final or fixed) that will be in effect during the funding period, the estimated amount of the base to which the rate is applied, and the total indirect expense.

Line 23 – Provide any other explanations or comments deemed necessary.

INSTRUCTIONS FOR STANDARD FORM 424A *(continued)*

EXHIBIT 11.6

---

tion design. You can determine which of these components to emphasize in your summary or abstract by reviewing the point or evaluation system the funding source will apply. Use your summary or abstract to show readers that they will find what they want in your proposal.

Many funding sources have explicit requirements concerning the summary or abstract. Some designate the space and number of words or characters that can be used, while others require potential grantees to underline a certain number of key words or phrases. Be sure to verify the rules before constructing this critical part of your proposal.

TITLE PAGE

Federal granting programs have a required face sheet or title page that must be attached to federal grant applications or proposals. The most common is Standard Form (SF) 424 (exhibit 11.7; instructions for completing the form are included in exhibit 11.8). Remember, you are dealing with a bureaucracy and, therefore, should double-check all requirements and make sure all necessary forms are completed per instructions.

The title of a proposal is very important. It is the first part of your proposal to be read by reviewers, and, if it is not good, it may be the only part read! Take the time to develop a title that ensures your proposal will get attention. The title of your proposal should:

- describe your project
- express your project's end results, not methods
- describe your project's benefits to clients
- be short and easy to remember

The best titles are like newspaper titles, descriptive and to the point. Titles that try to entice the reader by giving only part of the story seldom work.

Do not use biblical characters or Greek gods in your proposal title since you cannot be sure that the funding source will be familiar with your reference. For example, calling your solar energy project "Apollo's Flame" could work to your disadvantage if the reviewer does not know who Apollo is or fails to make the connection.

Acronyms should be used only if the funding source has a preference for them. Trying to develop a title that describes the benefits of your project is difficult enough without trying to use specific words that will result in a catchy acronym.

Since you have written the proposal, it is easy for you to develop tunnel vision and attribute more meaning to the words in the title than a person reading it for the first time would. To make sure this does not happen, read your title to other people who know little or nothing about your proposal, and then ask them what they think the proposal is about based on the title. You may find that you are not the best person to write the title. Have friends read the proposal and ask them for title suggestions.

Titles can vary in length and can be up to 10 to 13 words. Some federal programs have rules on the number of characters or spaces used in a title. Check the rules.

The key to writing a good title is to ask funding officials what they prefer and to examine a list of titles used by past grantees. This will give you a more accurate idea of what the funding source really likes.

FUTURE FUNDING

Most funding sources are buying a piece of the future. It is in their best interest to see any project they fund continue. This way, they are able to take credit for the project and its benefits over a greater length of time. Unfortunately, many grantseekers ignore the funding sources' need to keep their investment alive and neglect to mention a future financing plan in their proposal. If you cannot

APPLICATION FOR FEDERAL ASSISTANCE

OMB Approval No. 0348-0043

2. DATE SUBMITTED		Applicant Identifier

1. TYPE OF SUBMISSION:		3. DATE RECEIVED BY STATE	State Application Identifier

Application
- ☐ Construction
- ☐ Non-Construction

Preapplication
- ☐ Construction
- ☐ Non-Construction

4. DATE RECEIVED BY FEDERAL AGENCY	Federal Identifier

5. APPLICANT INFORMATION

Legal Name:

Organizational Unit:

Address (give city, county, state, and zip code):

Name and telephone number of the person to be contacted on matters involving this application (give area code)

6. EMPLOYER IDENTIFICATION NUMBER (EIN):

☐☐ — ☐☐☐☐☐☐☐

7. TYPE OF APPLICANT: (enter appropriate letter in box) ☐

- A State
- B County
- C Municipal
- D Township
- E Interstate
- F Intermunicipal
- G Special District
- H Independent School Dist.
- I State Controlled Institution of Higher Learning
- J Private University
- K Indian Tribe
- L Individual
- M Profit Organization
- N Other (Specify) _____

8. TYPE OF APPLICATION:

☐ New ☐ Continuation ☐ Revision

If Revision, enter appropriate letter(s) in box(es): ☐ ☐

- A Increase Award
- B Decrease Award
- C Increase Duration
- D Decrease Duration Other (specify): _____

9. NAME OF FEDERAL AGENCY:

10. CATALOG OF FEDERAL DOMESTIC ASSISTANCE NUMBER: ☐☐ – ☐☐☐

TITLE: ☐☐ ☐

11. DESCRIPTIVE TITLE OF APPLICANT'S PROJECT:

12. AREAS AFFECTED BY PROJECT (cities, counties, states, etc.):

13. PROPOSED PROJECT:		14. CONGRESSIONAL DISTRICTS OF:	
Start Date	Ending Date	a. Applicant	b. Project

15. ESTIMATED FUNDING:

a. Federal	$	.00
b. Applicant	$	.00
c. State	$	.00
d. Local	$	.00
e. Other	$	.00
f. Program Income	$	.00
g. TOTAL	$	.00

16. IS APPLICATION SUBJECT TO REVIEW BY STATE EXECUTIVE ORDER 12372 PROCESS?

a. ☐ YES. THIS PREAPPLICATION/APPLICATION WAS MADE AVAILABLE TO THE STATE EXECUTIVE ORDER 12372 PROCESS FOR REVIEW ON

DATE _____

b. NO. ☐ PROGRAM IS NOT COVERED BY E.O. 12372

☐ OR PROGRAM HAS NOT BEEN SELECTED BY STATE FOR REVIEW

17. IS THE APPLICANT DELINQUENT ON ANY FEDERAL DEBT?

☐ Yes If "Yes," attach an explanation. ☐ No

18. TO THE BEST OF MY KNOWLEDGE AND BELIEF, ALL DATA IN THIS APPLICATION/PREAPPLICATION ARE TRUE AND CORRECT. THE DOCUMENT HAS BEEN DULY AUTHORIZED BY THE GOVERNING BODY OF THE APPLICANT AND THE APPLICANT WILL COMPLY WITH THE ATTACHED ASSURANCES IF THE ASSISTANCE IS AWARDED

a. Typed Name of Authorized Representative	b. Title	c. Telephone number
d. Signature of Authorized Representative		e. Date Signed

Previous Editions Not Usable

G-2

Authorized for Local Reproduction

Standard Form 424 REV 4 88)
Prescribed by OMB Circular A-102

STANDARD FORM 424

EXHIBIT 11.7

INSTRUCTIONS FOR THE SF 424

This is a standard form used by applicants as a required facesheet for preapplications and applications submitted for Federal assistance. It will be used by Federal agencies to obtain applicant certification that States which have established a review and comment procedure in response to Executive Order 12372 and have selected the program to be included in their process, have been given an opportunity to review the applicant's submission.

Item: **Entry:**

1. Self-explanatory.

2. Date application submitted to Federal agency (or State if applicable) & applicant's control number (if applicable).

3. State use only (if applicable).

4. If this application is to continue or revise an existing award, enter present Federal identifier number. If for a new project, leave blank.

5. Legal name of applicant, name of primary organizational unit which will undertake the assistance activity, complete address of the applicant, and name and telephone number of the person to contact on matters related to this application.

6. Enter Employer Identification Number (EIN) as assigned by the Internal Revenue Service.

7. Enter the appropriate letter in the space provided.

8. Check appropriate box and enter appropriate letter(s) in the space(s) provided:

    —"New" means a new assistance award.

    —"Continuation" means an extension for an additional funding/budget period for a project with a projected completion date.

    —"Revision" means any change in the Federal Government's financial obligation or contingent liability from an existing obligation.

9. Name of Federal agency from which assistance is being requested with this application.

10. Use the Catalog of Federal Domestic Assistance number and title of the program under which assistance is requested.

11. Enter a brief descriptive title of the project. If more than one program is involved, you should append an explanation on a separate sheet. If appropriate (e.g., construction or real

Item: **Entry:**

property projects), attach a map showing project location. For preapplications, use a separate sheet to provide a summary description of this project.

12. List only the largest political entities affected (e.g., State, counties, cities).

13. Self-explanatory.

14. List the applicant's Congressional District and any District(s) affected by the program or project.

15. Amount requested or to be contributed during the first funding/budget period by each contributor. Value of in-kind contributions should be included on appropriate lines as applicable. If the action will result in a dollar change to an existing award, indicate *only* the amount of the change. For decreases, enclose the amounts in parentheses. If both basic and supplemental amounts are included, show breakdown on an attached sheet. For multiple program funding, use totals and show breakdown using same categories as item 15.

16. Applicants should contact the State Single Point of Contact (SPOC) for Federal Executive Order 12372 to determine whether the application is subject to the State intergovernmental review process.

17. This question applies to the applicant organization, not the person who signs as the authorized representative. Categories of debt include delinquent audit disallowances, loans and taxes.

18. To be signed by the authorized representative of the applicant. A copy of the governing body's authorization for you to sign this application as official representative must be on file in the applicant's office. (Certain Federal agencies may require that this authorization be submitted as part of the application.)

think of ways to finance your project after your federal grant funds run out, think again. Perhaps you could continue your project through

- service fees
- membership fees
- support from agencies like the United Way
- big gift campaigns aimed at wealthy individuals
- an endowment program
- foundation and corporate grants
- a direct-mail campaign
- other fund-raising mechanisms

Include the cost of one or more of these activities in your expenses, and budget them in the grant. You are not automatically considered an ingrate for doing this; rather, you may come across as a good executor of the funding source's estate. You are planning for continuation.

DISSEMINATION

In addition to the good that will come from meeting the objectives and closing the gap established in your needs statement, much good can come from letting others know what you and the funding source have accomplished. Others in your field will come to know your name and ask you to enter into consortia with them. In addition, other funding sources will solicit your application.

You can disseminate the results of your grant by

- mailing a final report, quarterly journal, or newsletter to others in your field
- sponsoring a seminar or conference on the topic
- attending a national or international conference to deliver the results of the project (many government funding officials cannot travel to conferences, but they can fund you to go and disseminate the results)
- producing a film or slide/tape presentation of the project

Activities aimed at disseminating project results are viewed positively by most funding sources. In general, they want their name up in lights and are willing to pay for it. So, build the costs related to dissemination into your budget.

ATTACHMENTS (APPENDIX)

The attachments section can provide the "winning edge" when your proposal is compared to a competitor's. Throughout the proposal development process, you should be gathering materials that could be used in the attachments section of your proposal. Your final task is to select which materials to include.

Naturally, you want to choose those that will best support your proposal and build credibility. Whether the funding source skims over them or examines them in detail, attachments may include:

- studies or research, tables, and graphs
- vitae of key personnel
- minutes of advisory committee meetings
- list of board members
- auditor's report or statement
- letters of recommendation or endorsement
- copy of your IRS tax-exempt designation
- pictures or architect's drawings
- copies of your agency's publications
- list of other funding sources you will approach for support

Check funding source rules to determine how long your attachments section can be. Guidelines may state that the attachments can be up to twice as long as the proposal. Also check funding source rules for the appropriate appendix format. Provide a separate table of contents for your appendix, and number the pages for easy reference.

WRITING YOUR FEDERAL OR STATE PROPOSAL

Your proposal must reflect what the funding source wants and what the reviewers will be looking for. In general:

- follow the guidelines exactly (even when they seem senseless)
- fill in all the blanks
- double-check all computations
- include anything the funding source asks for, even if you think you already provided the information under another section of your proposal

When writing your proposal, keep in mind that it must be readable and easy to skim. Place special emphasis on vocabulary, style, and visual attractiveness.

Vocabulary

Your contact with a past reviewer will have given you an idea of the reviewers' level of expertise and their depth of knowledge in your subject area. Be sure your proposal uses language appropriate to the reviewers. Shorter words are generally better than long, complex words, and avoid buzzwords unless you are sure the reviewer expects them. Define all acronyms.

Writing Style

By now you should know the background of the typical reviewer selected by the grantor agency and how much time the reviewers spend reading each proposal. These peer reviewers are under pressure to use their time efficiently, so you must produce a proposal that is poignant, yet organized and easy to read.

- Use simple sentences (no more than two commas) and short paragraphs (five to seven lines).
- Begin each section with a strong motivating "lead" sentence.
- Make sure your writing style cannot be construed as cute or offensive to the reader. Avoid stating the obvious and talking down to the reviewer.
- Develop a "user-friendly" proposal. One of the peer reviewers may be chosen to defend your proposal to the rest of the review panel. In this case, you want to be certain to make the reviewer your friend by organizing and referencing attachments in such a way that they can be used to mount a good defense and to answer the other panelists' questions.

Visual Attractiveness

Even scientific research need not look boring to the reviewer. To enhance the "readability" of your proposal and make your points stand out, use:

- underlining
- bullets
- different typefaces
- various margins and spacing
- bold headings
- pictures
- charts and graphs
- handwriting

While you must follow the grantor's rules regarding font, number of characters per inch, line spacing, and so on, your computer and laser printer can provide you with a wealth of creative ways to make your proposal more readable.

You will understand how important readability, writing style, and visual attractiveness are after you read several samples of funded proposals followed by your own. Tired reviewers need all the help you can give them to locate and score the important sections of your proposal. Avoid creativity for its own sake, but think of the reader and your goal as you write, type, and print your proposal.

Keep foremost in your mind that these federal funds are the result of taxes paid by individuals like you, as well as corporations. It is your responsibility to make the plan for how you propose to spend these monies as precise and as clearly related to the project outcome as possible. The tendency to "round up" numbers and pad budgets is a threat to your credibility and could affect your ability to gain the peer reviewers' and federal staff's confidence.

Remember, do not leave anything to chance. All required forms *must* be completed precisely.

CHAPTER 12

• • • • • • • • •

Improving Your Federal Proposal

The Grants Quality Circle

Proactive grantseekers initiate proposal development early in the federal grants cycle and therefore have sufficient time to have their proposals reviewed by their peers before submission. You will improve your proposal and significantly increase your chances for success by asking several colleagues or members of your grants advisory committee to voluntarily role-play the review team that will ultimately pass judgment on your proposal. This pre-submission review process is really a test run or mock review, and the group conducting it is, in essence, your quality circle, as described in Walter Edwards Deming's work in total quality management (TQM).[1] If you follow the TQM model, you will not pay your mock reviewers to take part in the activity. They should be motivated by their desire to help you improve your proposal, increase its probability of acceptance, and, thus, enhance the image of your organization.

The most significant factor in the success of this improvement exercise is how closely each aspect of the mock review resembles the actual federal or state review. The benefits you can derive from this technique are directly related to your ability to create the scenario in which the actual reviewers will find themselves. To arrange a mock review that is similar to what the actual review will be like, procure a list of last year's reviewers, a copy of the scoring system that will be used, and a sample of an exemplary proposal. You should also gather information about the setting in which your proposal will be reviewed.

To make this exercise as valuable as possible, provide your mock review group or grants quality circle with data on the following:

- The training each reviewer receives.
- The setting in which proposals are reviewed (the federal agency, the reviewer's home, both sites, and so on).
- The review process. (Does one reviewer defend the proposal while others try to locate flaws or weaknesses?)
- The scoring system. (Are scores averaged? Are the highest and lowest scores eliminated and the remainder averaged?)
- The amount of time spent reviewing each proposal.

It is essential that you instruct the members of your grants quality circle to spend only the same amount of time reviewing your proposal as the actual reviewers will. Some of your mock reviewers may mistakenly think they will be helping you by taking an inordinate amount of time to read your proposal carefully. You must inform them right away that this would be counterproductive to the end results. If actual reviewers will skim parts of the proposal, then your mock reviewers should do the same. Remind your quality circle participants that they should be trying to *mirror* the actual reviewers, not to do a better job than them! If the actual reviewers will invest over 90 minutes reviewing and scoring each proposal, consider distributing your draft proposal to the members of your grants quality circle before they come together.

The sample letter inviting an individual to participate in a grants quality circle (exhibit 12.1) and the grants quality circle worksheet (exhibit 12.2) will help you carry out this valuable exercise. After the suggestions from your mock review have been incorporated into your final proposal, you are ready to move on to submission.

In some cases it is not feasible to assemble a group of volunteers for a quality circle. There may be too few colleagues in your organization to conduct a role-playing activity such as this, or confidentiality may be an issue if personality problems exist or if competition in the field is fierce. One option in these instances is to ask one or two individuals you trust to review your proposal. Provide them with the same data and worksheets discussed above, and, if necessary, offer them an honorarium for their efforts ($100 or $200 is common). Request that they sign a nondisclosure agreement. Most university grant offices have these agreement forms and will be happy to share a copy with you. This way you can tailor the agreement to your organization with minimal effort.

Few techniques suggested in this book will have a more dramatic effect on the quality of your proposals than the grants quality circle. Support for this activity will be rewarded through the promotion of a better image with reviewers and federal staff, as well as an increase in quality proposals from staff members participating in the activity.

Date

Name
Address

Dear _____:

I would like to take this opportunity to request your input in helping our organization submit the very best grant proposal possible. We are asking that you review the enclosed proposal from the point of view of the federal reviewer. The attached materials will help you role-play the actual manner in which this proposal will be evaluated.

Please read the information on the reviewers' backgrounds and the scoring system and limit the time you spend reading the proposal to the time constraints that the real reviewers will observe. A grants quality circle worksheet has been provided to assist you in recording your scores and comments.

A meeting of all mock reviewers comprising our quality circle has been scheduled for [date _____]. Please bring your grants quality circle worksheet with you to this meeting. The meeting will last less than one hour. Its purpose is to analyze the scores and brainstorm suggestions to improve this proposal.

Sincerely,

Name
Phone Number

SAMPLE LETTER INVITING AN INDIVIDUAL TO PARTICIPATE IN A GRANTS QUALITY CIRCLE

EXHIBIT 12.1

The following information is designed to help you develop the proper focus for the review of the attached proposal.

1.   The Review Panelists

     Proposals are read by review panelists with the following degrees and backgrounds:

     Degrees: _____
     _____
     _____

     Backgrounds (Age, Viewpoints, Biases, and So On): _____
     _____
     _____
     _____

GRANTS QUALITY CIRCLE WORKSHEET

EXHIBIT 12.2

2.   The Time Element and Setting

Number of proposals read by each reviewer: _____

Average length of time spent reading each proposal _____

Proposals are read at the: _____ reviewer's home
                                  _____ reviewer's work
                                  _____ funder's location
                                  _____ other site

3.   The Scoring System
   a.   The scoring system that will be employed is based on a scale of. _____
   _____

   b.   The areas to be scored are (list or include attachment):

   Area   *Total Possible Points*   *Your Score*
   _____
   _____
   _____

   c.   According to the total points per area, how many points represent an outstanding,
        superior, adequate, weak, or poor score? For example, if the total points possible for
        one area are 25, 0-8 = poor, 9-12 = weak, 13-19 = adequate, 20-23 = superior, and
        24-25 = outstanding.
        _____
        _____
        _____

   d.   After recording your scores, list the positive points of the proposal that may appeal to
        the actual reviewer. Also list those areas that seem weak and may cost valuable points.
        List suggestions for improvement.
        _____
        _____
        _____
        _____

GRANTS QUALITY CIRCLE WORKSHEET *(continued)*

EXHIBIT 12.2

REFERENCE

1. Gary Fellers, *The Deming Vision: SPC/TQM for Administrators* (Milwaukee: ASQC Quality Press, 1992).

CHAPTER 13

• • • • • • • • • •

Submission

What to Do and What Not to Do

Although this chapter addresses the federal grants arena, much of the information it contains can also be applied to other government funding sources such as state, county, and city. Irrespective of which type of public funding source you are submitting your proposal to, you do not want to do anything at this late stage that may have a negative impact on your proposal's outcome.

WHAT TO DO

Submit your proposal early. Do not position yourself as a "last-minute applicant." Follow all instructions and every rule. Do not wait until your proposal has been written, has undergone a mock review, and is ready to be sent out before you read the submission rules. Review the submittal requirements early to make sure you have enough time to comply with them. After all of your hard work, it would be ridiculous to jeopardize your chances for success by failing to show funders that you can read and comply with their rules for submission.

Since each government agency and even some of the grant programs within agencies have different submittal procedures, they cannot all be listed here. Several federal programs require you to initial a special sign-off section and provide signatures next to each of the requirements that are most often overlooked. Others call for the inclusion of notarized copies of the board minutes and resolutions that authorized your organization's approval to submit the proposal (especially when matching or in-kind contributions are required). Many agencies require letters of commitment from consortia members.

Unfortunately, many grantseekers read the requirements too late and find that their board will not meet again before the grantor's deadlines. They then include a note with their proposal saying that they will forward the necessary documents at a later date. This is a red flag to grantors and alerts them that an applicant may be a problem.

Even with extensive instructions, grantseekers make mistakes in signing, page length, number of copies, assurances, and so on. In fact, it would be too time-consuming to list all of the problems federal grantors have in gaining compliance with their rules. Review and follow the submittal procedures contained in your application package carefully.

Keep the cover clear and simple. If the grantor requires a special cover sheet, use it. If the grantor does not require a special cover sheet, make sure the cover you place on the application does not interfere with the handling of your proposal. Your cover should act as a luggage tag, allowing for the easy identification of where your proposal is going. The cover should clearly designate the office, division, mail stop, and so on; the program title and CFDA number; the name and phone number of the program officer; your organization's name and return address; and your name.

WHAT NOT TO DO

If possible, do not use elected representatives in the grants process, especially at submittal time. Federal bureaucrats view the use of congresspeople and their aides as potentially unethical. Elected officials want to be viewed by you, the voter, as ready to help in any way, but their assistance should be limited to pre-proposal contact and gathering information about past grantees and reviewers when you are unable to get the information on your own.

Do not ask for extra time or a later submittal date, and do not ask to send in any parts of the proposal after the deadline. Do not contact federal bureaucrats after submission. This is viewed as an attempt to influence their review process and decision.

OTHER SUBMISSION TECHNIQUES

Several optional techniques may be helpful.

1. You could hand deliver your proposal (and all the copies the agency could use) to the designated grants logging center for that agency. While doing so, stop by the program office to thank staff members for their assistance.
2. You could send (or deliver) a copy of your proposal abstract or summary to your congressperson's office. Advise the congressperson that you do not want or expect any intervention at this point, but let

him or her know the approximate or anticipated date of the notice of award (usually several months away). Many times, federal granting officials will inform the congressperson of awards before they notify the grantee. Therefore, it is important to alert your congressperson that you have submitted a proposal and that you will contact him or her again closer to the notification date.

3. A few federal programs encourage and accept proposals submitted electronically. This does not mean by facsimile machine, but rather by computer, using a modem and a telephone line. As this method of submission develops, reviewers will eventually receive proposals by computer and their comments will be returned via e-mail.

Check with your program officer or contact person to confirm the preferred method of submission.

Submission is the final step in demonstrating your ability and desire to comply with the federal granting source's rules and regulations. Hopefully your attention to detail will lead the grantor to believe that you will be equally precise in executing your funded grant. One thing is certain, however; if you fail to comply with all submission rules you will lose your credibility and drastically diminish your chances of being funded.

CHAPTER 14
· · · · · · · · · ·

Federal Grant
Requirements

Many nonprofit agencies exhibit great fear and trepidation over the rules regarding federal grant monies. These fears are basically unwarranted and should be of concern only to nonprofit organizations that do not have adequate fiscal rules and regulations. The restrictions governing usage of federal funds are understandable and in most cases reasonable. Yes, there are instances of disallowed expenditures two or three years after a grant has been completed, but they are avoidable. Most people remember the exception rather than the rule. Over $80 billion in federal grant funds are awarded each year, and only a small fraction of grantees have their expenditures disallowed or experience a problem with an audit. Most likely, your existing personnel, accounting, and purchasing procedures will be adequate. If you must make changes in your system to ensure the adequate handling of federal funds, however, do so. Such changes will increase the credibility of your system.

The federal grants requirement worksheet (see exhibit 14.1) will help you comply with most federal grant requirements. If your organization has a grants administration office, this worksheet may not be necessary, but you, the project director, still need to know the facts so that you can help in the overall administration of your grant.

FEDERAL GRANTS REQUIREMENT WORKSHEET

The federal grants requirement worksheet will help you familiarize yourself with and keep abreast of the basic obligations your nonprofit organization agrees to fulfill by accepting federal grant funds.

1. Complete the first section of the worksheet when you receive notice of funding. Include the federal account identification number and all other information you can supply. It is critical that you record the actual start date or date funded so that you do not change any part of the grant before its official award date. Review your project planner and record the dates on which you must supply progress indicators.
2. List the Office of Management and Budget (OMB) circulars that will govern your grant expenditures and where the circulars are located.
3. Record any information about the number of years of funding that can be applied for.
4. Indicate the percentage and dollar total of the cost-sharing requirements, where the records will be kept, and who will be responsible for keeping them.
5. List the office or person responsible for approval of projects that involve the use of human and animal subjects and for ensuring compliance with federal regulations. If you work for an organization that already has a human subjects review committee, be sure to check with that committee. If your organization does not have a human subjects review committee, do not initiate one. Instead, involve a university- or college-related individual on your grants advisory committee. Ask to have access to his or her institution's review committee. Even though your proposal may not call for the performance of hard-core research, the federal government is very broad in its interpretation of what activities pose a potential danger to humans. In fact, federal officials even require human subjects approval for some needs assessment surveys, model projects, and demonstration grants.
6. Acceptance of federal funds requires that your organization have a policy regarding drug use and counseling of employees.
7. If your grant calls for the creation of unique materials, make note of the rules regarding ownership and use. Noting these in advance reduces problems later.
8. The fair and equal employment rules are reasonable and should pose no problems for most nonprofit organizations.

RAISING AND DOCUMENTING MATCHING FUNDS

One of the most common characteristics of federal grants is the requirement of matching funds or in-kind contributions (also known as cost sharing). An organization can be asked to supply either cash, services, or facilities to match a percentage of the grant. This requirement may change over the years that

Project Title: _____

Project Director: _____

Federal Account Identification Number: _____

Agency Staff: _____

Agency Phone No.: _____ Agency Fax No.: _____

Notification of Award Received On (Date): _____

Start Date of Project: _____

End Date of Project: _____

Dates Reports Are Due: _____

Final Report Due On (Date): _____

Number of Years Funding Can Be Applied For: _____

Matching or In-Kind Requirements: _____% $ _____

Where Matching or In-Kind Records Will Be Kept: _____

Who Will Be Responsible for Keeping Them: _____

Federal Rules Governing This Grant

- OMB Circulars/Guidelines Governing Grant Expenditures:
  _____
  _____
  _____
  _____

- Location of OMB Circulars/Guidelines Governing Grant Expenditures: _____
  _____
  _____
  _____
  _____

- Special Rules and Federal Management Circulars (List from Assurances Section of Proposal): _____
  _____
  _____
  _____
  _____

- Location of Special Rules and Federal Management Circulars:
  _____
  _____
  _____
  _____

- Federal Rules and Your Organization's Policy On

  Copyrights:

  Patents:

FEDERAL GRANTS REQUIREMENT WORKSHEET

EXHIBIT 14.1

144

Human Subjects Review (Include Person Responsible for Compliance and Approval):

Drug Usage and Counseling:

Ownership and Use:

Fair and Equal Employment:

Other:

FEDERAL GRANTS REQUIREMENT WORKSHEET *(continued)*

EXHIBIT 14.1

federal funds support the project. For example, year one may require a 20 percent match, year two a 40 percent match, and year three a 50 percent match.

The worksheet on sources of matching funds (see exhibit 14.2) can help you plan a successful matching funds campaign before you approach federal agencies. The worksheet contains several standard methods for cost sharing and provides an evaluation system for each method. (This worksheet can also be useful when working with foundations and corporations that request matching support.)

Project Title: _____

Total Project Cost: _____

Match Required: _____% $ _____

Review each of the following sources of matching funds. Check with federal officials to ensure that your match is in compliance with their rules and will be accepted. Make sure that nothing listed under your match has been provided from federal funds.

1.   Personnel—List the percentage of time and effort of each individual who will be contributing to the match. Include salaries, wages, and fringe benefits.

WORKSHEET ON SOURCES OF MATCHING FUNDS

EXHIBIT 14.2

Options:

- Include the time and effort of volunteers, consultants, and/or corporate sponsors if allowable by the grantor.

- If the project calls for staff training or development, will your organization be required to increase salaries? If so, check with the grantor to see whether this can be listed as a match.

2. Equipment—List any equipment that will be purchased primarily to carry out this project. Include the cost of each piece and the total equipment cost.

3. Facilities—List the location, square footage, and cost per foot for each facility and the total facilities (space) cost.

4. Foundation/Corporate Grantors—What other grantors could you approach for a grant to match this grant?

- Foundations:

- Corporations:

5. Fund-Raising Activities—In some cases you may have to resort to fund-raising activities to develop your matching portion. List the activities and the net return expected from each.

- Special Events (Dance, Raffle, etc.):

- Sales of Products:

- Other:

WORKSHEET ON SOURCES OF MATCHING FUNDS *(continued)*

EXHIBIT 14.2

FEDERAL GRANTS MANAGEMENT CIRCULARS

The highly regulated, detailed rules about grant management are probably the most imposing characteristic of federal grants. These rules may specify allowable costs, indirect cost rates, accounting requirements, and the like. Before getting involved in government grants, you and/or your accounting department should review the appropriate grants management circulars. Such a review usually diminishes fears about your organization's ability to comply with federal grants requirements. In most cases you will find that your organization has safeguards in effect that meet the requirements.

The Office of Management and Budget produces circulars outlining uniform standards for financial dealings with government granting agencies. These circulars, which are described in table 14.1, can be ordered from the Superintendent of Documents, Government Printing Office, Washington, DC 20402-9238, (202) 783-3238.

The following section is a broad description of OMB Circular A-114. State and local governments must also review OMB Circulars A-87 and A-142.

OMB Circular A-114

OMB Circular A-114 is entitled "Grants and Agreements with Institutions of Higher Education, Hospitals, and Other Nonprofit Organizations." The 30-page circular, along with its updates and attachments, budget forms, and cash request instructions, is a guide to the rules regarding federal grants. Attachments to the circular cover the following areas:

- cash depositories
- bonding and insurance
- retention and custodial requirements for records
- program income
- cost sharing and matching
- standards for financial management systems
- financial reporting requirements
- monitoring and reporting program performance
- payment requirements
- revision of financial plans
- close-out procedures
- suspension and termination
- standards for applying
- property management standards
- procurement standards

Please be advised that you should always refer to the most current circular for the specific rules and regulations in these areas.

Fears concerning the expenditure of federal grant funds are reduced when you request the appropriate OMB circulars for your type of organization and review the rules with your fiscal staff. From purchasing to personnel, your organization will most likely already have the necessary safeguards in place. Those areas that look as if they will pose a problem can be addressed in a general manner, for all federal grants, or handled separately, case by case, to avoid any problems.

TABLE 14.1

A Description of OMB Circulars

Name	What It Does	Areas Covered	Special Ramifications
OMB Circular A-21	Defines cost principles for federal research and development grants to educational institutions	Cost definition, allowable costs, unallowable costs	Long and complex circulars; wide range of allowable costs
OMB Circular A-95	Designates a procedure of review by local government before dispursing federal funds	Any grant area covered is listed in CFDA by program number	Get on the local committee or develop a "friend" who is on it; call your county planning department for information
OMB Circular A-102	Sets administrative standards for federal agencies in management of grants to state and local governments	Application forms, grant payments, eligibility, matching share, financial management system, property management procurement standards	Although different federal agencies may set their own guidelines, they are usually in harmony with the standard set down in this circular
OMB Circular A-110	Set administrative standards for federal agencies in the management of grants to nonprofit organizations	Application forms, grant payment, matching shares, procurement standards	No federal agency may set more rigid standards than those outlined in the circular; exceptions to this rule are allowed when grantee has weak financial history
OMB Circular A-111	Sets out guidelines for joint funding of grant programs		Tells how to get funding from agency for more than one agency for your project
Federal Management Circular 74-4	Establishes principles and standards for determining costs applicable to grants and contracts to state and local government	Outlines what costs are allowable under grants and contracts	Tells what rules apply to lease and rental of equipment, etc.

CHAPTER 15

••••••••

Dealing with the Decision of Public Funding Sources

The federal government is attempting to streamline the grants process. This includes making award determinations that are understandable and the same across all granting programs. Instead of making confusing determinations (such as "supportable but not fundable"), the federal government in now using these determinations:

- accepted (as written)
- accepted with modifications (usually budget modifications, which will affect some activities)
- rejected (the proposal did not reach the level or score required for funding)

ACCEPTED

If your proposal is accepted, consider taking the following steps:

1. Thank the grantor. Whether you are notified by phone, by letter, or electronically, send the program or project officer a thank-you letter showing your appreciation for the time and effort staff and reviewers expended on your proposal.
2. Request the reviewers' comments, and include a self-addressed label for the funding source's convenience.
3. Ask the federal official for insight into what you could have done better.
4. Invite the program or project officer for a site visit.

5. Ask the official what mistakes successful grantees often make in carrying out their funded grant so you can be sure to avoid these errors.

6. Review the reporting structure. What does the grantor require and when? Will your dates for milestones and progress indicators be helpful?

ACCEPTED WITH BUDGET MODIFICATIONS

Should your proposal receive this response, do the following:

1. Send the funding source a thank-you letter.
2. Call the funding source and suggest that the program officer refer to your project planner to negotiate the budget terms.
3. Discuss the option of eliminating some of the project's methods or activities.
4. If several activities must be eliminated, consider dropping the accomplishment of an objective or reducing the expected degree of change.
5. If you are forced to negotiate away the supporting structure necessary to achieve your objectives, be prepared to turn down the funds. After all, you do not want to enter into an agreement that will cause you to lose credibility later.

REJECTED

If your proposal is rejected, take the following actions aimed at developing insight into the changes you need to make in your proposal for the next submission cycle:

1. Send the funding official a thank-you letter in appreciation for his or her time and effort as well as that of the reviewers and staff. Let the funding official know that although you were aware of the risk of failure before you invested your time in applying, you would appreciate assistance in reapplying.
2. Request the reviewers' comments. Enclose a self-addressed stamped envelope for their convenience.
3. Ask the funding official for his or her suggestions.
4. Find out whether your proposal could possibly be funded as a pilot project, as a needs assessment, or in some other way.
5. Ask whether there are any ways the funding source could assist you in getting ready for the next submission cycle, such as conducting a preliminary review.

6. Ask whether it would be wise for you to reapply. What are your chances and what would you have to change?
7. Ask whether you could become a reviewer to learn more about the review process.

By examining the reviewers' comments you may find that some reviewers scored a section of your proposal as outstanding, while others gave the same section a low score. This situation can create a dilemma. Changing your proposal to reflect one reviewer's comments may negate another reviewer's comments, and your changes could result in resubmission scores that are just average. Ask the grantor what you can do about this situation. Also, ask an outside expert to review your proposal; even if you must pay someone to review the proposal, you need insight into what is causing this discrepancy.

Recently, some federal agencies have started informing grantseekers at the time of rejection whether they should change their proposal and reapply or avoid re-submittal and change their approach entirely.

Your response to your grant application's outcome must be positive. Whether you are jubilant or depressed, thank the grantor and seek to learn as much as possible from the experience. Demonstrate your willingness to learn from the funding source's feedback. You will find reinforcement for your positive behavior and become aware of how to avoid making the same mistakes.

CHAPTER 16

•••••••••

Follow-Up with Government Funding Sources

The object of following up is to position yourself as an asset to funding sources and not as a pest. You want to develop professional relationships and maintain contact with funding sources throughout the grants process, not just at award time. In addition to advising funders of your willingness to serve as a reviewer, consider:

- forwarding notes on special articles or books in your area to them
- inviting them to visit your organization
- asking whether they would like to speak at your professional group or association's conference, or at a special grants conference
- asking them what meetings or conferences they will be attending so that you can look them up
- requesting information about what you can do to have an impact on legislation affecting their funding levels or allocations

By remaining on grantors' mailing lists and reviewing the *Federal Register,* you will gain advance knowledge of the next funding opportunity. Do not wait until next year's deadline to begin thinking about your ensuing application. Start to plan for next year right after funding decisions are made for the current year.

The best way to learn what is going on is to visit the funding source personally. Keep in touch. Watch for meeting announcements in the *Federal Register.* Testify at committee hearings that will affect the agency and its funding level. Send the agency blind copies of your efforts to have an impact on legislation for them (and yourself). Use your association memberships and legislative committees to push for changes that benefit the particular agency, and write to Senate and House appropriations committees.

DEVELOPING CONTINUED GRANT SUPPORT

The key to continued success is to repeat the steps that have brought you to this point. If you have used the concepts presented in this manual to develop a proactive grants process, you have a system that alerts you to changes in program rules, deadlines, and the like through the *Federal Register,* mailing lists, personal contacts, and established links.

Although federal officials may change jobs and positions, they seem to reappear again and again. A systematic approach to recording research on funding sources and officials will prove useful as you come across old friends and make new ones. By maintaining your relationship, whether you have received funding or not, you demonstrate to funding sources that you plan to be around for a while and that you will not forget them as soon as you receive their check. Unfortunately, changes in staffing at government agencies make maintaining contacts more difficult. Just when things are going great, the program officers you have been working with will move on. But take heart, they may appear again somewhere down the grants road, so keep on their good side!

PART
3

• • • • • • • • •

Private Funding
Sources

CHAPTER 17

• • • • • • • • •

The Differences between Private and Public Funding

The private marketplace consists of two major segments—2.3 million corporations and 35,765 foundations. Estimates are that only 30 to 40 percent of corporations are contributors in this marketplace; therefore, the *total* number of potential private grantors is approximately 800,000 corporations and 35,765 foundations.

The foundation marketplace can be divided into several categories:

- national general purpose
- special purpose
- community
- family
- corporate

Foundations in each of these categories not only fund different types of proposals, they also look for different characteristics in those organizations they select as grantees.

Another important, but sometimes overlooked, private funding type is nonprofit organizations. This group includes professional associations, Hellenic groups, business groups, service clubs, and membership groups. Like foundations, corporations, and government grantors, nonprofit organizations have specific funding preferences and needs.

In 1993 foundations and corporations awarded over $15 billion in grants, while the government awarded approximately $80 billion. Total amount awarded is one of the major differences between the two marketplaces. The amount of federal money awarded is over five times the amount of private money awarded, which is one of the reasons why it is always good practice to check out federal funds first.

The private grants marketplace is very different from the public market-place in many other ways too. For example, the federal government has many bureaucrats involved in awarding and monitoring its $80 billion. The private sector, on the other hand, is characterized by having little to no staff. Even some of the largest foundations have only small, part-time, or shared staff. In fact, fewer than 1,000 foundations have an office, and there are only 1,500 professionals and 1,700 support staff members in all 35,765-plus foundations.

GRANTSEEKERS' DECISION MATRIX

The grantseekers' decision matrix (see table 17.1) will help you develop your knowledge of the principal types of funding sources and their differences and similarities. It summarizes the major funding characteristics and preferences of federal funding programs, state funding programs, foundations, corporations, and nonprofit organizations.

Column 1 of the matrix lists the major funding source types. Columns 2 through 10 provide information on variables such as geographic area/need, type of project, and award size. This information will help you select the best type of funding source for your project. Please note that the matrix is meant to point you in the right direction only. Follow-up research will allow the proactive grantseeker to determine the funder's interest, the appropriateness of the project, and the proper request amount before proposal preparation and submission.

To achieve grants success you must be vigilant in attempting to consider your proposal, including the amount of your request, from the grantor's point of view. It should be increasingly evident that the "one proposal fits all" method of grantseeking will not meet with a positive response from such a diverse group of private grantors.

TABLE 17.1

GRANTSEEKERS' DECISION MATRIX

Type Funder	Geographic/Need	Type of Project	Grant award size For Field on Int	Image	Credentials of P.I. or P.D.	Preproposal contact ·Any face to face is·	Proposal contact	Review System	Grants Administration (Rules)
Government									
1. Federal	Varies—but must have national/international	Model Innovation Research	Large	Very national image+	National image	Write, phone, go and see	Extensive—many forms long	Staff and peer review Human subjects and animals	Many / complies OMB cir audits + match $
2. State	State / local need	Model and Replication	Medium Small	Statewide image+	Statewide image	Write, phone, go and see	Extensive—many forms long	Staff and some peer review	Many / complex audits + match $
Foundation									
3. National General Purpose	National need—local regional population	Model Innovative	Large Medium	National image+	National+	Write, phone	Short—concept paper—longer form if interested	Staff and some peer review	Few audits and rules
4. Special Purpose	Need in area of interest	Model Innovative Research	Large to Small	Image not as critical as solution is	Image in field of interest+	Write, phone	Short—concept paper—longer form if interested	Board review (some staff)	Few audits and rules
5. Community	Local need	Operation Replication Building Equipment	Small	Local image+	Respected locally	Write, phone, go and see	Short—letter proposal	Board review	Few audits and rules
6. Family	Varies—but geographic concern for need	Innovation Replication Building/Equipment Some Research	Medium Small	Regional image+	Local/regional	Write, phone	Short—letter proposal	Board	Very few audits and rules
Corporate									
7. Corporate—Large	Near plants or offices	Product Development Replication Building Equipment	Medium Small	Local image+ Employee involvement	Local, national	Write, phone, go and see	Short—letter proposal	Contributions committee	Very few audits and rules
8. Corporate—Small	Very near to company	Same	Medium Small	Local image critical	Local	Write, phone, go and see	Short—letter proposal	Owner/Family	Very few audits and rules
Other									
9. Nonprofit Organizations and Service Clubs	Local	Replication Building Equipment Scholarship	Small	Local image and member involvement	Local	Write, phone, present to committee or to members	Short—letter proposal	Committee review and/or member vote	Few rules and audit

CHAPTER 18

· · · · · · · · · ·

How to Record Research and Information

A key to successful grantseeking with foundations and corporations is to gather the most complete and accurate information possible on funding sources before you approach them. The corporate and foundation research form (see exhibit 18.1) will help you do this. Complete one worksheet for each granting agency you research. Try to provide as much information on the form as possible, but, remember, even a partially completed worksheet will help you make a more intelligent decision on whether you should solicit grant support from a particular funding source. Enlist volunteers to ferret out the information you need. Let your research guide your solicitation strategy and proposal development process.

Bauer Associates' Winning Links software program has been designed to assist you in recording and accessing data in an efficient manner. (For ordering information, see the list of resources available from Bauer Associates at the end of the book.)

In addition to the research you conduct on grant-making organizations, you should also uncover and record as much information as possible on the decision makers in those organizations. The funding executive research worksheet (see exhibit 18.2) is designed to help you do this.

Do not ask funding executives for the information on the worksheet. Instead, use books such as *Trustees of Wealth, Dun & Bradstreet's Directory of Corporate Management,* and *Who's Who* publications to find information on private funding officials (see chapter 20). Also check periodical indexes, newspapers, and funding source publications such as newsletters and annual reports. Ask your advisory committee members whether they know the funding executives, know of them, or know a person who has firsthand knowledge of

The following form outlines the data you need to collect in order to make a decision to seek funds from this grant source. Your attempts to collect as much of this information as possible will prove rewarding.

*Source/Date

1. Name of Corp./Fdn.: _____

   Address: _____

   Phone: _____

2. Contact Person: _____
   Title: _____
   Links from Our Organization to Contact Person: _____
   _____
   _____
   _____

3. Grantor's Areas of Interest: _____
   _____
   _____

4. Eligibility Requirements/Restrictions:
   a. Activities Funded: _____
   _____
   _____

   b. Organizations Funded: _____
   _____
   _____

   c. Geographic Funding Preferences: _____
   _____
   _____

   d. Other Requirements/Restrictions: _____
   _____
   _____
   _____

5. Information Available:

	Sent For	Received
Guidelines	_____	_____
Newsletter	_____	_____
Annual Report	_____	_____
_____	_____	_____
_____	_____	_____

CORPORATE AND FOUNDATION RESEARCH FORM

EXHIBIT 18.1

6.	a. Contributions Committee Members/Board of Directors/Officers:

_____
_____
_____

	b. Staff Full Time Part Time

_____   _____   _____
_____   _____   _____
_____   _____   _____

7.	Deadline: _____
	Application Process/Requirements: _____
	_____
	_____

8.	Financial Information: Fiscal Year 19___
	Corporation (Not Corporate Foundation): _____
	Sales: $_____ Parent Company: _____
	Corp. Sites: _____ # Employees: _____
	_____
	_____

	Credit Rating:_____ Source: _____
	Private or Publicly Held: _____
	If Publicly Held: Stock Price: $ _____
	                     Dividend: $ _____

	Products Produced/Distributed: _____
	_____
	_____

	Foundation: Corporate_____ Private _____
	Asset Base: $ _____
	Are there current gifts to build the asset base?
	yes _____ no _____
	If yes, how much in the most recent year? $ _____

	Total No. of Grants Awarded in 19____: _____
	Total Amt. Awarded in Grants in 19____: $ _____
	High Grant: $ _____
	Low Grant: $ _____
	Avg. Grant: $ _____
	In our area of interest there were _____, totaling $_____

	High Grant in Our Interest Area: $ _____
	Low Grant in Our Interest Area: $ _____
	Avg. Grant in Our Interest Area: $ _____

9.	Number of Proposals Received in 19_____: #
	Number of Proposals Awarded in 19_____: #

CORPORATE AND FOUNDATION RESEARCH FORM *(continued)*

EXHIBIT 18.1

```
Sample Grants in Our Area of Interest:
Recipient Organization                          Amount

_____          _____

_____          _____

_____          _____


* Please indicate the source of information and the date it was recorded.
```

CORPORATE AND FOUNDATION RESEARCH FORM (continued)

EXHIBIT 18.1

them. You can also pick up useful information from telephone conversations and personal visits. If you visit a grantor in person, be sure to use your observation skills. Look for favorite pictures, memorabilia, college diplomas, certificates, notices of appreciation, and so on.

Naturally, you do not have to have funding executive information in order to consider submitting a proposal, but it will increase your chances of success. The information you collect and record on your funding executive research worksheet will help you in two major ways.

1. It will allow you to determine, in advance, likely preferences and biases you will encounter at an in-person grant interview.
2. It will make it easier to locate links between your organization and a funding source.

Recording accurate research on foundation and corporate decision makers will raise your chances of success. In addition, your ability to attract future funding will increase as you develop a history and file on each of the grantors you are interested in.

```
                                                        Source/Date
1. Funding Source Name: _____
2. Name of Contact Person/Director/Contributions Officer: _____
   _____
3. Title: _____   Birth Date: _____
4. Business Address: _____
   _____
5. Home Address: _____
   _____
6. Education:
   Secondary: _____
   College: _____
   Post Graduate: _____
7. Military Service: _____
```

FUNDING EXECUTIVE RESEARCH WORKSHEET

EXHIBIT 18.2

8. Clubs/Affiliations: _____

_____

9. Corporate Board Memberships: _____

10. Business History (Promotions, Other Firms, etc.): _____

_____

_____

_____

11. Religious Affiliation: _____
12. Other Philanthropic Activities: _____

_____

13. Newspaper/Magazine Clipping Attached:
    Yes: _____
14. Contacts in Our Organization: _____

_____

15. Recent Articles/Publications: _____

_____

16. Awards/Honors: _____

_____

_____

_____

FUNDING EXECUTIVE RESEARCH WORKSHEET *(continued)*

EXHIBIT 18.2

CHAPTER 19

Foundation Funding Source Research Tools

Basic research tools for developing your list of potential foundation grantors can be accessed at little or no charge and usually within a short distance from your workplace. The foundations themselves have developed a network of libraries where foundation grantseekers can access foundation grant information. A list of this network can be found at the end of this chapter.

Before you begin searching for your best possible grantor, review the following resources. Although you may purchase resources or access them through electronic transmission, first explore the hard-copy versions to determine your level of usage and the cost-effectiveness of purchasing versus traveling to a cooperating collection or the public library.

The whole point of your research effort is to focus on the sources most likely to fund your proposal. Even if you are a novice grantseeker, do not be tempted to send letters to any and all foundations that are even remotely related to your project area. If pre-proposal contact is allowed or a proposal format is provided or suggested, take every opportunity to develop an individualized, tailored proposal for each of your best prospects.

THE FOUNDATION DIRECTORY

The Foundation Directory, the major source of information on larger foundations, covers 6,785 of the 35,765 foundations. These 6,785 foundations hold assets in excess of $162 billion, leaving the remaining 29,065 foundations with $8 billion in total assets. The foundations described in *The Foundation Directory* make grants totaling over $8 billion, or 90 percent of all foundation funding.

To be included in *The Foundation Directory* a foundation must:

* hold assets of a least $2 million, or
* distribute $200,000 or more in grants each year.

The directory contains information on independent, community, and company-sponsored foundations. (Company-sponsored foundations are foundations that corporations have initiated as part of their philanthropy program. Only those company-sponsored foundations that meet the criteria outlined above appear in the directory.) Foundations included in the directory appear in numerical order, and each has its own entry number.

The directory contains six indexes to assist you in your search for appropriate funding sources:

1. Index to donors, officers, and trustees
2. Geographic index
3. Types of support index
4. Subject index
5. Foundations new to edition index
6. Foundation name index

One technique that will add a whole new dimension to your foundation grants effort is to become adept at using the index to donors, officers, and trustees. When your organization's "friends" provide you with their links, pay special attention to those people who list board memberships or friends on foundation boards. In most cases, your "friend" will be willing to discuss your project with fellow board members or with friends who serve on other boards.

The Foundation Directory Part 2 is also available for your use. This supplemental directory includes over 4,000 midsize foundations with annual grant programs from $50,000 to $200,000. Both directories are published by the Foundation Center, 79 Fifth Avenue, Dept. ME, New York, NY 10003-3076, (800) 424-9836.

Using *The Foundation Directory*

The most productive approach to using the directory is to first review chapter 5 on redefining your project idea. After identifying key words and fields of interest (e.g., children, Native Americans, music), you can use the directory's subject index to determine which foundations have an active interest in the area for which you are seeking grant support. Another approach is to use the types of support index to identify foundations interested in your type of project (e.g., conferences, building funds, equipment, matching funds).

Before you rush into reviewing the actual foundation entries, remember that a significant portion of foundations possess a geographic homing device. In other words, they give only where they live. The directory's geographic index will point you in the direction of those foundations that may be interested in your project because of its location.

The best match will be a foundation that funds your subject area, type of project, and geographic area. Do not despair if the use of the geographic index produces limited prospects. Many foundations have a national and even international interest in certain subject areas. While these foundations may not have granted funds in your state or community before, they may do so if approached properly.

As you do your research, be sure to record the name of the foundation, the state, and the directory entry number for each foundation you are interested in. Recording this information will help you refer to the foundation quickly.

Entries in *The Foundation Directory* consist of

- Entry number.
- Name, address, and telephone number.
- Date and place of establishment.
- Donors.
- Foundation type.
- Financial data: Including assets, expenditures, total number of grant dollars, number of grants made, and high and low grant awards. (One important variable that is not covered in this section is which areas of interest received the high and low grants. You will need to do more in-depth research to uncover this information.)
- Purpose and activities: What areas the foundation prefers to support. (This information does not include how much of the foundation's grant money is attributed to each area.)
- Fields of interest: The stated interests of the funding source. (Use this information to narrow down your funding source choices by comparing your proposal to the foundation's stated interests.)
- Types of support: The funding mechanisms used by the grantor to support its stated fields of interest. (Use this information to match your proposal with the type of grant the foundation supports. For example, if the foundation prefers research over model or demonstration grants, you could consider adding a research component to your proposal.)
- Limitations: Including geographic preferences, restrictions by subject or type of recipient, and specific types of support the foundation does not provide.
- Application information: Including the name of the contact person, the preferred form of application, the number of copies of proposals requested, application deadlines, frequency and dates of board meetings, and the general amount of time the foundation takes to notify applicants of the board's decision. Some foundations will indicate that they contribute to preselected organizations only, that applications are not being accepted, or that their funds are currently committed to ongoing

projects. When this occurs, your only chance for a grant is to review the list of officers and trustees with your grants advisory group to see whether you have a link to the foundation. In other instances, foundations will state that they do not allow pre-proposal contact and that the desired contact is by letter only. The letter they are referring to and its development are the focus of chapter 22.

- Officers, principal administrators, trustees, or directors: Names and titles of members of the foundation's governing body.
- Number of staff: Number of professional and support staff employed by the foundation and the part-time or full-time status of these employees.
- EIN: Employer Identification Number assigned by the Internal Revenue Service.

A fictitious *Foundation Directory* entry is provided in exhibit 19.1. For the purpose of explanation, assume that the grantseeker is interested in securing grants for projects related to developmental disabilities. Entry number 5025, Flubocker Foundation, is a good choice for the prospective grantee to examine further because the grantseeker's project falls within the foundation's stated fields of interest and will take place in the foundation's preferred geographic funding area—New York State. The prospective grantee will have to conduct more in-depth research to discover how much money the Flubocker Foundation has actually awarded to projects related to people with developmental disabilities and the high and low grants in that particular area.

THE FOUNDATION GRANTS INDEX

The Foundation Grants Index contains over 65,000 descriptions of grants of $10,000 or more, and each grant description has an identification number. You can use this reference book to search for the right grantor before consulting *The Foundation Directory* or after you have located a prospective grantor to see exactly what grant awards it has made in your field of interest. In either case, the goal is to find accurate information on the size, number, and recipients of grants awarded by each foundation you anticipate approaching.

The Foundation Grants Index is divided into seven sections:

1. Grants: Contains the main listing of grants and is arranged by major subject fields. The grants are listed alphabetically by state, foundation name, and recipient organization name within the foundation. Grant descriptions are arranged in numerical order for easy reference.
2. Recipient name index: An alphabetical index of domestic and foreign recipients.
3. Subject index: Will be particularly helpful if you begin your search for prospective grantors with *The Foundation Grants Index*. By us-

5025 Flubocker Foundation
20 Money Place
New York, NY 10005   (212)234-1234

Established in 1952 in NY.

Donor(s): Members of Flubocker Family
Foundation type: Independent
Financial data (yr. ended 12/31/94): Assets,
$27,137,892 (M); expenditures, $936,152;
including $756,300 for 32 grants
(high: $37,000; low: $1,500)
Fields of interest: Education, youth, social
services, higher education, handicapped.
Types of support: Operating budgets, special
projects, research, seed money.
Limitations: Giving primarily in NY. No
grants to individuals.
Application Information: Application form not
required.
Initial approach: Letter
Copies of proposal: One
Board meeting date(s): October
Write: Mary J. Flubocker, V.P.
Officers: Melvin J. Flubocker, Pres.; Mary J.
Flubocker, V.P.; Sylvia Skim, Secy.; Jonathan
S. Bills, Treas.
Trustees: Irving Flood, Laurel Lisez, Maxwell
Litesky, Luch Maddox, William Martin, C. Pape,
A. Rankin, Anna Slide, Arthur Flubocker, M.
Stillwater, Jr.
Number of staff: None.
EIN: 979171152

FOUNDATION DIRECTORY ENTRY (FICTITIOUS DATA)

EXHIBIT 19.1

ing the subject index in conjunction with the key words you have
developed, you can discover what grants have been awarded in your
area of interest and by what foundations. The more varied your key
words are, the greater the likelihood of locating an interested grantor.

4. Type of support/geographic index: Useful in locating those founda-
    tions whose geographic preference coincides with your location.

5. Recipient category index: Provides insight into what foundations
    fund your competitors and other organizations with similar inter-
    ests. This index is useful in educating your administration about the
    role that foundation grants play in organizations similar to yours.

6. Index to grants by foundation: Lists all the grants found in section 1
    alphabetically by foundation state, then by foundation name.

7. Foundations (addresses and limitations): Alphabetically lists the foundations included in the book, along with their addresses, telephone numbers, and limitations, including geographic, program, and type of support restrictions.

In our example, we can use a variety of key terms to uncover foundations that have funded projects on developmental disabilities in the past or have given to a related field. For instance, we could look in section 3, the subject index, under *developmentally disabled, education, mental health,* or *human services.* Let's assume we look under *developmentally disabled* and find several grants, including entry numbers 33688, 33689, and 33690. By looking for these identification numbers in section 1, Grants, we can find the funding sources that awarded these grants.

Unfortunately, the entries under these identification numbers will not provide you with the same information you will find in *The Foundation Directory.* In fact, in section 1 of *The Foundation Grants Index* you will not even be able to ascertain the complete address of a funding source; however, you can locate this information in section 7. Once you have done so, you should go to *The Foundation Directory* to gather more information on the potential grantor.

If you locate a prospective funding source in *The Foundation Directory* first, then you can use *The Foundation Grants Index* to find out how many of the foundation's grants in excess of $10,000 went to each area of interest. For example, using the subject index in *The Foundation Grants Index,* you could look up relatively quickly the grants awarded by the fictitious Flubocker Foundation. In the subject index, the entry "disabled" has 23 subentries for different areas of disability. The subentry "education" would lead us to the Flubocker Foundation.

As you can see from the hypothetical *Foundation Grants Index* entry in exhibit 19.2, you can find the grants for over $10,000 awarded by the Flubocker Foundation first under the subject field ("Disabled/Education"), then by the state in which the foundation is located ("New York"), and then by the foundation name ("Flubocker"). A review of the list of grants and the information already gathered from *The Foundation Directory* indicates that the Flubocker Foundation does indeed value the area of developmental disabilities since its high grant of $37,000 (taken from the financial data provided in *The Foundation Directory*) was awarded in this area.

INTERNAL REVENUE SERVICE TAX RETURNS

Federal law requires that all foundations provide their tax returns for public information purposes. A foundation's 990-PF return gives fiscal details on receipts and expenditures, compensation of officers, capital gains or losses, and other financial matters. Form 990-AR includes information on foundation managers, assets, and grants paid or committed for future payment.

Disabled/Education

New York

Flubocker Foundation

    33688. **Zap University, Ithaca, NY.** $37,000, 1994. For center to rehabilitate developmentally disabled in Ithaca area. 01/94 NL.

    33689. **Community Development League, NYC, NY.** $18,500, 1994. For programs to find employment for the developmentally disabled. 01/94 NL.

    33690. **SUNY at Bayshore, Bayshore, NY.** $10,000, 1994. For research into developmental disabilities. 01/94 NL.

FOUNDATION GRANTS INDEX ENTRY (FICTITIOUS DATA)

EXHIBIT 19.2

Exhibit 19.3 is a sample of the form that all private foundations must return to the Internal Revenue Service. While *The Foundation Directory* and *The Foundation Grants Index* are useful reference tools, they are basically compilations of information from many sources, and there is no guarantee as to the accuracy of the information provided. In fact, *The Foundation Grants Index* is based on only 50 percent of the actual total foundation grants.

The Internal Revenue Service, however, deals in specifics. By reviewing the returns of the private foundations you believe to be your best funding prospects, you can find valuable information such as the actual amount of assets, new gifts received, total grants paid out, and so on. Most important, you can view a list of all the grants they have paid, including grants for less than $10,000.

Copies of tax returns for the past three years for all 35,765 foundations can be viewed for free at the Foundation Center's national reference collections in New York City and Washington, DC. In addition, the Foundation Center has designated libraries as cooperating collections. These cooperating collections have tax returns for private foundations located in their state and, in some cases, surrounding states.

THE FOUNDATION CENTER

Incorporated as a nonprofit organization in 1953, the Foundation Center was formed by foundations as an independent national service center. Part of the Foundation Center's mission is to provide accurate information on philanthropy, with special emphasis on foundation grant making. The center covers its operating expenses through grants from foundations and corporations, the sale of publications, and fee-based subscriber services. The center operates four reference collections, one in New York, one in Washington, DC, one in Cleveland, and one in San Francisco. Each of these is staffed by Foundation Center employees. As previously mentioned, the New York and Washington collections have the Internal Revenue Service records for all foundations. The Cleveland and San Francisco collections focus on foundations located in the Midwest and the West.

Exhibit 19.4 shows the locations of the reference collections operated by the Foundation Center, as well as the 200 cooperating collections operated by libraries, community foundations, and other nonprofit agencies. Those cooperating collections marked with a bullet have Internal Revenue Service returns on microfiche for their state or region.

Locate the collection nearest you and make a visit. In addition to having the most current editions of *The Foundation Directory, The Foundation Grants Index,* and IRS tax returns, the collection probably will have several other valuable grants resource materials including

- computer-generated printouts or guides that list grants by subject area
- state foundation directories
- other publications from the Foundation Center and other sources (see the list of resources for more detail).

ELECTRONIC RETRIEVAL AND DATABASE SEARCHES

Many public libraries, university libraries, and higher education grants offices are able to perform electronic searches of *The Foundation Directory, Foundation Grants Index,* and other resources containing foundation grants information. Explore the possibility of computer search and retrieval by contacting an established grants office near you.

Knight-Ridder Information Services is a commercial organization that provides access to hundreds of databases in a range of subject areas. The Foundation Center offers *The Foundation Directory* file and *The Foundation Grants Index* file online through Knight-Ridder. In addition, there are several comprehensive grants databases, including *KR Information OnDisc: The GRANTS Database,* that contain information on government and corporate grants as well as foundation grants (see the list of resources for more information).

Research to locate your most likely foundation grantor need not be labor-intensive or costly. Using electronic databases in your search will save you time, but the actual information you will find is identical to that in the print form. The key is to locate the data that will enable you to estimate your chances for success before you invest any more time in seeking a foundation grant.

Form **990-PF**	**Return of Private Foundation**	**PAGE 1**
Department of the Treasury Internal Revenue Service	or Section 4947(a)(1) Charitable Trust Treated as a Private Foundation (See separate instructions.) **Note:** You may be able to use a copy of this return to satisfy state reporting requirements.	**19 91**

For the calendar year 1991, or fiscal year beginning _____ , 1991, and ending _____ , 19 ___

Please type, print, or attach label. See Specific Instructions.

Name of organization **NAME**

Number, street, and room (or P.O. box number) **ADDRESS**

City or town, state, and ___

A Employer identification number

B State registration number (see instruction F)

C If application pending, check here . . ▶ ☐

D Foreign organizations, check here . . . ▶ ☐

H Check type of organization: ☐ Exempt private foundation
☐ 4947(a)(1) trust (see instruction C) ☐ Other taxable private foundation

I Fair market value ... end of year **ASSETS** ... col. (c), line 16)

J Accounting method: ☐ Cash ☐ Accrual ☐ Other (specify) _____ (Part I column (d) must be on cash basis.)

E If your private foundation status terminated under section 507(b)(1)(A), check here . ▶ ☐

F If the foundation is in a 60-month termination under section 507(b)(1)(B), check here . ▶ ☐

G If address changed, check here. . . . ▶ ☐

Part I	**Analysis of Revenue and Expenses** (The total of amounts in columns (b), (c), and (d) may not necessarily equal the amounts in column (a) (see instructions).)	**(a)** Revenue and expenses per books	**(b)** Net investment income	**(c)** Adjusted net income	**(d)** Disbursements for charitable purposes
Revenue	1 Contributions, gifts, grants, etc., received (attach schedule)				
	2 Contributions from split-interest trusts				
	3 Interest on savings and temporary cash investments				
	4 Dividends and interest from securities				
	5a Gross rents				
	b (Net rental income or (loss) _____)				
	6 Net gain or (loss) from sale of assets not on line 10				
	7 Capital gain net income (from Part IV, line 2) . .				
	8 Net short-term capital gain				
	9 Income modifications				
	10a Gross sales minus returns and allowances				
	b Minus: Cost of goods sold				
	c Gross profit or (loss) (attach schedule)				
	11 Other income (attach schedule)				
	12 **Total** (add lines 1 through 11).				
Operating and Administrative Expenses	13 Compensation of officers, directors, trustees, etc.				
	14 Other employee salaries and wages				
	15 Pension plans, employee benefits				
	16a Legal fees (attach schedule)				
	b Accounting fees (attach schedule)				
	c Other professional fees (attach schedule). . . .				
	17 Interest				
	18 Taxes (attach schedule).				
	19 Depreciation (attach schedule) and depletion . .				
	20 Occupancy				
	21 Travel, conferences, and meetings				
	22 Printing and publications				
	23 Other expenses (attach schedule)				
	24 **Total** operating and administrative expenses (add lines 13 through 23)				
	25 Contributions, gifts, grants paid . . . . . . **GRANTS PAID**				
	26 **Total** expenses and disbursements (add lines 24 and 25)				
	27a Excess of revenue over expenses and disbursements (line 12 minus line 26)				
	b Net investment income (if negative, enter "-0-")				
	c Adjusted net income (if negative, enter "-0-") .				

For Paperwork Reduction Act Notice, see page 1 of the instructions.   Cat. No. 11289X   Form **990-PF** (1991)

*If blank, see page 2, line 16, column (c)

SMALL IRS FORM (only page 1 of 4 is shown here)

EXHIBIT 19.3

FOUNDATION CENTER COOPERATING COLLECTIONS   FREE FUNDING INFORMATION CENTERS

The Foundation Center is an independent national service organization established by foundations to provide an authoritative source of information on foundation and corporate giving. The New York, Washington, D.C., Atlanta, Cleveland, and San Francisco reference collections operated by the Foundation Center offer a wide variety of services and comprehensive collections of information on foundations and grants. Cooperating Collections are libraries, community foundations, and other nonprofit agencies that provide a core collection of Foundation Center publications and a variety of supplementary materials and services in areas useful to grantseekers. The core collection consists of:

THE FOUNDATION DIRECTORY 1 AND 2, AND SUPPLEMENT	THE FOUNDATION GRANTS INDEX QUARTERLY	THE LITERATURE OF THE NONPROFIT SECTOR
THE FOUNDATION 1000	FOUNDATION GRANTS TO INDIVIDUALS	NATIONAL DIRECTORY OF CORPORATE GIVING
FOUNDATION FUNDAMENTALS	GUIDE TO U.S. FOUNDATIONS, THEIR TRUSTEES, OFFICERS,	SELECTED GRANT GUIDES
FOUNDATION GIVING	AND DONORS	USER-FRIENDLY GUIDE
THE FOUNDATION GRANTS INDEX	THE FOUNDATION CENTER'S GUIDE TO PROPOSAL WRITING	

Many of the network members make available for public use sets of private foundation information returns (IRS Form 990-PF) for their state and/or neighboring states. A complete set of U.S. foundation returns can be found at the New York and Washington, D.C., offices of the Foundation Center. The Atlanta, Cleveland, and San Francisco offices contain IRS Form 990-PF returns for the southeastern, midwestern, and western states, respectively. Those Cooperating Collections marked with a bullet (■) have sets of private foundation information returns for their state and/or neighboring states.

Because the collections vary in their hours, materials, and services, *it is recommended that you call the collection in advance.* To check on new locations or current information, call toll-free 1-800-424-9836.

REFERENCE COLLECTIONS OPERATED BY THE FOUNDATION CENTER

THE FOUNDATION CENTER	THE FOUNDATION CENTER	THE FOUNDATION CENTER	THE FOUNDATION CENTER	THE FOUNDATION CENTER
8th Floor	312 Sutter St., Rm. 312	1001 Connecticut Ave., NW	Kent H. Smith Library	Suite 150, Grand Lobby
79 Fifth Avenue	San Francisco, CA 94108	Washington, DC 20036	1422 Euclid, Suite 1356	Hurt Bldg., 50 Hurt Plaza
New York, NY 10003	(415) 397-0902	(202) 331-1400	Cleveland, OH 44115	Atlanta, GA 30303
(212) 620-4230			(216) 861-1933	(404) 880-0094

ALABAMA

■ BIRMINGHAM PUBLIC LIBRARY
Government Documents
2100 Park Place
Birmingham 35203
(205) 226-3600

HUNTSVILLE PUBLIC LIBRARY
915 Monroe St.
Huntsville 35801
(205) 532-5940

■ UNIVERSITY OF SOUTH ALABAMA
Library Building
Mobile 36688
(205) 460-7025

■ AUBURN UNIVERSITY AT
MONTGOMERY LIBRARY
7300 University Drive
Montgomery 36117-3596
(205) 244-3653

ALASKA

■ UNIVERSITY OF ALASKA AT
ANCHORAGE
Library
3211 Providence Drive
Anchorage 99508
(907) 786-1848

JUNEAU PUBLIC LIBRARY
Reference
292 Marine Way
Juneau 99801
(907) 586-5267

ARIZONA

■ PHOENIX PUBLIC LIBRARY
Business & Sciences Unit
12 E. McDowell Rd.
Phoenix 85004
(602) 262-4636

■ TUCSON PIMA LIBRARY
101 N. Stone Ave.
Tucson 87501
(602) 791-4010

ARKANSAS

■ WESTARK COMMUNITY
COLLEGE—BORHAM LIBRARY
5210 Grand Avenue
Ft. Smith 72913
(501) 788-7200

■ CENTRAL ARKANSAS LIBRARY
SYSTEM
700 Louisiana
Little Rock 72201
(501) 370-5952

PINE BLUFF-JEFFERSON COUNTY
LIBRARY SYSTEM
200 E. Eighth
Pine Bluff 71601
(501) 534-2159

CALIFORNIA

HUMBOLDT AREA FOUNDATION
P.O. Box 99
Bayside 95524
(707) 442-2993

■ VENTURA COUNTY COMMUNITY
FOUNDATION
Funding and Information Resource
Center
1355 Del Norte Rd.
Camarillo 93010
(805) 988-0196

■ CALIFORNIA COMMUNITY
FOUNDATION
Funding Information Center
606 S. Olive St., Suite 2400
Los Angeles 90014-1526
(213) 413-4042

OAKLAND COMMUNITY FUND
Nonprofit Resource Center
1203 Preservation Pkwy., Suite 100
Oakland 94612
(510) 834-1010

■ GRANT & RESOURCE CENTER OF
NORTHERN CALIFORNIA
Building C, Suite A
2280 Benton Dr.
Redding 96003
(916) 244-1219

LOS ANGELES PUBLIC LIBRARY
West Valley Regional Branch Library
19036 Van Owen St.
Reseda 91335
(818) 345-4393

RIVERSIDE CITY & COUNTY PUBLIC
LIBRARY
3021 Franklin Ave.
Riverside 92502
(714) 782-5201

NONPROFIT RESOURCE CENTER
Sacramento Public Library
828 I Street, 2nd Floor
Sacramento 95814
(916) 552-8817

■ SAN DIEGO COMMUNITY
FOUNDATION
Funding Information Center
101 West Broadway, Suite 1120
San Diego 92101
(619) 239-8815

■ NONPROFIT DEVELOPMENT CENTER
Library
1762 Technology Dr., #225
San Jose 95110
(408) 452-8181

■ PENINSULA COMMUNITY
FOUNDATION
Funding Information Library
1700 S. El Camino Real, R301
San Mateo 94402-3049
(415) 358-9392

LOS ANGELES PUBLIC LIBRARY
San Pedro Regional Branch
9131 S. Gaffey St.
San Pedro 90731
(310) 548-7779

■ VOLUNTEER CENTER OF GREATER
ORANGE COUNTY
Nonprofit Management Assistance
Center
1000 E. Santa Ana Blvd., Ste. 200
Santa Ana 92701
(714) 953-1655

■ SANTA BARBARA PUBLIC LIBRARY
40 E. Anapamu St.
Santa Barbara 93101
(805) 962-7653

SANTA MONICA PUBLIC LIBRARY
1343 Sixth St.
Santa Monica 90401-1603
(310) 458-8600

SONOMA COUNTY LIBRARY
3rd & E Streets
Santa Rosa 95404
(707) 545-0831

SEASIDE BRANCH LIBRARY
550 Harcourt St.
Seaside 93955
(408) 899-8131

COLORADO

PIKES PEAK LIBRARY DISTRICT
20 N. Cascade
Colorado Springs 80901
(719) 531-6333

■ DENVER PUBLIC LIBRARY
Social Sciences & Genealogy
1357 Broadway
Denver 80203
(303) 640-8870

CONNECTICUT

DANBURY PUBLIC LIBRARY
170 Main St.
Danbury 06810
(203) 797-4527

GREENWICH PUBLIC LIBRARY
101 West Putnam Ave.
Greenwich 06830
(203) 622-7921

■ HARTFORD PUBLIC LIBRARY
500 Main St.
Hartford 06103
(203) 293-6000

D.A.T.A.
70 Audubon St.
New Haven 06510
(203) 772-1345

FOUNDATION CENTER COOPERATING COLLECTIONS

EXHIBIT 19.4

DELAWARE

■ UNIVERSITY OF DELAWARE
Hugh Morris Library
Newark 19717-5267
(302) 831-2432

FLORIDA

VOLUSIA COUNTY LIBRARY CENTER
City Island
Daytona Beach 32014-4484
(904) 255-3765

■ NOVA UNIVERSITY
Einstein Library
3301 College Ave.
Fort Lauderdale 33314
(305) 475-7050

INDIAN RIVER COMMUNITY
COLLEGE
Charles S. Miley Learning Resource
Center
3209 Virginia Ave.
Fort Pierce 34981-5599
(407) 462-4757

■ JACKSONVILLE PUBLIC LIBRARIES
Grants Resource Center
122 N. Ocean St.
Jacksonville 32202
(904) 630-2665

■ MIAMI-DADE PUBLIC LIBRARY
Humanities/Social Science
101 W. Flagler St.
Miami 33130
(305) 375-5575

■ ORLANDO PUBLIC LIBRARY
Social Sciences Department
101 E. Central Blvd.
Orlando 32801
(407) 425-4694

SELBY PUBLIC LIBRARY
Reference
1001 Blvd. of the Arts
Sarasota 34236
(813) 951-5501

■ TAMPA-HILLSBOROUGH COUNTY
PUBLIC LIBRARY
900 N. Ashley Drive
Tampa 33602
(813) 273-3628

■ COMMUNITY FOUNDATION OF
PALM BEACH & MARTIN COUNTIES
324 Datura St., Suite 340
West Palm Beach 33401
(407) 659-6800

GEORGIA

■ ATLANTA-FULTON PUBLIC LIBRARY
Foundation Collection—Ivan Allen
Department
1 Margaret Mitchell Square
Atlanta 30303-1089
(404) 730-1900

■ DALTON REGIONAL LIBRARY
310 Cappes St.
Dalton 30720
(706) 278-4507

HAWAII

■ UNIVERSITY OF HAWAII
Hamilton Library
2550 The Mall
Honolulu 96822
(808) 956-7214

HAWAII COMMUNITY FOUNDATION
Hawaii Resource Center
222 Merchant St., Second Floor
Honolulu 96813
(808) 537-6333

IDAHO

■ BOISE PUBLIC LIBRARY
715 S. Capitol Blvd.
Boise 83702
(208) 384-4024

■ CALDWELL PUBLIC LIBRARY
1010 Dearborn St.
Caldwell 83605
(208) 459-3242

ILLINOIS

■ DONORS FORUM OF CHICAGO
53 W. Jackson Blvd., Suite 430
Chicago 60604-3608
(312) 431-0265

■ EVANSTON PUBLIC LIBRARY
1703 Orrington Ave.
Evanston 60201
(708) 866-0305

ROCK ISLAND PUBLIC LIBRARY
401 - 19th St.
Rock Island 61201
(309) 788-7627

■ SANGAMON STATE UNIVERSITY
Library
Shepherd Road
Springfield 62794-9243
(217) 786-6633

INDIANA

■ ALLEN COUNTY PUBLIC LIBRARY
900 Webster St.
Ft. Wayne 46802
(219) 424-0544

INDIANA UNIVERSITY NORTHWEST
LIBRARY
3400 Broadway
Gary 46408
(219) 980-6582

■ INDIANAPOLIS-MARION COUNTY
PUBLIC LIBRARY
Social Sciences
40 E. St. Clair
Indianapolis 46206
(317) 269-1733

IOWA

■ CEDAR RAPIDS PUBLIC LIBRARY
Foundation Center Collection
500 First St., SE
Cedar Rapids 52401
(319) 398-5123

■ SOUTHWESTERN COMMUNITY
COLLEGE
Learning Resource Center
1501 W. Townline Rd.
Creston 50801
(515) 782-7081

■ PUBLIC LIBRARY OF DES MOINES
100 Locust
Des Moines 50309-1791
(515) 283-4152

■ SIOUX CITY PUBLIC LIBRARY
529 Pierce St.
Sioux City 51101-1202
(712) 252-5669

KANSAS

■ DODGE CITY PUBLIC LIBRARY
1001 2nd Ave.
Dodge City 67801
(316) 225-0248

■ TOPEKA AND SHAWNEE COUNTY
PUBLIC LIBRARY
1515 SW 10th Ave.
Topeka 66604-1374
(913) 233-2040

■ WICHITA PUBLIC LIBRARY
223 S. Main St.
Wichita 67202
(316) 262-0611

KENTUCKY

WESTERN KENTUCKY UNIVERSITY
Helm-Cravens Library
Bowling Green 42101-3576
(502) 745-6125

■ LOUISVILLE FREE PUBLIC LIBRARY
301 York Street
Louisville 40203
(502) 574-1611

LOUISIANA

■ EAST BATON ROUGE PARISH LIBRARY
Centroplex Branch Grants Collection
120 St. Louis
Baton Rouge 70802
(504) 389-4960

■ BEAUREGARD PARISH LIBRARY
205 S. Washington Ave.
De Ridder 70634
(318) 463-6217

■ NEW ORLEANS PUBLIC LIBRARY
Business & Science Division
219 Loyola Ave.
New Orleans 70140
(504) 596-2580

■ SHREVE MEMORIAL LIBRARY
424 Texas St.
Shreveport 71120-1523
(318) 226-5894

MAINE

■ UNIVERSITY OF SOUTHERN MAINE
Office of Sponsored Research
246 Deering Ave., Rm. 628
Portland 04103
(207) 780-4871

MARYLAND

■ ENOCH PRATT FREE LIBRARY
Social Science & History
400 Cathedral St.
Baltimore 21201
(410) 396-5430

MASSACHUSETTS

■ ASSOCIATED GRANTMAKERS OF
MASSACHUSETTS
294 Washington St., Suite 840
Boston 02108
(617) 426-2606

■ BOSTON PUBLIC LIBRARY
Soc. Sci. Reference
666 Boylston St
Boston 02117
(617) 536-5400

WESTERN MASSACHUSETTS
FUNDING RESOURCE CENTER
65 Elliot St.
Springfield 01101-1730
(413) 732-3175

■ WORCESTER PUBLIC LIBRARY
Grants Resource Center
Salem Square
Worcester 01608
(508) 799-1655

MICHIGAN

■ ALPENA COUNTY LIBRARY
211 N. First St.
Alpena 49707
(517) 356-6188

■ UNIVERSITY OF MICHIGAN-ANN
ARBOR
Graduate Library
Reference & Research Services
Department
Ann Arbor 48109-1205
(313) 764-9373

■ BATTLE CREEK COMMUNITY
FOUNDATION
Southwest Michigan Funding Resource
Center

2 Riverwalk Centre
34 W. Jackson St.
Battle Creek 49017-3505
(616) 962-2181

■ HENRY FORD CENTENNIAL LIBRARY
Adult Services
16301 Michigan Ave.
Dearborn 48126
(313) 943-2330

■ WAYNE STATE UNIVERSITY
Purdy/Kresge Library
5265 Cass Avenue
Detroit 48202
(313) 577-6424

■ MICHIGAN STATE UNIVERSITY
LIBRARIES
Social Sciences/Humanities
Main Library
East Lansing 48824-1048
(517) 353-8818

■ FARMINGTON COMMUNITY LIBRARY
32737 West 12 Mile Rd.
Farmington Hills 48018
(810) 553-0300

■ UNIVERSITY OF MICHIGAN—FLINT
Library
Flint 48502-2186
(810) 762-3408

■ GRAND RAPIDS PUBLIC LIBRARY
Business Dept.—3rd Floor
60 Library Plaza NE
Grand Rapids 49503-3093
(616) 456-3600

MICHIGAN TECHNOLOGICAL
UNIVERSITY
Van Pelt Library
1400 Townsend Dr.
Houghton 49931
(906) 487-2507

SAULT STE. MARIE AREA PUBLIC
SCHOOLS
Office of Compensatory Education
460 W. Spruce St.
Sault Ste. Marie 49783-1874
(906) 635-6619

■ NORTHWESTERN MICHIGAN
COLLEGE
Mark & Helen Osterin Library
1701 E. Front St.
Traverse City 49684
(616) 922-1060

MINNESOTA

■ DULUTH PUBLIC LIBRARY
520 W. Superior St.
Duluth 55802
(218) 723-3802

■ SOUTHWEST STATE UNIVERSITY
University Library
Marshall 56258
(507) 537-6176

■ MINNEAPOLIS PUBLIC LIBRARY
Sociology Department
300 Nicollet Mall
Minneapolis 55401
(612) 372-6555

ROCHESTER PUBLIC LIBRARY
11 First St. SE
Rochester 55904-3777
(507) 285-8002

ST. PAUL PUBLIC LIBRARY
90 W. Fourth St.
St. Paul 55102
(612) 292-6307

FOUNDATION CENTER COOPERATING COLLECTIONS *(continued)*

EXHIBIT 19.4

■ JACKSON/HINDS LIBRARY SYSTEM
300 N. State St.
Jackson 39201
(601) 968-5803

■ CLEARINGHOUSE FOR
MIDCONTINENT FOUNDATIONS
University of Missouri
5315 Rockhill Rd.
Kansas City 64110
(816) 235-1176

■ KANSAS CITY PUBLIC LIBRARY
311 E. 12th St.
Kansas City 64106
(816) 221-9650

■ METROPOLITAN ASSOCIATION FOR
PHILANTHROPY, INC.
5615 Pershing Avenue, Suite 20
St. Louis 63112
(314) 361-3900

■ SPRINGFIELD-GREENE COUNTY
LIBRARY
397 E. Central
Springfield 65802
(417) 869-9400

■ MONTANA STATE
UNIVERSITY—BILLINGS
Library—Special Collections
1500 North 30th St.
Billings 59101-0298
(406) 657-1662

BOZEMAN PUBLIC LIBRARY
220 E. Lamme
Bozeman 59715
(406) 586-4787

■ MONTANA STATE LIBRARY
Library Services
1515 E. 6th Ave.
Helena 59620
(406) 444-3004

■ UNIVERSITY OF MONTANA
Maureen & Mike Mansfield Library
Missoula 59812-1195
(406) 243-6800

■ UNIVERSITY OF
NEBRASKA—LINCOLN
Love Library
14th & R Streets
Lincoln 68588-0410
(402) 472-2848

■ W. DALE CLARK LIBRARY
Social Sciences Department
215 S. 15th St.
Omaha 68102
(402) 444-4826

■ LAS VEGAS-CLARK COUNTY LIBRARY
DISTRICT
833 Las Vegas Blvd. North
Las Vegas 89101
(702) 382-5280

■ WASHOE COUNTY LIBRARY
301 S. Center St.
Reno 89501
(702) 785-4010

■ NEW HAMPSHIRE CHARITABLE FDN.
37 Pleasant St.
Concord 03301-4007
(603) 225-6641

■ PLYMOUTH STATE COLLEGE
Herbert H. Lamson Library
Plymouth 03264
(603) 535-2258

CUMBERLAND COUNTY LIBRARY
New Jersey Room
800 E. Commerce St.
Bridgeton 08302
(609) 453-2210

■ FREE PUBLIC LIBRARY OF ELIZABETH
11 S. Broad St.
Elizabeth 07202
(908) 354-6060

■ COUNTY COLLEGE OF MORRIS
Learning Resource Center
214 Center Grove Rd.
Randolph 07869
(201) 328-5296

■ NEW JERSEY STATE LIBRARY
Governmental Reference Services
185 West State St.
Trenton 08625-0520
(609) 292-6220

ALBUQUERQUE COMMUNITY
FOUNDATION
3301 Menual NE, Ste. 30
Albuquerque 87176-6960
(505) 883-6240

■ NEW MEXICO STATE LIBRARY
Information Services
325 Don Gaspar
Santa Fe 87501
(505) 827-3824

■ NEW YORK STATE LIBRARY
Humanities Reference
Cultural Education Center
Empire State Plaza
Albany 12230
(518) 474-5355

SUFFOLK COOPERATIVE LIBRARY
SYSTEM
627 N. Sunrise Service Rd.
Bellport 11713
(516) 286-1600

NEW YORK PUBLIC LIBRARY
Fordham Branch
2556 Bainbridge Ave.
Bronx 10458
(718) 220-6575

BROOKLYN IN TOUCH
INFORMATION CENTER, INC.
One Hanson Place—Room 2504
Brooklyn 11243
(718) 230-3200

BROOKLYN PUBLIC LIBRARY
Social Sciences Division
Grand Army Plaza
Brooklyn 11238
(718) 780-7700

■ BUFFALO & ERIE COUNTY PUBLIC
LIBRARY
Business & Labor Dept.
Lafayette Square
Buffalo 14203
(716) 858-7097

HUNTINGTON PUBLIC LIBRARY
338 Main St.
Huntington 11743
(516) 427-5165

QUEENS BOROUGH PUBLIC LIBRARY
Social Sciences Division
89-11 Merrick Blvd.
Jamaica 11432
(718) 990-0761

■ LEVITTOWN PUBLIC LIBRARY
1 Bluegrass Lane
Levittown 11756
(516) 731-5728

NEW YORK PUBLIC LIBRARY
Countee Cullen Branch Library
104 W. 136th St.
New York 10030
(212) 491-2070

PLATTSBURGH PUBLIC LIBRARY
19 Oak St.
Plattsburgh 12901
(518) 563-0921

ADRIANCE MEMORIAL LIBRARY
Special Services Department
93 Market St.
Poughkeepsie 12601
(914) 485-3445

■ ROCHESTER PUBLIC LIBRARY
Business, Economics & Law
115 South Avenue
Rochester 14604
(716) 428-7328

ONONDAGA COUNTY PUBLIC
LIBRARY
447 S. Salina St.
Syracuse 13202-2494
(315) 448-4700

UTICA PUBLIC LIBRARY
303 Genesee St.
Utica 13501
(315) 735-2279

■ WHITE PLAINS PUBLIC LIBRARY
100 Martine Ave.
White Plains 10601
(914) 422-1480

■ COMMUNITY FDN. OF WESTERN
NORTH CAROLINA
Learning Resources Center
14 College Street
Asheville 28801
(704) 254-4960

■ THE DUKE ENDOWMENT
200 S. Tryon St., Suite 1100
Charlotte 28202
(704) 376-0291

DURHAM COUNTY PUBLIC LIBRARY
301 North Roxboro
Durham 27702
(919) 560-0110

■ STATE LIBRARY OF NORTH CAROLINA
Government and Business Services
Archives Bldg., 109 E. Jones St.
Raleigh 27601
(919) 733-3270

■ FORSYTH COUNTY PUBLIC LIBRARY
660 W. 6th St.
Winston-Salem 27101
(910) 727-2680

BISMARCK PUBLIC LIBRARY
515 North Fifth St.
Bismarck 58501
(701) 222-6410

■ FARGO PUBLIC LIBRARY
102 N. 3rd St.
Fargo 58102
(701) 241-1491

STARK COUNTY DISTRICT LIBRARY
Humanities
715 Market Ave. N.
Canton 44702
(216) 452-0665

■ PUBLIC LIBRARY OF CINCINNATI &
HAMILTON COUNTY
Grants Resource Center
800 Vine St.—Library Square
Cincinnati 45202-2071
(513) 369-6940

COLUMBUS METROPOLITAN LIBRARY
Business and Technology
96 S. Grant Ave.
Columbus 43215
(614) 645-2590

■ DAYTON & MONTGOMERY COUNTY
PUBLIC LIBRARY
Grants Resource Center
215 E. Third St.
Dayton 45402
(513) 227-9500 x211

■ TOLEDO-LUCAS COUNTY PUBLIC
LIBRARY
Social Sciences Department
325 Michigan St.
Toledo 43624-1614
(419) 259-5245

■ YOUNGSTOWN & MAHONING
COUNTY LIBRARY
305 Wick Ave.
Youngstown 44503
(216) 744-8636

MUSKINGUM COUNTY LIBRARY
220 N. 5th St.
Zanesville 43701
(614) 453-0391

■ OKLAHOMA CITY UNIVERSITY
Dulaney Browne Library
2501 N. Blackwelder
Oklahoma City 73106
(405) 521-5072

■ TULSA CITY-COUNTY LIBRARY
400 Civic Center
Tulsa 74103
(918) 596-7944

OREGON INSTITUTE OF
TECHNOLOGY
Library
3201 Campus Dr.
Klamath Falls 97601-8801
(503) 885-1773

■ PACIFIC NON-PROFIT NETWORK
Grantsmanship Resource Library
33 N. Central, Suite 211
Medford 97501
(503) 779-6044

■ MULTNOMAH COUNTY LIBRARY
Government Documents
801 SW Tenth Ave.
Portland 97205
(503) 248-5123

OREGON STATE LIBRARY
State Library Building
Salem 97310
(503) 378-4277

NORTHAMPTON COMMUNITY
COLLEGE
Learning Resources Center
3835 Green Pond Rd.
Bethlehem 18017
(215) 861-5360

ERIE COUNTY LIBRARY SYSTEM
27 South Park Row
Erie 16501
(814) 451-6927

FOUNDATION CENTER COOPERATING COLLECTIONS *(continued)*

EXHIBIT 19.4

DAUPHIN COUNTY LIBRARY SYSTEM
Central Library
101 Walnut St.
Harrisburg 17101
(717) 234-4976

LANCASTER COUNTY PUBLIC
LIBRARY
125 N. Duke St.
Lancaster 17602
(717) 394-2651

■ FREE LIBRARY OF PHILADELPHIA
Regional Foundation Center
Logan Square
Philadelphia 19103
(215) 686-5423

■ CARNEGIE LIBRARY OF PITTSBURGH
Foundation Collection
4400 Forbes Ave.
Pittsburgh 15213-4080
(412) 622-1917

POCONO NORTHEAST
DEVELOPMENT FUND
James Pettinger Memorial Library
1151 Oak St.
Pittston 18640-3755
(717) 655-5581

READING PUBLIC LIBRARY
100 South Fifth St.
Reading 19602
(215) 655-6355

■ MARTIN LIBRARY
159 Market St.
York 17401
(717) 846-5300

RHODE ISLAND

■ PROVIDENCE PUBLIC LIBRARY
150 Empire St.
Providence 02906
(401) 455-8088

SOUTH CAROLINA

■ ANDERSON COUNTY LIBRARY
202 East Greenville St.
Anderson 29621
(803) 260-4500

■ CHARLESTON COUNTY LIBRARY
404 King St.
Charleston 29403
(803) 723-1645

■ SOUTH CAROLINA STATE LIBRARY
1500 Senate St.
Columbia 29211
(803) 734-8666

SOUTH DAKOTA

NONPROFIT GRANTS ASSISTANCE
CENTER
Business & Education Institute
Washington Street, East Hall
Dakota State University
Madison 57042
(605) 256-5555

■ SOUTH DAKOTA STATE LIBRARY
800 Governors Drive
Pierre 57501-2294
(605) 773-5070
(800) 592-1841 (SD residents)

SIOUX FALLS AREA FOUNDATION
141 N. Main Ave., Suite 310
Sioux Falls 57102-1132
(605) 336-7055

TENNESSEE

■ KNOX COUNTY PUBLIC LIBRARY
500 W. Church Ave.
Knoxville 37902
(615) 544-5700

■ MEMPHIS & SHELBY COUNTY
PUBLIC LIBRARY
1850 Peabody Ave.
Memphis 38104
(901) 725-8877

■ NASHVILLE PUBLIC LIBRARY
Business Information Division
225 Polk Ave.
Nashville 37203
(615) 862-5843

TEXAS

ABILENE CENTER FOR NONPROFIT
MANAGEMENT
Funding Information Library
500 N. Chestnut, Suite 1511
Abilene 79604
(915) 677-8166

■ AMARILLO AREA FOUNDATION
700 First National Place
801 S. Fillmore
Amarillo 79101
(806) 376-4521

■ HOGG FOUNDATION FOR MENTAL
HEALTH
3001 Lake Austin Blvd.
Austin 78703
(512) 471-5041

TEXAS A & M UNIVERSITY AT
CORPUS CHRISTI
Library
Reference Dept.
6300 Ocean Dr.
Corpus Christi 78412
(512) 994-2608

■ DALLAS PUBLIC LIBRARY
Urban Information
1515 Young St.
Dallas 75201
(214) 670-1487

EL PASO COMMUNITY FOUNDATION
1616 Texas Commerce Building
El Paso 79901
(915) 533-4020

■ FUNDING INFORMATION CENTER
OF FORT WORTH
Texas Christian University Library
2800 S. University Dr.
Ft. Worth 76129
(817) 921-7664

■ HOUSTON PUBLIC LIBRARY
Bibliographic Information Center
500 McKinney
Houston 77002
(713) 236-1313

■ LONGVIEW PUBLIC LIBRARY
222 W. Cotton St.
Longview 75601
(903) 237-1352

LUBBOCK AREA FOUNDATION, INC.
502 Texas Commerce Bank Building
Lubbock 79401
(806) 762-8061

■ FUNDING INFORMATION CENTER
530 McCullough, Suite 600
San Antonio 78212-8270
(210) 227-4333

NORTH TEXAS CENTER FOR
NONPROFIT MANAGEMENT
624 Indiana, Suite 307
Wichita Falls 76301
(817) 322-4961

UTAH

■ SALT LAKE CITY PUBLIC LIBRARY
209 East 500 South
Salt Lake City 84111
(801) 524-8200

VERMONT

■ VERMONT DEPT. OF LIBRARIES
Reference & Law Info. Services
109 State St.
Montpelier 05609
(802) 828-3268

VIRGINIA

■ HAMPTON PUBLIC LIBRARY
4207 Victoria Blvd.
Hampton 23669
(804) 727-1312

■ RICHMOND PUBLIC LIBRARY
Business, Science & Technology
101 East Franklin St.
Richmond 23219
(804) 780-8223

■ ROANOKE CITY PUBLIC LIBRARY
SYSTEM
Central Library
706 S. Jefferson St.
Roanoke 24016
(703) 981-2477

WASHINGTON

■ MID-COLUMBIA LIBRARY
405 South Dayton
Kennewick 99336
(509)586-3156

■ SEATTLE PUBLIC LIBRARY
Science, Social Science
1000 Fourth Ave.
Seattle 98104
(206) 386-4620

SPOKANE PUBLIC LIBRARY
Funding Information Center
West 811 Main Ave.
Spokane 99201
(509) 838-3364

■ UNITED WAY OF PIERCE COUNTY
Center for Nonprofit Development
734 Broadway
P.O. Box 2215
Tacoma 98401
(206) 597-6686

GREATER WENATCHEE COMMUNITY
FOUNDATION AT THE WENATCHEE
PUBLIC LIBRARY
310 Douglas St.
Wenatchee 98807
(509) 662-5021

WEST VIRGINIA

■ KANAWHA COUNTY PUBLIC LIBRARY
123 Capitol St.
Charleston 25301
(304) 343-4646

WISCONSIN

■ UNIVERSITY OF
WISCONSIN-MADISON
Memorial Library
728 State St.
Madison 53706
(608) 262-3242

■ MARQUETTE UNIVERSITY MEMORIAL
LIBRARY
Funding Information Center
1415 W. Wisconsin Ave.
Milwaukee 53233
(414) 288-1515

UNIVERSITY OF
WISCONSIN—STEVENS POINT
Library—Foundation Collection
99 Reserve St.
Stevens Point 54481-3897
(715) 346-3826

WYOMING

■ NATRONA COUNTY PUBLIC LIBRARY
307 E. 2nd St.
Casper 82601-2598
(307) 237-4935

■ LARAMIE COUNTY COMMUNITY
COLLEGE
Instructional Resource Center
1400 E. College Dr.
Cheyenne 82007-3299
(307) 778-1206

■ CAMPBELL COUNTY PUBLIC LIBRARY
2101 4-J Road
Gillette 82716
(307) 682-3223

■ TETON COUNTY LIBRARY
320 S. King St.
Jackson 83001
(307) 733-2164

ROCK SPRINGS LIBRARY
400 C St.
Rock Springs 82901
(307) 362-6212

PUERTO RICO

UNIVERSITY OF PUERTO RICO
Ponce Technological College Library
Box 7186
Ponce 00732
(809) 844-8181

UNIVERSIDAD DEL SAGRADO
CORAZON
M.M.T. Guevara Library
Santurce 00914
(809) 728-1515 x 4357

Participants in the Foundation Center's Cooperating Collections network are libraries or nonprofit information centers that provide fundraising information and other funding-related technical assistance in their communities. Cooperating Collections agree to provide free public access to a basic collection of Foundation Center publications during a regular schedule of hours, offering free funding research guidance to all visitors. Many also provide a variety of services for local nonprofit organizations, using staff or volunteers to prepare special materials, organize workshops, or conduct orientations.

The Foundation Center welcomes inquiries from libraries or information centers in the U.S. interested in providing this type of public information service. If you are interested in establishing a funding information library for the use of nonprofit organizations in your area or in learning more about the program, please write to: Judith Margolin, Vice President for Public Services, The Foundation Center, 79 Fifth Avenue, New York, NY 10003-3076.

9/94

FOUNDATION CENTER COOPERATING COLLECTIONS (*continued*)

EXHIBIT 19.4

CHAPTER

• • • • • • • • • •

Researching Corporate Grant Opportunities

Although there are over 2.3 million corporations in the United States, your research into corporations that will fund your project will be simplified and narrowed when you consider the following facts:

- Of the 2.3 million corporations in the United States, only 35 percent make any philanthropic contributions at all.
- Of those that make contributions, only 6 percent contribute over $500 a year.
- Of the $124.3 billion contributed to nonprofit organizations through private philanthropy in 1993, corporate giving accounted for approximately 4.8 percent or $6 billion.
- Corporate *foundation* giving accounted for only $1.49 billion of the $6 billion reported in 1993.[1]

The Foundation Center is a good resource for information on corporate foundation grants. Its publication *National Directory of Corporate Giving* provides information on over 1,700 corporate foundations and over 600 direct-giving programs. *Corporate Foundation Profiles,* also published by the Foundation Center, contains grants information on over 228 of the largest corporate foundations in the United States.

You will find much less information available on corporate grants awarded by companies that do not use a foundation to make their grants. And the information you do find will be much less reliable. The reason for the lack of sound data on corporate giving is that there are no laws allowing public review of corporate contributions programs. Companies must record their corporate charitable contributions on their Internal Revenue Service tax return, but no one, not even a stockholder, has the right to see the return.

The data on corporate giving are derived from self-reported, voluntary responses to surveys and questionnaires. Even the corporate contributions data reported in *Giving USA* are based on a voluntary survey conducted by the Conference Board, a nonprofit organization with a reputation for keeping corporate responses confidential.

Armed with the knowledge that corporate giving is based on a "quid-pro-quo," or "this-for-that," approach, your foremost strategy should be to look at your proposal idea and redefine it, if necessary, in a way that could attract corporate support. Do not start by purchasing an expensive national reference book on corporate giving unless you plan to move your organization to another city. Corporations usually give where they live. Corporate plants, workers, product development, and other vested interests such as geographic proximity all play a role in motivating corporate contributions. Your best bet is to draw a circle with a 25-mile radius around your organization, identify the larger employers in the circle (companies employing 100 or more), and determine which of these corporations your project could most easily be related to.

While it still makes sense to check out the corporate grant resource books available in your local public library and Foundation Center regional collection, a more important source for data is your local chamber of commerce. The chamber of commerce can provide you with a list of local corporations and information on number of employees, total value of payroll, and products and services provided.

Those local companies whose products, employees, communities, or families would be affected by your proposal are your best choices for pre-proposal contact. Since corporate contributions depend on a company's profitability, your corporate research should include information on revenue. One way to obtain accurate data on profitability is to ask a corporate member of your grants advisory committee who subscribes to Dun and Bradstreet's financial services to request a Dun and Bradstreet report on the prospective corporate grantor. This report will rate the fiscal stability of the company and give you a sense of the company's ability to support your proposal.

Another technique for keeping abreast of local corporations is to purchase one share of stock in each publicly held company in your area. If you receive a dividend check, you will know the company made money! Using this technique, you will also get information on top corporate administrators and board member changes.

If your corporate proposal involves research, product development, or product positioning with your clients, you can move beyond local boundaries and corporate locations. To do so, refer to *The Standard Industrial Classification Manual,* which should be available at your local public library or college library. Better known as the *SIC Manual,* this publication references companies by the types of goods they produce. The *SIC Manual* can be a valuable resource if you have a project that can either position a company's products or provide a model that others could follow to increase sales and profits. For example, if your project uses innovative ways to educate people with vision impairments, you might use the *SIC Manual* to locate companies that manufacture state-of-the-art telecommunications equipment that could be used in your solution.

Your public library or local college library will have information about the companies you identify. Any one of the Dun and Bradstreet research tools or Standard and Poor's publications will provide the basic information you will need to determine your best prospects for funding.

Exhibit 20.1 is an example of what an entry in *Dun and Bradstreet's Million Dollar Directory* looks like. As you can see, entries in the directory include the following information on corporations:

- address and phone number of the corporation
- subsidiary relationships
- sales
- employees
- divisions and products
- officers

All entries in the directory are indexed alphabetically, geographically, and by product classifications.

Volume 1 of *Standard and Poor's Register of Corporations, Directors and Executives* provides similar information (see exhibit 20.2). Entries include:

- corporate name, address, and phone number
- an extensive list of officers
- sales volume
- number of employees
- a description of products

Since a corporation's executives often make up its contributions committee, I have chosen to show a list of officers for volume 1 of *Standard and Poor's Register of Corporations, Directors and Executives* sample entry in exhibit 20.2.

In both *Dun and Bradstreet's Million Dollar Directory* and volume 1 of *Standard and Poor's Register of Corporations, Directors and Executives,* the names designated with an asterisk appear in each publication's companion book (or volume) on directors and executives. For example, after searching in volume 1 of *Standard and Poor's Register of Corporations, Directors and Executives,* you may decide you want to locate more information on William S. Chasel Jr., vice chairman and chief financial officer of American Communications Company. There is an asterisk next to his name in volume 1 of the *Register,* so you can look for further information in volume 2. Exhibit 20.3 is a sample of what you might find.

As you can see from the sample, the information provided in volume 2 of *Standard and Poor's Register of Corporations, Directors and Executives* includes the age, educational background, and residence of the corporate execu-

American Communications Co* (NY)
ACC
099 Brady Ave., New York, NY 10007
Tel (212) 897-8888 Sales 58888MM Emp 877342
ACC
    SIC 4822 3822 7811
Communications Holding Company

*	C L Brown	Ch Bd
*	W S Chasel Jr	V Ch B
*	J E Olson	V Ch B
*	W M Ellinghouse	Pr
	T E Bolger	Ex VP
	R R Hough	Ex VP
	C E Hugel	Ex VP
	K J Whaling	Ex VP
	R W Kleinert	VP
	A von Auw	VP
	R E Allen	VP Bus Svcs
	J A Baird	VP Network Plng & Design
	J R Billings	VP Federal Regulatory Matters
	E M Block	VP Pb Rl & Employee Info
	R J Marano	VP Staff
	H W Clarke Jr	VP Human Resources
	J G Fox	VP Pb Affairs
	D E Quinn	VP Network Svcs
	W B Kelly	VP Tariffs Costs
	A J McGill	VP Bus Mktg
	R V Reed	VP Labor Rls
		Corporate Personnel & Policy
		Seminar
	J L Segally	VP Financial Mgt
	W G Sharell	VP Plng & Admn
	A G Hartoll	VP State Regulatory Matters
	J L Clendenin	VP Residence Mktg Sls & Svce
	V A Dwyer	VP Tr
	R N Flint	VP Comp
	H J Trienens	VP Genl Counsel
	F A Hutson Jr	Sec

Directors

Edward W Carter	Catherine M Bleary
Archie K Davis	John D deButts
James H Evens	Peter E Hass
Edward M Hanify	William H Dewitt

ENTRY FROM *DUN & BRADSTREET'S MILLION DOLLAR DIRECTORY* (FICTITIOUS DATA)

EXHIBIT 20.1

AMERICAN COMMUNICATIONS CO.
099 Brady Ave., New York, NY 10007
Tel. 212-897-8888

* Chrm & Chief Exec Officer—Charles L. Brown
* Pres & Chief Oper Officer—William M. Ellinghouse
* Vice-Chrm & Chief Fin Officer—William S. Chasel, Jr.
* Vice-Chrm—James E. Olson
  Exec V-P (Business)—Thomas E. Bolger
  Exec V-P (Network)—Richard R. Hough
  Exec V-P—Charles E. Hugel
  Exec V-P—Morris Tanenbaum
  Exec V-P (Residence)—Kenneth J. Whaling
  Exec V-P—S.R. Wilcox
  V-P & Asst to Chrm—Alvin von Auw
  V-P (Bus Services)—Robert E. Allen
  V-P (Network Plan & Design)—Jack A. Baird
  V-P (Fed Reg Matters)—James R. Billings
  V-P (Pub Rel & Empl Inf)—Edward M. Block
  V-P (Human Resources)—H. Weston Clarke, Jr.
  V-P (Residence Mktg Sales & Serv)—John L. Clendenin
  V-P &Treas—Virginia A. Dwyer
  V-P (Pub Affairs)—John G. Fox
  V-P (Pres-Long Lines Dept)—Robert W. Kleinert
  V-P (Tariffs & Costs)—Walter B. Kelly
  V-P (Bus Mktg)—Archie J. McGill
  V-P (State Reg Matters)—Alfred G. Hartoll
  V-P (Labor Rel Cor Per & Policy Seminar)—Rex V. Reed
  V-P—Bruce G. Schwartzburg
  V-P (Fin Mgt)—John L. Segally
  V-P (Plan & Admin D)—William G. Sharell
  V-P & Gen Coun—Howard J. Trienens
  V-P (Network Services)—Paul M. Billard
  V-P & Compt—Robert N. Flint
  Secy—Frank A. Hutson, Jr.
  Accts—Coopers & Lybrand
  Revenue: $45.41 Bil Employees 984,000
  Stock Exchange(s): NYS, BST, PAC, MID, CIN, PSE
* ALSO DIRECTORS—Other Directors Are:

Edward W. Carter	Catherine M. Bleary
Archie K. Davis	John D. de Butts
James P. Hannie	Betty Johnson

BUSINESS: Communications
  S.I.C. 4844; 4833

ENTRY FROM VOLUME 1 OF *STANDARD AND POOR'S REGISTER OF CORPORATIONS, DIRECTORS AND EXECUTIVES* (FICTITIOUS DATA)

EXHIBIT 20.2

CHASEL, WILLIAM S., JR. (b. 1940 Brooklyn—Dartmouth Coll. (Amos Tuck Sch. of Bus. Admin.), 1962)—Vice-Chrm, Chief Fin Officer & Dir, American Communications Co., 099 Brady Ave., New York, NY 10007
    Campbell Soup Co., Dir
    Southside Telephone Company, Dir
    Manufacturers Hanner Corp. & Trust Co., Dir
    Philadelphia Fund Savings Group, Trustee

CHASHELL, GEORGE R. (b. 1939 Mansfield, OH—BPOE)—Secy, Bopping Paines Inc., 664 S. West St., Mannington, OH 44902—Res: 355 Oak St., Mannington 45654
    Bopping Paines Inc. (California), Secy
    Bopping Paines Inc. (Delaware), Secy
    Bopping Disc Inc., Asst Secy
    Smiths Water System Co., Secy
    National Construction Sacky Credit Group, Mem

CHASIN, EDWARD A. (b. 1930 Duluth, MN—Univ. of Chicago, 1952)—Exec. V-P & Dir (Mktg Sales), Complete Controls Inc., 6777 Washington St., Minneapolis 56654—Res: 5555 Shoreside Ave., Wayzata, MN 55392
    Fireside County Club, 1st V-P & Dir

CHASMAN, EDMUND JOSEPH (b. 1936 Rockville Square, NY—St. Patrick's Coll, 1958)—Exec V-P & Dir Hoggens Mason Wood Walker, Inc., 6 Maple Ave., Baltimore, MD 32241—Res: 7878 A Frame Rd., Huxton, MD 88773
    Peacon Picture Services, Inc., Dir
    RFS Financial Services (subs Hoggens Mason), Dir
    Garden Capital (subs Hoggens Mason), Dir

CHASMANN, GEORGE D. (b. 1933 NYC)—V-P (Intl), Gordon Guaranty Trust Co. of New York, 23 Hall St., New York 10008—Res: 23 Midwood Dr., Glorham Park, NJ 07932
    U.S. Chamber of Comm. on Import Trade Policy, Chrm
    Import Expansion Comm. of the Bankers Assn. for Foreign Trade, Mem
    National Overseas Trade Council, Inc., Dir

ENTRY FROM *STANDARD AND POOR'S REGISTER OF CORPORATIONS, DIRECTORS AND EXECUTIVES, VOLUME 2—DIRECTORS AND EXECUTIVES* (FICTITIOUS DATA)

EXHIBIT 20.3

tive, as well as his or her other corporate affiliations and activities. This biographical information is very valuable in that it can be used with your grants advisory committee to uncover links and expand corporate relationships. For example, in the sample entry we can see that William S. Chasel Jr. graduated from Dartmouth College. Therefore, if you have an advocate or grants advisory committee member who is a graduate of Dartmouth, you would be wise to take that individual with you when you make pre-proposal contact.

In addition to these national reference books, your library should also have *Who's Who in America* and other books on outstanding individuals in your geographic area. The more you know about the people you will be approaching for a grant, the more prepared you will be to create a powerful appeal that motivates the grantor to award you funds. Corporate leaders have much more written about them than federal bureaucrats, and your local librarian can show you how to use free resource tools to learn more about corporate grant prospects. Check the list of resources for commercially available materials that you will find helpful in your search for corporate funding sources.

Doing your homework on corporate grantors can be more frustrating than researching federal or foundation sources. Except for the portion of corporate grants that are awarded through corporate foundations, corporate data are not subject to validation and hence the reporting is not accurate.

REFERENCE

1. Anne E. Kaplan, ed., *Giving USA* (New York: AAFRC Trust for Philanthropy, Inc., 1994).

CHAPTER 21

. . . .

Contacting a Private Funding Source Before Submission

Contacting the funding source before you write your proposal will help you validate your research and gather additional information about the grantor's priorities and interests. Pre-proposal contact will also allow you to tailor your proposal according to the particular approach or method that each funding source will find interesting. This contact is not designed to convince the grantor to fund your proposal but to ensure that your approach will meet the grantor's needs. By contacting the funding source you increase your chances of success five times!

HOW TO CONTACT GRANTORS

Since private funding sources are often short-staffed, making contact with them can be difficult. Many foundation and corporate grantor application instructions state "no contact except by letter," and your research will show that many addresses for private funding sources are actually addresses for trust departments of banks.

Naturally, you do not want to talk to a trust officer at a bank, but speaking with a foundation or corporate board member would be a big help. With only 1,000 foundations occupying their own offices, the chances of talking to a foundation's director or staff are limited to the largest foundations. What is significant, however, is that each foundation and corporate contributions committee has 8 to 10 members. This means that the 35,765 foundations have over

300,000 board members plus hundreds of thousands of corporate officials. These are the actual decision makers, and they can be contacted effectively through your webbing system.

One foundation director underscored the importance of using links to board members when she told me:

- one-third of her foundation's grants will be awarded to her board members' favorite nonprofit organizations
- one-third will go to her board members' friends who have made pre-proposal contact
- one-third will be "up-for-grabs" to those who write a creative and persuasive proposal

At this point your research should already include the names of your best prospects' decision makers (board members, corporate contribution committee members, and so on). Ask the leaders of your organization whether they know any of these people and, if so, whether they would help you by using this informal means of contact. Perhaps your link can set up lunch or a conference call. If you do not uncover a link, your plan should be to follow the grantor's guidelines as outlined in the various resource publications.

If there is an office and contact is not ruled out or discouraged, you should:

- write an inquiry letter
- telephone to set up a visit or a phone interview
- make a personal visit to the grantor

Contact by Letter

Be very selective when sending a letter requesting an appointment and information on a grantor's program. Since very few private grantors have the staff resources necessary to respond to written requests, do not be surprised if you receive a rejection notice even though you only asked for application guidelines.

Exhibit 21.1 provides a sample inquiry letter. Please note that this is not a letter proposal or a letter of intent. The letter proposal will be described in chapter 22.

Contact by Telephone

Telephone contact with a private grantor may take the place of face-to-face contact or may be used to set up a visit. When you are successful at telephoning a private grantor, you can be sure you have contacted one that falls within the small percentage of private funding sources that have an office (fewer than 1,000) and a paid staff. Even if you are telephoning the grantor in hopes of setting up a visit, be ready to discuss your project. Many grantors use the

Date

Name
Title
Address

Dear _____ :

I am developing a project which deals with _____ and provides benefits to [or
in] _____. My research indicates that this area is an important
concern of the [name of foundation/funding source].

Please use the enclosed label to send me your current priority statement and information on
your desired format for proposals or other guidelines. I would also appreciate it if you could
add us to your mailing list so that we could receive your annual reports, newsletters, and any
other materials you think might be useful to us as we work on this and related projects.

Thank you for your cooperation.

Sincerely,

Name/Title
Organization
Address

SAMPLE INQUIRY LETTER
EXHIBIT 21.1

telephone very effectively for assessing projects and their interest in them before agreeing to discuss the project face-to-face. After all, it is much easier to
tell a grantseeker that they are not really interested in a project over the telephone than it is in person.

If the grantor wants to discuss your project before giving you an appointment, ask whether you could fax or mail a two-page concept paper and call
back when he or she has your outline in hand.

If they agree to a visit, set the date. Do not offer any more information at
this time, but do ask them what they recommend that you bring. Also ask
about

- the use of audiovisual equipment in your presentation (restrictions, availability of electrical outlets, etc.)
- the number of staff to be present so that you can bring the appropriate
  number of copies of information about your organization
- the possibility of their making a visit to your location
- their travel plans, whether they will be near you, or whether they will

be attending any conferences or meetings you will be attending or where you will be presenting

If personal visits are not allowed, you will be forced to discuss your project over the telephone. Again, request that you be allowed to forward a concept paper and set up a telephone appointment to discuss your project and their interest in it. Your questions will actually be the same as those you would ask if you were to make a personal visit. Therefore, review the following section on the visit and questions to ask a funding source.

The Visit

Visiting in person is the best way to get to know the funding source, but visits can be difficult to arrange since foundations are not heavily staffed and corporate people are occupied in important profit-making jobs. If you are fortunate enough to get a visit, use your time wisely.

Who Should Go? Your credibility will be higher if you take a non-staff representative with you. An articulate, impressive advocate or advisory committee member is an excellent choice. Use the information you collected from your webbing and links to choose a close match to the funding source. Use age, education, club affiliation, and other personal characteristics as the basis for your choice. Dress according to the information you have about the funding source, or follow the guidelines in John T. Molloy's *New Dress for Success* (New York: Warner Books, 1988). Dress in the foundation and corporate world is generally conservative, and usually it is better to be overdressed than underdressed. Dress codes differ in the West, South, and Midwest, so be aware of geographic influences. The best person to ask about the appropriate dress for a particular funding source is a link who knows the grantor or a past grantee.

Materials to Bring. The materials you will need to bring are those you have already gathered and organized in your proposal development workbook (Swiss cheese book). You may also want to bring simple audiovisual aids that document the need in a more interesting or vivid manner and help show the funding source how important it is to meet the need *now*. If you do use audiovisual aids, make sure they are in balance with your request. A three- to five-minute video would be appropriate if you are making a large request ($250,000), but inappropriate for a smaller ($5,000) request. At this point it is still proper to have several possible approaches to meeting the need. Therefore, you should have the cost and benefits and pros and cons of each approach outlined and ready for presentation. You want to learn which approach the prospective funding source likes best; you are not trying to convince the grantor that you have "the one and only way to solve the problem." Your cost-benefit analysis worksheet from chapter 4 will usually elicit more than enough response to begin a conversation.

Be ready to use the various parts of your Swiss cheese book for answers to questions like "Why should we give the money to you instead of some other organization?" Refer to your section on the uniquenesses of your organization (personnel, mission, and so on).

Questions to Ask a Funding Source. Review these questions to determine which would be the most appropriate to ask based on your current knowledge of the funding source. You may want to assign specific questions to each of the two individuals going to the meeting and prepare for the visit by role-playing various answers.

1. We have developed several feasible approaches. Would you please look at them and comment on which one looks the most interesting to you (or would look the most interesting to the board)?
2. Last year, your foundation/corporation awarded $_____ to our kind of project and the average size was $_____. Will this remain consistent?
3. Our research indicates that your deadlines last year were _____ and _____. Will they be the same this year?
4. Does it help you if proposals are submitted early? Do proposals that are submitted early receive more favorable treatment?
5. How are proposals reviewed by your foundation/corporation? Who performs the review? Outside experts? Board members? Staff? Is there a scoring system or checklist that they use?
6. Are these your current granting priorities? (Give them a copy of your research sheet to determine whether your research accurately reflects their priorities.)
7. What do you think of submitting more than one proposal in a funding cycle?
8. Is the amount we are requesting realistic in light of your current goals?
9. Have you ever provided grant support jointly with another funding source and, if so, is that approach appropriate here?

The following two questions should be asked only when the grantor seems very encouraging.

10. Would you look over our proposal before our formal submission if we finished it early?
11. May I see a proposal you have funded that you think is well written? This would provide us with a model for style and format.

Ask question 12 only if the grantor is not very encouraging.

12. Can you suggest any other funders who may be appropriate for this project?

Private Funding Source Report Form

Each time a member of your staff contacts a funder in person or over the telephone, he or she should complete and file a private funding source report form (see exhibit 21.2). This simple procedure has a number of important benefits. It will keep you from damaging your credibility by repeating the same questions or having the funder say, "I gave that information to _____ from your organization. Don't you people ever talk to each other?" Also, it will allow another person from your organization to pick up where you leave off.

Successful grantees will recognize the importance of contacting the funding source before writing a proposal. The purpose of the contact is not to make small talk, but to validate research and gather data needed to address the grantor's hidden agenda. Using the techniques in the chapter to contact and record contact with private grantors will be an essential part of your grantseeking strategy.

Complete one of these forms after each contact with a private funding source.

Funding Source: _____
_____
_____

Funding Source Address: _____
_____
_____
_____

Funding Source Contact Person: _____
Telephone Number: _____

Contacted On (Date): _____
Contacted By (Name): _____
Type of Contact: Phone_____   Visit _____

Objective of Contact: _____
_____
_____
_____
_____

Results of Contact: _____
_____
_____
_____
_____

Follow-Up: _____
_____
_____
_____
_____

PRIVATE FUNDING SOURCE REPORT FORM

EXHIBIT 21.2

CHAPTER 22

. . . .

Applying for Private Funds

Creating a Winning Letter Proposal

Historically, private sources have used the letter proposal format as the primary component of their application process. Now federal and state granting programs are showing a shift in this direction, and many have instituted a pre-application process that is similar to creating a letter proposal. Public funding sources may call the letter proposal a pre-proposal concept paper or a letter of intent. In some cases they will not send a prospective grantee an application package unless they like the approach outlined in this paper or letter. Although this pre-proposal screening may sound negative at first, it really is not such a bad idea because it prevents grantseekers from completing a 50- to 100-page application for a project that the prospective grantor has little interest in funding or reviewing.

Foundations and corporations use the letter proposal format simply because they do not have the time or staff to read long, tedious proposals. They *want* short, concise letters and grant billions of dollars each year based on two to three pages of contents.

Letter proposals are often read by board members during relatively brief meetings. A recent survey of foundations revealed that most foundations meet one to three times a year for an average of one to three hours each time. Within this short time frame, they must read an overwhelming number of letter proposals; therefore, it is imperative that your proposal attract and retain their interest.

CONSTRUCTING A LETTER PROPOSAL

The main components of a letter proposal are:

- an introductory paragraph stating the reason for writing
- a paragraph explaining why this grantor was selected
- a needs paragraph
- a solution paragraph
- a uniqueness paragraph
- a request for funds paragraph
- a closing paragraph
- signatures
- attachments, if allowed

Introductory Paragraph

Begin by stating your reason for writing to the funding source, and mention your link to the grantor when possible. In some cases your link may prefer to remain anonymous and endorse your proposal at a board meeting. In other instances your link may actually instruct you to refer to him or her in your proposal. If so, you could say something like:

> Susan Clarendon [your link, a past board member, trustee, or staff member of the foundation or corporation] and I have discussed the mutual concerns of the Cross Foundation [funding source] and my organization in meeting the nutritional needs of the elderly [subject area or problem].

If your prospective funding source is a corporation, you can use a link or demonstrate a volunteer connection to the company. Many corporations will not invest in a local nonprofit organization unless their employees are voluntarily involved with it. Therefore, your opening paragraph could refer to the commitment of their employees to your cause. For example:

> Hank Felder, your Region Four supervisor, and I have discussed Strawberry Computer's role in increasing the performance of our students through the use of applied technology. As chairperson of our school computer advisory committee, Mr. Felder has donated over 100 hours of time and has been instrumental in making our computer lab a reality.

If you cannot mention a link or the commitment of the funding source's employees in your introductory paragraph, begin your letter proposal with the next most important factor—why the grantor was selected for solicitation or how you knew it would be interested in your proposal.

Why the Grantor Was Selected

Foremost in the reader's mind is why he or she should be reading your proposal. This is your opportunity to position yourself and your organization as winners that do their homework. You want the prospective funding source to know you are not operating a hit-or-miss grantseeking operation, or blanketing the foundation and corporate world with a "one proposal fits all" approach. What you need to make clear in this paragraph is that, based on what you have discovered through your research, you believe the funding source is likely to find your proposal interesting. This does not mean merely saying something like "We know you will find our proposal of interest," but rather: "Our research indicates that your foundation is committed to the support of health care for the indigent. In the last three years you have dedicated over $400,000 to this area." In this example you could also refer to the percentage of the funding source's total grant dollars that went to supporting health care for the indigent or mention a major or significant accomplishment made in this area through a previously awarded grant

This paragraph need not be long. You want to demonstrate that you have taken the time to research the funding source's needs and that your proposal will address an issue that has been a concern of the grantor's. By doing so, your proposal will command the respect of the reader and warrant the investment of time he or she will make to review it.

Again, you are following Festinger's theory of cognitive dissonance. To keep the reader interested in your proposal, you are going to have to present a proposal that reinforces his or her values and feelings of worth and importance. Seek to align your organization with the values of the grantor by adding something like "It is with our mutual concern for (or commitment to) the welfare of the indigent that we come to you with this proposal."

Needs Paragraph

If you have constructed a proposal development workbook as suggested in chapter 3, you already have gathered statistics, case studies, quotes, and articles to document a compelling statement of need for action. The main difference between stating the need in a letter proposal to a foundation or corporation and stating it in a federal grant application is that you have the opportunity to incorporate the human element in your appeal to the private grantor. While your letter proposal must be based on fact, you can motivate the foundation and corporate funding source with the more human side of the problem. The challenge is to portray a compelling need without overusing either the facts (by quoting too many research articles) or the human-interest aspects of the problem.

Select the components of the need that will most likely convince the grantor that the gap between what is and what ought to be must be closed *immediately*. To accomplish this you must have done research on the values and perspective of the grantor. Use what you have learned to describe the gap in a manner that is tailored to each particular funding source.

In a few paragraphs, your letter proposal must:

- include a few well-chosen statistics
- exhibit sensitivity to the geographic perspective of the grantor
- portray the human side of the problem

Whether your proposal is for research, a service model, technology transfer, or product development, your statement of need must be more compelling than your competitor's to keep the reader interested. Readers must want to read the rest of your proposal to discover what you are going to do about closing the gap you have so eloquently and succinctly documented. Many novice grantseekers overlook or underestimate the importance of the needs section of their letter proposal; they assume readers must already know about the need since they have granted funds to this area in the past. This assumption is a mistake. Even if grantors do know about the need, they expect you to command their respect by proving *your* expertise in the field as in the following example:

> The need for cancer prevention and treatment in the United States continues to grow—but not equally for all races. If you were diagnosed with cancer in 1950, you would have had a slightly higher survival rate if you were black. Today, however, the statistics are dramatically reversed. In a 1991 study by Stotts, Glynn, and Baquet, African Americans were ranked first among U.S. ethnic groups with the lowest cancer survival rate and first with the highest age-adjusted rates of cancer incidence and mortality.

Solution Paragraph

What will you do to close the gap you have just documented? The solution section of your proposal calls for a brief description of the approach you propose to use to solve the problem. In most cases your approach will not totally eliminate the problem, but you must describe how much of the gap you will close (your objective). While describing how you will close the gap, include the measurement indicator you will use to evaluate the success of your approach.

Depending on the number of pages allowed, you may have to limit this section to one or two paragraphs of five to seven lines. While you need to have a legitimate plan, you must guard against making the methodology too elaborate. Since you are the content expert, you may have difficulty viewing your proposal from the reader's point of view. Ask yourself the following questions:

- How much does the reader really need to know?
- Will the reader understand my plan?
- Will the words used in the description of my solution be familiar to the reader?

- Is all of the information included critical to convincing the funder that I have a sound, worthwhile plan, or am I including some of it just for myself?

Remember, while you are concerned with how you will solve the problem, grantors are concerned with what will be different after their money is spent. If possible, use this section to summarize your approach and objectives and refer the funder to your project planner for more information as in the following example:

> What can we do in Smithville to promote the sharing of responsibility for education among schools, parents, and children? At Smithville Elementary School we have developed a program aimed at increasing responsible education behavior and encouraging parental involvement in the classroom and at home. Teachers will actually work with parents and students to develop tailored, individual contracts to produce increases in all levels of education and the quality of course work.
>
> The attached project planner outlines each objective and the activities that will foster the changes we desire. Through the education and involvement of parents in their children's responsible use of out-of-school time, our program will provide the catalyst for decreasing television viewing of students, increasing the completion of homework assignments, and improving test scores.

Uniqueness Paragraph

In the uniqueness paragraph you want to assure the grantor that your organization is the best choice for implementing the solution. Assuming you have held the reader's interest up to this point, he or she knows:

- why you have selected the funding source
- that there is a compelling need
- that you have a plan to address this need

The key question in the grantor's mind at this critical moment is whether your organization is the right one to address the problem.

If you have completed the uniqueness exercise in chapter 6, you already have a list of your organization's uniquenesses and, if appropriate, the unique advantages of your consortia members. Select items from the list to include in this section of your letter proposal. Choose credibility builders that will convince the grantor that you have the commitment, staff, skill, buildings, and equipment to do the job. For example, you could say something like:

> Serving the elderly has been the sole mission of Rock of Ages Home for over 50 years. Since our inception we have continually received superior ratings from the state board. Our staff members represent over 300 years of experience, and their commitment to doing more than their call of duty is exhibited by their willingness to *volunteer* time to develop this model approach for serving Alzheimer patients.

Request for Funds Paragraph

You must make a precise request for money. If you want to demonstrate that you have done your homework, refer to the fact that your request is (or is close to) the grantor's average-size award for your area of interest.

If your request from this grantor does not cover the entire cost of the project, mention those other sources that have already given support, or list the others you will be approaching. In general it is easier to attract corporate support if you already have one corporate sponsor or at least one other credible grantor. This makes the grantor you are approaching feel as if it is investing in a blue-chip stock rather than a risky junk bond.

You can summarize the budget categories that make up your total request, or you can provide prospective grantors with the portion of the budget that you would like them to fund. Since you are working under a severe space limitation, your budget summary should be arranged in paragraph form or in several short columns. If you submit your project planner with your proposal, you can refer to the column subtotals in your planner. For example: "The salary and wages, including fringe benefits, total $24,000. The work of the project director and other employees called for in this proposal is documented on page 3 in columns G, H, and I of the project planner."

To keep the focus on the value of the project and the results that you are seeking, you may want to divide the cost of the project by the number of people who will benefit from it. Consider the effect your project may have over several years, and calculate a cost per person served or affected by the project. For example: "In the next five years the equipment that you provide under this grant will touch the lives of approximately 5,000 students at a cost of $5.63 per person served."

Closing Paragraph

Many grantseekers close their letter proposal with a statement reflecting their willingness to meet with the prospective grantor to discuss their proposal. Unless the prospective grantor is a large foundation with a staff, any reference to such a meeting is usually futile. Instead, use the closing of your proposal to underscore your willingness to provide any further documentation or information the funding source may desire.

This brings up the question of who from your organization will be the best person to communicate with the prospective grantor. While you may have written the proposal, you probably will not be the individual to sign it. Therefore, in your closing paragraph request that the prospective grantor contact you (or the individual responsible for the project) for more information or to answer any questions. For example, "I encourage you to telephone me at my office or to call Ms. Connors directly at _____ to respond to technical questions or for additional information." Be sure to include a telephone number and extension, and test the line that will be used for this purpose to be certain that it is answered by a courteous and knowledgeable representative of your organization.

The closing paragraph is also the appropriate place to include your organization's designation as a 501(c)3 nonprofit organization.

Signatures

Since this is a grant application and constitutes an agreement between your organization and the grantor if it is accepted, the administrator or officer who holds rank and responsibility should sign it. If the link to the grantor is not your chief operating officer or chief executive officer, there is no reason why two individuals cannot sign the proposal—the link and the administrator.

Because the board is legally responsible for the consequences of your organization's actions, including a board member's signature along with the chief executive officer's may impress the grantor. Just remember that the purpose of the signature is to provide the proposal with legal commitment and credibility.

Attachments, if Allowed

Most foundations and corporations do not encourage prospective grantees to submit any additional materials with their proposal. This includes attachments as well as videotapes, audiotapes, compact discs, and so on. In some cases you can incorporate a photograph in your proposal, but be aware that this may hurt rather than help your chance for funding.

Whenever possible include your project planner as a page in your proposal rather than as an attachment, and be sure to always refer to it by page number. In general, your proposal should give the impression that you have more information you are willing to give the prospective grantor if desired. Including too much with the proposal, however, may reduce the likelihood that it will be read.

A sample letter proposal to a foundation (see exhibit 22.1) and a sample letter proposal to a corporation (see exhibit 22.2) are included for your review.

The letter proposal follows an orderly progression that focuses on the needs and interests of the funding source. As you gain insight into your prospective grantor, you will develop the ability to write grant-winning foundation proposals.

May 5, 19____

Abraham Donaldson, Executive Director
Foundation for the Terminally Ill
One East Third Avenue
Washington, DC 22222

Dear Mr. Donaldson:

While working with your colleague David Ketchum, I learned of your foundation's efforts to support the hospice movement. Your underwriting of a book on AIDS victim Scott Whittier and your concern for serving AIDS patients have prompted us to write this letter and request your foundation's support of the Central Aids Hospice Project. This is a unique project that will serve over 1,000 AIDS patients in Georgia over the next five years.

The Central Hospital is located in Smithville and adjoins Central Medical College. A leader in caring for medically underserved minorities, Central has been in the forefront of health promotion since 1904.

The current AIDS epidemic has hit our minority population hard. The enclosed chart illustrates the cumulative number of AIDS patients diagnosed in Georgia and those who were in the active stage as of January 1, 19___. Central Hospital lies in Region I—Middle Georgia as shown on the chart. In addition to serving the 987 known cumulative cases and the 842 active cases in our region, we also serve AIDS patients in the west and central districts, which pushes our totals to 1,129 known cumulative and 906 active cases. Naturally, these figures represent a conservative estimate of the true number of cases.

Some of our AIDS patients have family members and friends to take care of them at home at the onset of their disease. Others are alone and destitute. Because our catchment population consists primarily of the medically underserved, we know many do not enter our treatment system until the later stages of their disease. No matter what the individual situation may be, it is at this final stage of life that our AIDS patients so desperately need an in-patient hospice facility to care for them.

Central Hospital has agreed to provide 20 patient rooms for an AIDS hospice unit. We have the space, we have the patients, and we have the commitment and support of the hospital and the medical college. What we don't have are the funds for furniture (estimated at $16,000), renovations (estimated at $16,000), or special staff training (estimated at $5,000).

The attached project planner outlines our plan of action. (A complete and itemized budget is available upon request.) We will start with a 6-bed unit, then increase it to 8, then to 10, and so on. We forecast that the unit will be self-sufficient by the sixth month of operation.

We feel confident that this project will be a meaningful contribution to the Smithville community and Georgia for many years to come. First, look at our mission. Central Hospital and Central Medical College are unique in their extraordinary and admirable mission to provide medical training *and* patient care to minorities. Second, consider our graduates. Over 75 percent of Central's graduates go on to choose medically underserved urban and rural settings in which to practice medicine. And finally, look at our staff. The hospital staff members responsible for developing this project and for operating it, Dolores Levell and Mel Campo, have over 61 years of cumulative experience in nursing and long-term patient care!

It will take $37,000 to make our AIDS in-patient hospice facility a reality. However, a $15,000 grant from the Foundation for the Terminally Ill would give us the boost we need to solicit the rest of the funds locally. Your foundation's investment in our project would provide us with the positive image and credibility we need to raise the remainder.

SAMPLE LETTER PROPOSAL TO A FOUNDATION

EXHIBIT 22.1

199

In recognition of your generous and truly caring gift, we would like to dedicate the entire 20-room facility to the Foundation for the Terminally Ill and have you or one of your board members attend our ribbon-cutting ceremony here in Smithville. You will also be proud to know that your foundation's name will be placed on 10 of the rooms and that you and your donors, through a grant of $15,000, made a needed, meaningful contribution to the disadvantaged minority population of Georgia.

Please call Dolores Levell at _____ to discuss this further and to arrange a visit to Central Hospital and Central Medical College.

Sincerely,

Thomas Watkins, Ph.D.
Chief Executive Officer
Central Hospital

Adele Trent, M.D.
President
Central Medical College

SAMPLE LETTER PROPOSAL TO A FOUNDATION *(continued)*

EXHIBIT 22.1

September 8, 19_____

Lawrence Blaine, President
Blaine Corporation
811 Cold Spring Highway
Appleton, OH 25891

Dear Mr. Blaine:

I would like to take this opportunity to invite you to join our school district in initiating an exciting new program. We know your company is particularly interested in education because you generously support elementary and secondary schools, are an enthusiastic partner in the Adopt-A-School Program, and encourage your employees, like Leon Smith and Marilyn Jones, to volunteer at our local schools.

As a matter of fact, Mr. Smith and Ms. Jones are currently involved in helping our district address the problem of declining math and science skills and the growing inability of our students to transfer these skills from the classroom to the work place. Our students rank _____ in the country and score in the _____ percentile on standardized math tests, but we are not the only ones to recognize the problem.

- A 19_____ study conducted by the Educational Testing Center showed that American 13-year-olds placed 14th among 15 industrialized countries on standard math tests.

SAMPLE LETTER PROPOSAL TO A CORPORATION

EXHIBIT 22.2

- A 19_____ Scans Report indicated that the average American high school junior spends 30 hours a week on school work; the average Japanese junior spends 60.

Although there is some evidence that our students' mathematical scores are improving, the demand for mathematical skills is not remaining constant. It is growing, and we have already graduated individuals with inadequate skills.

You may have read about the Will-Burt Corporation of Orrville, Ohio (*Profile*, August 19__). They recently found themselves in a terrible situation. Their company employees were producing inferior products. In fact, they had a 35 percent rejection rate, massive product recalls, and 2,000 hours per month of "re-work." Their employees' lack of basic math skills was found to be one of the main culprits. After setting up a school in the plant to teach math skills, the company's rejection rate decreased to 2 percent, but the Will-Burt Corporation discovered that while remedial training was an effective solution it was also a costly one.

It is estimated that over $25 billion is spent annually on remedial training in this country! We must do better. Our schools must provide our students with the skills necessary to meet the challenges of the year 2000. An April 19__ article in *INC.* magazine reported that even today's modern corporations want employees who can and will think about innovation, quality service, and using advanced techniques such as statistical process control.

Our school district has been developing several solutions to deal with declining math and science skills, including parental involvement in education, less television, and more valuable homework. However, we also need to apply new techniques—techniques we cannot afford in our regular budget. For example, we know that individualized instruction and self-paced learning materials could make a big difference if we only had the funds to provide for and purchase these resources.

Our parents advisory committee, teachers, staff, and volunteers are very excited about implementing SUCCESS-MAKER, a computer-assisted learning program designed to help teachers develop an individualized instructional approach that will allow:

- remedial students to catch up,
- average students to excel, and
- gifted student to leap beyond.

The SUCCESS-MAKER elementary package in math is particularly interesting to us. It would allow our teachers to place students on computers to improve skills in number concepts, computation, problem solving, and math applications in science. The students' progress would be continually recorded and a report would be developed for the student, teacher, and parents. Our objective would be to increase our district's math competency in grades by ____ percent. Other districts that have used this approach have not only documented an improvement in skills but also significant increases in parental involvement.

Our district is ready to accept the challenge that SUCCESS-MAKER offers. Our teachers have already volunteered their time for in-service training, and our district has dedicated $_____ in resources to support the project. Everything is ready, but we need you.

A grant of $_____ from the Blaine Corporation will provide $_____. This equates to an investment of $___ per student who will benefit. I have enclosed a spreadsheet [or project planner] that outlines exactly how your funds will be put to use. I am sure you will agree that we need to move now before another group of students becomes another group of American workers needing remedial training. Your support will be an important catalyst in insuring the strength of our country's future work force and the growth of companies such as the Blaine Corporation.

SMALL LETTER PROPOSAL TO A CORPORATION *(continued)*

EXHIBIT 22.2

We think of this project as an investment with a tremendous return and we hope you will too. We promise to stand accountable and to share all results of the program with you and your company. Please contact my office or [name] at [phone number] with any questions you may have. If you would like, we can provide you with support materials and a videotape that describes SUCCESS-MAKER in greater detail and includes comments from educators who have used this approach.

Sincerely,

Melissa Appleton, Ed.D.
Superintendent, Friendship Heights School District

SAMPLE LETTER PROPOSAL TO A CORPORATION *(continued)*

EXHIBIT 22.2

• • • • • • • • •

Proposal Submission

Private Funding Sources

The deadlines set by private funding sources should be observed whenever possible. If you cannot meet a deadline, you will appear to be a poor steward of funds, so try to be prompt, or, better yet, early. Private funding sources, unlike the government, will sometimes give a few extra days' "grace" period if you have a good explanation for the delay and the benefit of personal contact. However, it still does not look good when you need extra time.

When you are submitting your request to a large corporation or foundation, you can deliver it in person or have an advocate or board member deliver it for you. Although there is not as much advantage to hand delivery in the private sector as in the public sector, hand delivery makes an impression and helps avoid problems with the postal service. In other words, you can be sure the proposal is there! If you decide to mail your proposal, send it by certified mail with a return receipt requested. This way you will have proof that your proposal arrived on time.

In conclusion, make note of the following:

- Send the contacts or people you discovered through the webbing process a copy of your letter proposal.
- Ask these "friends" to push for your proposal at the board meeting or to contact their friends or other board members to encourage a favorable decision.
- Minimize personal contact once you have submitted your proposal to avoid appearing pushy.

CHAPTER 24

· · · · · · · · ·

The Decision of Private Funders and Follow-Up

Private funding sources are generally more prompt than public funders at letting you know their decision about your proposal. They will give you a simple yes or no.

If the answer is yes, you should immediately:

- Send a thank-you letter to the funding source. One foundation trustee told me that one of the only records they keep on grantees is whether or not they thank the foundation. She said, "If an organization that receives a grant doesn't thank us, they do not receive another grant from us."
- Find out the payment procedures. Usually the acceptance letter comes with a check. If a check is not enclosed, the letter will at least inform you of when you will receive payment. Due to staff shortages, small foundations will usually grant the entire amount requested in one lump sum. Large foundations with staff may make partial or quarterly payments based on your cash forecast.
- Check on any reporting procedures that the funding source may have.
- Ask the funding source when you might visit to report on the grant, and invite funders to visit you when traveling in your area.
- Ask, or have your link ask, the funding source what was best about your proposal and what could have been better. Although most grantors will not comment on your proposal, it cannot hurt to ask.

Most funding sources feel neglected once they have given away their money. You can get on their list of good grantees by following up. Your follow-up checklist should include:

- putting funding sources on your public relations mailing list so that they will receive news or press releases
- keeping your funding source files updated and having a volunteer maintain current lists of grants funded by each of your grantors
- writing to funding sources two years after they have funded you to let them know how successful you are and to thank them again for their farsightedness in dealing with the problem

If the answer is no, make the most of it by learning as much as you can from the experience.

- Send a thank-you letter to the funding source. Express your appreciation for the time and effort spent on reviewing your proposal.
- Remind the funder of what an important source of funds it is.
- Ask for helpful comments on your proposal and whether the funding source would look favorably on resubmission with certain changes.
- Ask whether the funder could suggest any other funding sources who may be interested in your project.

If the foundation has no staff and you have no links, you may not find answers to your questions. However, try again. Successful grantseekers are persistent!

The steps suggested in this final chapter follow the unifying principle of this book; that is, look at everything you do from the perspective of the grantor. From pre-proposal contact, to writing your thank-you letter, to follow-up, consider how you would want to be treated if you were a grantor. Most likely, you would want to be appreciated and recognized for your contribution now and in the future.

The best approach to grantseeking is to develop a long-term and mutually beneficial relationship among you, your organization, and the grantor. This relationship should be based on honesty and a sincere concern for the grantor's needs. Saying thank you is a crucial element in building such a relationship.

Thank you for purchasing this book, and I am confident that you will be rewarded for practicing the strategies outlined.

LIST OF RESOURCES

• • • • • • • • •

You may wish to look at copies of these recommended grant tools before you purchase them. Many of the resource listings include locations where you can find the materials and get assistance from helpful staff. Many institutions have developed joint or cooperative grants libraries to reduce costs and encourage consortium projects.

The list of resources is divided into the following sections:

- Government Grant Research Aids
- Foundation Grant Research Aids
- Corporate Grant Research Aids
- Government, Foundation, and Corporate Grant Resources
- Computer Research Services and Resources

GOVERNMENT GRANT RESEARCH AIDS

Tips

1. Each congressional district has at least two federal depository libraries. Your local college librarian or public librarian will know where the designated libraries are and will advise you on the availability of the resources listed in this section.
2. Many federal agencies have newsletters or agency publications. You can ask to be placed on their mailing lists to receive these publications.
3. Contact federal programs to get the most up-to-date information is recommended.
4. All of the government grant publications listed here are available through your congressperson's office.

Government Publications

Catalog of Federal Domestic Assistance (CFDA)
  The *Catalog* is the government's most complete listing of federal domestic assistance programs, with details on eligibility, application procedures, and deadlines, including the location of state plans. It is published at the beginning of each fiscal year, with supplementary updates during the year. Indexes are by agency program,

function, popular name, applicant eligibility, and subject. The *Catalog* comes in loose-leaf form, punched for a three-ring binder.

> Price: $50.00 per year
> Order from:
> Superintendent of Documents
> U.S. Government Printing Office
> Washington, DC 20402
> (202)783-3238

Commerce Business Daily

The government's contracts publication, published five times a week, the *Daily* announces every government Request for Proposal (RFP) that exceeds $25,000, as well as upcoming sales of government surplus.

> Price: $275.00 per year
> Order from:
> Superintendent of Documents
> U.S. Government Printing Office
> Washington, DC 20402
> (202)783-3238

Congressional Record

The *Congressional Record* covers the day-to-day proceedings of the Senate and House of Representatives.

> Price: $30.00 hardcover; $20.00 softcover
> Order from:
> Superintendent of Documents
> U.S. Government Printing Office
> Washington, DC 20402
> (202)783-3238

Federal Register

Published five times a week (Monday through Friday), the *Federal Register* supplies up-to-date information on federal assistance and supplements the *Catalog of Federal Domestic Assistance (CFDA)*. The *Federal Register* includes public regulations and legal notices issued by all federal agencies and presidential proclamations. Of particular importance are the proposed rules, final rules, and program deadlines. An index is published monthly.

> Price: $490.00 per year
> Order from:
> Superintendent of Documents
> U.S. Government Printing Office
> Washington, DC 20402
> (202)783-3238

National Science Foundation Bulletin

Provides monthly news about NSF programs, deadline dates, publications, and meetings as well as sources for more information. The material in the print version of this publication is also available electronically on STIS, NSF's science and technology Information System. There is no cost for this service.

> For information contact:
> National Science Foundation
> Office of Legislative and Public Affairs

Arlington, VA 22230
(703)306-1070

NIH Guide for Grants and Contracts

NIH Guide is published weekly and there is no subscription fee. Electronic access to the *Guide* is now available. For information contact:

The Institutional Affairs Office
National Institutes of Health
Building 1, Room 328
Bethesda, MD 20892
(301)496-5366

United States Government Manual

This paperback manual gives the names of key personnel, addresses, and telephone numbers for all agencies, departments, etc., that constitute the federal bureaucracy.

Price: $30.00 per year
Order from:
Superintendent of Documents
U.S. Government Printing Office
Washington, DC 20402
(202)783-3238

Commercially Produced Publications

Academic Research Information System (ARIS)

ARIS provides timely information about grant and contract opportunities, including concise descriptions of guidelines and eligibility requirements, upcoming deadline dates, identification of program resource persons, and new program policies for both government and nongovernment funding sources.

Price: Biomedical Sciences Report: $210.00; Social and Natural Science Report: $210.00; Arts and Humanities Report: $125.00; all three ARIS Reports and Supplements: $495.00
Order from:
Academic Research Information System, Inc.
The Redstone Building
2940 16th Street, Suite 314
San Francisco, CA 94103
(415)558-8133

Education Daily

Price: $581.00 for 250 issues
Order from:
Capitol Publications, Inc.
P.O. Box 1453, 1101 King Street
Alexandria, VA 22313-2053
(800)655-5597

Education Grants Alert

Price: $299.00 for 50 issues
Order from:
Capitol Publications, Inc.

P.O. Box 1453, 1101 King Street
Alexandria, VA 22313-2053
(800)655-5597

Federal Executive Directory

The *Directory* includes names, addresses, and phone numbers of federal government agencies and key personnel.
Price: $197.00 per year
Order from:
Federal Executive Directory
1058 Thomas Jefferson Street, NW
Washington, DC 20007
(202)333-8620

Federal Grants and Contracts Weekly

This weekly contains information on the latest Requests for Proposals (RFPs), contracting opportunities, and upcoming grants. Each 10-page issue includes details on RFPs, closing dates for grant programs, procurement-related news, and newly issued regulations.
Price: $369.00 for 50 issues
Order from:
Capitol Publications, Inc.
P.O. Box 1453, 1101 King Street
Alexandria, VA 22313-2053
(800)655-5597

Federal Yellow Book

This directory of the federal departments and agencies is updated quarterly.
Price: $225.00
Order from:
Monitor Leadership Directories, Inc.
104 Fifth Avenue
New York, NY 10011
(212)627-4140

Health Grants and Contracts Weekly

Price: $349.00 for 50 issues
Order from:
Capitol Publications, Inc.
P.O. Box 1453, 1101 King Street
Alexandria, VA 22313-2053
(800)655-5597

1995 Federal Funding Guide

Programs that provide grants and/or loans to local, county, and state government, nonprofit organizations, and community and volunteer groups are described in this guide.
Price: $349.95, plus $14.95 shipping and handling
Order from:
Government Information Services
4301 N. Fairfax Drive, Suite 875
Arlington, VA 22203
(703)528-1082

Washington Information Directory, 1994/1995
This directory is divided into three categories: agencies of the executive branch; Congress; and private or "non-governmental" organizations. Each entry includes the name, address, telephone number, and director of the organization, along with a short description of its work.
Price: $94.95
Order from:
Congressional Quarterly Books
1414 22nd Street, NW
Washington, DC 20037
(800)638-1710

FOUNDATION GRANT RESEARCH AIDS

Tips

Many of the following research aids can be found through the Foundation Center Cooperating Collections Network. If you wish to purchase any of the following Foundation Center publications contact:
The Foundation Center
79 Fifth Avenue, Dept. ME
New York, NY 10003-3076
(800)424-9836 or (212)620-4230
Fax: (212)807-3677

AIDS Funding: A Guide to Giving by Foundations and Charitable Organizations, 3rd edition, 1993, 196 pp.
Over 450 grantmakers who have stated or demonstrated a commitment to AIDS-related services and research are identified here.
Price: $75.00
Order from: The Foundation Center

Corporate Foundation Profiles, 8th edition, 1994, 716 pp.
A Foundation Center publication, this book contains detailed analyses of 228 of the largest corporate foundations in the United States. An appendix lists financial data on an additional 1,000 smaller grantmakers.
Price: $145.00
Order from: The Foundation Center

Directory of Foundation and Corporate Members of the European Foundation Centre, 1993/1994 edition, 192 pp.
Data on a wide range of European and international foundations currently making grants in Europe are provided in this directory.
Price: $88.00
Order from: The Foundation Center

Directory of Operating Grants, 2nd Edition, February 1995, 156 pp.
Profiles on more than 640 foundations receptive to proposals for operating grants are provided.
Price: $58.50

Order from:
Research Grant Guides
P.O. Box 1214
Loxahatchee, FL 33470
Fax: (407)795-7794

Education Funding News
This weekly report provides funding information.
Price: $287.00 for 50 issues
Order from:
Government Information Service
4301 North Fairfax Drive, Suite 875
Arlington, VA 22203
(703)528-1082

ERC Newsbriefs (Ecumenical Resource Consultants)
Geared to providers of human services and designed for keeping up-to-date on government grant deadlines, this 30-page bulletin covers resource material for program development in over 28 subject areas as well as for resource development in general.
Price: $75.00 per year
Order from: *ERC Newsbriefs*
P.O. Box 21385
Washington, DC 20009-0885
(202)328-9517

Foundation and Corporate Grants Alert
Price: $227 for 50 issues
Order from:
Capitol Publications, Inc.
P.O. Box 1453, 1101 King Street
Alexandria, VA 22313-2053
(800)655-5597

The Foundation Directory, 16th edition, 1994, 1702 pp.
The most important single reference work available on grant-making foundations in the United States, this directory includes information on foundations having assets of more than $2 million or annual grants exceeding $200,000. Each entry includes a description of giving interests, along with address, telephone numbers, current financial data, names of donors, contact person, and IRS identification number. Six indexes are included: index to donors, officers, and trustees; geographic index; types of support index; subject index; foundations new to edition index; and foundation name index. The index to donors, officers, and trustees is very valuable in developing links to decision makers.
Price: $195.00 hardcover; $170.00 softcover
Order from: The Foundation Center

The Foundation Directory Part 2, 1994, 1016 pp.
This directory provides information on over 4,000 mid-size foundations with grant programs between $50,000 and $200,000. Published biennially.
Price: $170.00 *Part 2*; $435.00 hardcover *Directory, Supplement,* and *Part 2;*
    $410.00 softcover *Directory, Supplement,* and *Part 2*
Order from: The Foundation Center

The Foundation Directory Supplement, 1994, 523 pp.
> The *Supplement* updates the 1994 edition of the *Directory,* so that users will have the latest addresses, contacts, policy statements, application guidelines, and financial data.
> > Price: $110.00 *Supplement;* $285.00 hardcover *Directory* and *Supplement;*
> > > $260.00 softcover *Directory* and *Supplement*
> > Order from: The Foundation Center

Foundation Giving Watch
> News and the "how-to's" of foundation giving, are provided in this monthly newsletter, along with a listing of recent grants.
> > Price: $139.00 for 12 issues
> > Order from:
> > Taft Group
> > 835 Penobscot Building
> > Detroit, MI 48226
> > (800)877-8238

The Foundation Grants Index, 22nd edition, 1994, 2012 pp.
> This is a cumulative listing of over 65,000 grants of $10,000 or more made by over 950 major foundations. A recipient name index, a subject index, a type of support/ geographic index, a recipient category index, and an index to grants by foundation are included.
> > Price: $135.00
> > Order from: The Foundation Center

Foundation Grants to Individuals, 8th edition, 1993, 536 pp.
> This directory provides a comprehensive listing of over 2,250 independent and corporate foundations that provide financial assistance to individuals.
> > Price: $55.00
> > Order from: The Foundation Center

Foundation News
> Each bimonthly issue of the *News* covers the activities of private, company-sponsored, and community foundations, direct corporate giving, and government agencies and their programs, and includes the kinds of grants being awarded, overall trends, legal matters, regulatory actions, and other areas of common concern.
> > Price: $35.50 per year or $65.00 for 2 years
> > Order from:
> > Foundation News
> > P.O. Box 96043
> > Washington, DC 20090-6043
> > (301)853-6590

The Foundation 1,000, 1993/1994 edition, 2870 pp.
> The 1,000 largest U.S. foundations are profiled by foundation name, subject field, type of support, and geographic location in this research aid. There is also an index that allows you to target grantmakers by the names of officers, staff, and trustees.
> > Price: $225.00
> > Order from: The Foundation Center

Foundation Reporter
This annual directory of the largest private charitable foundations in the United States supplies descriptions and statistical analyses.
Price: $365.00
Order from:
Taft Group
835 Penobscot Building
Detroit, MI 48226
(800)877-8238

Grant Guides
There are a total of 30 *Grant Guides* available in a variety of areas such as children and youth, alcohol and drug abuse, mental health, addictions and crisis services, minorities, the homeless, public health and diseases, and social services. Each guide provides descriptions of hundreds of foundation grants of $10,000 or more recently awarded in its subject area. Sources of funding are indexed by type of organization, subject focus, and geographic funding area.
Of the 30 guides, eight are in the field of education including elementary and secondary education, higher education, libraries and information services, literacy, reading and adult/continuing education, scholarships, student aid and loans, science and technology programs, and social and political science programs.
Price: $65.00 each
Order from: The Foundation Center

Guide to Funding for International and Foreign Programs, 2nd edition, 1994, 356 pp.
The guide includes over 650 funding sources that award grants to international non-profit institutions and projects, as well as over 5,600 grant descriptions.
Price: $85.00
Order from: The Foundation Center

Guide to U.S. Foundations, Their Trustees, Officers, and Donors, 1994 edition, 4416 pp.
Includes information on over 35,700 U.S. private, corporate, and community foundations and an index to the individuals who establish, manage, and oversee these foundations.
Price: $195.00
Order from: The Foundation Center

National Guide to Funding for Elementary and Secondary Education, 2nd edition, 1993, 589 pp.
Over 2,000 sources of funding for elementary and secondary education and over 4,700 grant descriptions listing organizations that have successfully approached these funding sources are included in this guide.
Price: $135.00
Order from: The Foundation Center

National Guide to Funding for the Environment and Animal Welfare, 2nd edition, 1994, 322 pp.
Includes over 1,100 sources of funding for environment- and animal welfare–related nonprofit institutions and projects, as well as over 2,700 grant descriptions.
Price: $85.00
Order from: The Foundation Center

National Guide to Funding in Arts and Culture, 3rd edition, 1994, 1035 pp.
This guide includes over 4,000 sources of funding for arts- and culture-related non-profit organizations and projects, as well as over 9,000 grant descriptions.
Price: $135.00
Order from: The Foundation Center

National Guide to Funding in Health, 3rd edition, 1993, 971 pp.
This guide includes over 3,300 funding sources for health-related projects and institutions and over 9,000 grant descriptions.
Price: $135.00
Order from: The Foundation Center

National Guide to Funding in Higher Education, 3rd edition, 1994, 1012 pp.
Over 3,600 sources of funding for higher education projects and institutions and over 10,000 grant descriptions are included in this source.
Price: $135.00
Order from: The Foundation Center

National Guides from The Foundation Center are also available in the following areas:
Aging, 1992, $80.00
Children, Youth and Families, 1993, $135.00
Economically Disadvantaged, 1993, $85.00
Library and Information Services, 1993, $85.00
Religion, 1993, $135.00
Women and Girls, 1993, $95.00

Who Gets Grants/Who Gives Grants, 2nd edition, 1994, 1353 pp.
This book includes over 18,400 nonprofit organizations and descriptions for more than 54,500 foundation grants they received. The introduction also lists the 1,000 largest recipients of foundation grant dollars and the 50 largest recipients in each of the 19 subject fields tested.
Price: $95.00
Order from: The Foundation Center

Private Foundation IRS Tax Returns

The Internal Revenue Service requires private foundations to file income tax returns each year. Form 990-PF provides fiscal details on receipts and expenditures, compensation of officers, capital gains or losses, and other financial matters. Form 990-AR provides information on foundation managers, assets, and grants paid or committed for future payment.

The IRS makes this information available on aperture cards that may be viewed for free at the reference collections operated by the Foundation Center (New York, San Francisco, Washington, DC, Cleveland, and Atlanta) or at the Foundation Center's regional cooperating collections (see chapter 19, exhibit 19.4). You may also obtain this information by writing to the appropriate IRS office (see accompanying list). Enclose as much information about the foundation as possible, including its full name, street address with zip code, employer identification number if available, and the year or years for which returns are requested. It generally takes four to six weeks for the IRS to respond, and the IRS will bill you for all charges, which vary depending on the office and length of the return.

Internal Revenue Service Center Regional Offices

- Central Region (Indiana, Kentucky, Michigan, Ohio, West Virginia):
  Public Affairs Officer
  Internal Revenue Service Center
  P.O. Box 1699
  Cincinnati, OH 45201

- Mid-Atlantic Region (District of Columbia, Maryland, Virginia, Pennsylvania [zip codes starting with 150-168 and 172]):
  Public Affairs Officer
  Internal Revenue Service Center
  11601 Roosevelt Boulevard
  Philadelphia, PA 19154

- Midwest Region (Illinois, Iowa, Minnesota, Missouri, Montana, Nebraska, North Dakota, Oregon, South Dakota, Wisconsin):
  Public Affairs Officer
  Internal Revenue Service Center
  P.O. Box 24551
  Kansas City, MO 64131

- North Atlantic Region (Connecticut, Delaware, Maine, Massachusetts, New Hampshire, New York, New Jersey, Rhode Island, Vermont, Pennsylvania [zip codes 169-171 and 173-196]):
  Public Affairs Officer
  Internal Revenue Service Center
  P.O. Box 400
  Brookhaven, NY 11742

- Southeast Region (Alabama, Arkansas, Georgia, Florida, Louisiana, Mississippi, North Carolina, South Carolina, Tennessee):
  Public Affairs Officer
  Internal Revenue Service Center
  P.O. Box 47-421
  Doraville, GA 30362

- Southwest Region (Arizona, Colorado, Kansas, New Mexico, Oklahoma, Texas, Utah, Wyoming):
  Public Affairs Officer
  Internal Revenue Service Center
  P.O. Box 934
  Austin, TX 78767

- Western Region (Alaska, California, Hawaii, Idaho, Nevada, Washington):
  Public Affairs Officer
  Internal Revenue Service Center
  P.O. Box 12866
  Fresno, CA 93779

Directories of State and Local Grant Makers

The second edition of *The "How To" Grants Manual* listed numerous state directories. However, the number of directories now available has increased significantly, and, therefore, all of them cannot be listed here. Visit the Foundation Center cooperating collection (see chapter 19, exhibit 19.4) closest to you to determine what directories are available for your state and surrounding region.

CORPORATE GRANT RESEARCH AIDS

Corporations interested in corporate giving often establish foundations to handle their contributions. Once foundations are established, their Internal Revenue Service returns become public information, and data are compiled into the directories previously mentioned under Foundation Grant Research Aids.

Corporate contributions that do not go through a foundation are not public information, and research sources consist of

- information volunteered by the corporation
- product information
- profitability information

Annual Survey of Corporate Contributions
Sponsored by the Conference Board and the Council for Financial Aid to Education, this annual survey of corporate giving includes a detailed analysis of beneficiaries of corporate support but does not list individual firms and specific recipients.
Price: $25.00 for associates; $100.00 for non-associates
Order from:
The Conference Board
845 Third Avenue
New York, NY 10022
(212)759-0900

Corporate Giving Watch
This newsletter reports on corporate giving developments.
Price: $139.00 for 16 issues

Order from:
Taft Group
838 Penobscot Building
Detroit, MI 48226
(800)877-8238

Directory of Corporate Affiliations, six volumes
This six-volume directory lists divisions, subsidiaries, and affiliates of thousands of companies with addresses, telephone numbers, key persons, employees, etc.
Price: $950.00, plus shipping and handling
Order from:
Reed Reference Publishing
P.O. Box 31
New Providence, NJ 07974
(800)323-6772

Dun and Bradstreet's Million Dollar Directory, 5 volumes
The five volumes list names, addresses, employees, sales volume, and other pertinent data for 160,000 of the largest businesses in the United States.
Price: $1,395.00
Order from:
Dun and Bradstreet Information Services
3 Sylvan Way
Parsippany, NJ 07054
(800)526-0651

National Directory of Corporate Giving, 3rd edition, 1993, 956 pp.
Information on over 1,700 corporate foundations, plus an additional 600 direct-giving programs, is provided in this directory. An extensive bibliography and six indexes are included to help you target funding prospects.
Price: $195.00
Order from:
The Foundation Center
79 Fifth Avenue, Dept. ME
New York, NY 10003-3076
(800)424-9836 or (212)620-4230
Fax: (212)807-3677

Standard and Poor's Register of Corporations, Directors and Executives, three volumes
This annual register is made up of three volumes (volume 1, *Corporations*; volume 2, *Directors and Executives;* and volume 3, *Indexes*). These volumes are available on a lease basis only. The volumes provide up-to-date rosters of over 400,000 executives of the 46,000 nationally known corporations they represent, along with their names, titles, and business affiliations.
Price: $595.00 per year, includes 3 supplements
Order from:
Standard and Poor's Corporation
Attn: Sales
25 Broadway, 17th Floor
New York, NY 10004
(212)208-8786

Standard Industrial Classification Manual
Developed for use in the classification of establishments by type of activity in which they are engaged.
Price: $30.00 plus $4.00 for handling
Order from:
National Technical Information Service
5285 Port Royal Road
Springfield, VA 22161
(703)487-4028

Taft Corporate Giving Directory, 16th edition, 1995
This directory provides detailed entries on 1,000 company-sponsored foundations. Included are nine indexes.
Price: $365.00 plus shipping and handling
Order from:
Taft Group
838 Penobscot Building
Detroit, MI 48226
(800)877-8238

Who's Who in America, 1994, 48th edition
Known for its life and career data on noteworthy individuals. The 48th edition has three volumes and more than 82,500 biographies.
Price $449.95
Order from:
Marquis Who's Who
121 Chanion Road
New Providence, NJ 07974
(800)521-8110

GOVERNMENT, FOUNDATION, AND CORPORATE GRANT RESOURCES

Many of the following research aids can be purchased from Oryx Press, 4041 N. Central Avenue, Suite 700, Phoenix, AZ 85012-3397, (800)279-6799, fax: (800)279-4663, Internet: info@oryxpress.com.

Administering Grants, Contracts, and Funds
Provides information on the roles and responsibilities of an effective grants office. Particularly useful for those in the process of setting up a new grants office or evaluating an existing one.
Price: $36.95
Order from: Oryx Press

Directory of Biomedical and Health Care Grants
This directory provides information on over 3,182 biomedical and health care–related programs sponsored by the federal government, corporations, professional associations, special interest groups, and state and local governments. Published annually.
Price: $84.50
Order from: Oryx Press

Directory of Building and Equipment Grants, 2nd edition
Aimed at aiding in the search for building and equipment grants, this directory profiles more than 900 foundations and also includes federal sources of support.
> Price: $49.50
> Order from:
> Research Grant Guides
> P.O. Box 1214
> Loxahatchee, FL 33470
> Fax: (407)795-7794

Directory of Computer and High Technology Grants, 2nd edition
This directory provides 3,000 funding entries, including profiles on 600 foundation and 33 federal programs, to help organizations obtain software and computer and high-tech equipment.
> Price: $52.50
> Order from:
> Research Grant Guides
> P.O. Box 1214
> Loxahatchee, FL 33470
> Fax: (407)795-7794

Directory of Funding Sources for Community Development
Descriptions of over 2,000 programs that offer funding opportunities for quality-of-life projects at the community level are included. Funding programs sponsored by both local and national sources are listed, including state, local, and federal government sources, nonprofit and corporate sponsors, foundations, and advocacy groups. Published annually.
> Price: $45.50
> Order from: Oryx Press

Directory of Grants for Organizations Serving People with Disabilities, 8th edition
Profiles on more than 1,000 foundations, 29 federal sources of support, and 4,100 funding entries are included. Foundations listed in the directory have a history of awarding grants that help organizations serving people with disabilities.
> Price: $47.50
> Order from:
> Research Grant Guides
> P.O. Box 1214
> Loxahatchee, FL 33470
> Fax: (407)795-7794

Directory of Grants in the Humanities
Nearly 4,000 programs sponsored by corporations, foundations, professional associations, and special interest groups are covered. Also included are programs funded by the National Endowment for the Arts, the National Endowment for the Humanities, and state and local arts and humanities councils. Published annually.
> Price: $84.50
> Order from: Oryx Press

Directory of Research Grants
Information on over 6,000 government, corporate, organizational, and private funding sources supporting research programs in academic, scientific, and technology related subjects is included. Published annually.

Price: $135.00
Order from: Oryx Press

Giving USA 94
Annual report on philanthropy for the year 1993.
Price: $45 without *Giving USA Update* newsletter; $75 annual report plus newsletter
Order from:
AAFRC Trust for Philanthropy
25 W. 43rd Street, Suite 820
New York, NY 10036
(212)354-5799

Grantseeking Primer for Classroom Leaders, Scholastic, Inc.
Systematic guide providing classroom leaders with a step-by-step approach to preparing a proposal and locating likely funders.
Price: $19.95
Order from: David G. Bauer Associates, Inc.
(800)836-0732

The Principal's Guide to Grant Success, Scholastic, Inc.
Practical techniques for developing an efficient and successful grant system and for helping teachers and staff produce on-target applications for grants.
Price: $24.95
Order from: David G. Bauer Associates, Inc.
(800)836-0732

Successful Grants Program Management, Scholastic, Inc.
Valuable tool for superintendents or central office administrators interested in evaluating the grants system in their districts and developing a grants program that saves time and produces needed funding.
Price: $29.95
Order from: David G. Bauer Associates, Inc.
(800)836-0732

COMPUTER RESEARCH SERVICES AND RESOURCES

There is a wealth of information available through databases and information retrieval systems. Check with your librarian and your grants office to locate those databases you may already have access to. Most large libraries and many smaller ones offer Knight-Ridder searches as part of their reference service for a fee.

Congressional Information Service Index (CIS Index)
CIS Index covers congressional publications and legislation from 1970 to date. Hearings, committee prints, House and Senate reports and documents, special publications, Senate executive reports and documents, and public laws are indexed. *CIS Index* includes monthly abstracts and index volumes. Hard copies of grant-related materials are also available from *CIS*, including *CIS Federal Register Index,* which covers announcements from the *Federal Register* on a weekly basis.

Price: $1,145.00 hardcover annual edition; monthly service (including hardcover annual edition) is on a sliding scale ranging from $1,145.00 to $4,845.00 depending on your library's annual book, periodical, and microform budget

Order from:

Congressional Information Services, Inc.

4520 East West Highway, Suite 800

Bethesda, MD 20814

(800)638-8380

Knight-Ridder Information Services

A commercial organization which provides access to 500 databases in a range of subject areas, Knight-Ridder has a one-time set-up fee of $290.00, which includes one day of training, and an annual fee of $75.00. Knight-Ridder Information Services also provides a CD-ROM version of the *Federal Register*. The price for this service is $750.00 annually, plus an additional $750.00 for a basic Local Area Network subscription.

For more information contact:

Knight-Ridder Information Services

3460 Hillview Avenue

Palo Alto, CA 94304

(800)334-2564

KR Information OnDisc: The GRANTS Database

The CD-ROM version of *The GRANTS Database* describes nearly 10,000 funding programs in more than 90 different areas and subjects, including grants from private and commercial organizations, as well as federal, state, and local governments. Updated bimonthly.

Price: $850.00 yearly subscription fee (without CD-ROM drive); $1,500.00 (with CD-ROM drive)

Order from:

Knight-Ridder Information Services

3460 Hillview Avenue

Palo Alto, CA 94304

(800)334-2564

Fax: (415)858-7069

For more information:

Oryx Press

4041 North Central Avenue, Suite 700

Phoenix, AZ 85012-3397

(800)279-6799

Fax: (800)279-4663

Internet: info@oryxpress.com

Federal Assistance Programs Retrieval System (FAPRS)

The *FAPRS* lists more than 1,250 federal grant programs. All states have *FAPRS* services available through state, county, and local agencies, as well as through federal extension services. For further information, call (202)708-5126 or write to your congressperson's office; he or she can request a search for you, in some cases at no charge.

For more information:
Federal Domestic Assistance Catalog Staff
GSA/IRMS/WKU
300 Seventh Street, SW
Reporters Building, Room 101
Washington, DC 20407

Foundation Center Databases

The Foundation Center offers the public two online computer databases—*The Foundation Directory* file and *The Foundation Grants Index* file. Both databases are available online through DIALOG. The cost for this service is $1.20 per connect minute and $.45 for each record printed.

Contact:
The Foundation Center
79 Fifth Avenue
New York, NY 10003-3076
(800)424-9836
In NY State: (212)620-4230
Fax: (212)807-3677

Grant Winner

Four diskettes designed to make the busy grantseeker more efficient by organizing the process. Contains many of the forms and letters in David Bauer's *The "How To" Grants Manual,* published by ACE/Oryx Press.

Price: $215.00
Order from: David G. Bauer Associates, Inc. at (800) 836-0732 or
Bauer and Ferguson
2225 Elevado Road
Vista, CA 92084
(800) 662-6642

The GRANTS Subject Authority Guide, 1991, 88 pp.

This guide includes 2,421 subject terms used to index *The GRANTS Database* and features "see" and "see also" references to help users target the most appropriate files.

Price: $29.50
Order from:
Oryx Press
4041 N. Central Avenue, Suite 700
Phoenix, AZ 85012-3397
(800)279-6799
Fax: (800)279-4663
Internet: info@oryxpress.com

GrantSearch CFDA

This is an electronic edition of the *Catalog of Federal Domestic Assistance,* including the full text of all federal grant programs included in the *CFDA.*

Price: $375.00
Order from:
Capitol Publications, Inc.
1101 King Street, Suite 444
Alexandria, VA 22314
(800)847-7772

The Sponsored Programs Information Network (SPIN)

SPIN is a database of federal and private funding sources. A microversion is available as well as an online version.

Price: Online: $500.00 annually, plus $10.00 per search, or $3,500.00 annually with unlimited searches; microversion: $2,995.00 for biweekly updates, $1,995.00 for monthly updates, or $1,195.00 for quarterly updates

Order from:
InfoEd
453 New Karner Road
Albany, NY 12205
(800)727-6427

Winning Links

Software for recording information on links to funding sources provided by your board members, staff members, and volunteers.

Price $139.00
Order from:
David G. Bauer Associates at (800)836-0732 or
Bauer and Ferguson
2225 Elevado Road
Vista, CA 92084
(800) 662-6642

INDEX

• • • • • • • • • •

by Linda Webster

ORDERING
INFORMATION

• • • • • • • • •

Order the following materials from Oryx Press

The Oryx Press
Attn: Customer Service
4041 North Central, Suite 700
Phoenix, AZ 85012-3397

Call toll free 800-279-6799
Fax toll free 800-279-4663
Outside the U.S. call 602-265-2651 or
Fax 602-265-6250

Administering Grants, Contracts, and Funds—248 pages examining each aspect of a grants office from evaluation, objectives, and mission to support services. $36.95.

The Complete Grants Sourcebook for Higher Education, 2nd Edition—465 pages of research on funding sources for higher education. Excellent source of information on funders and their higher education expenditures. $85.00.

The Complete Grants Sourcebook for Nursing and Health—A practical guide that includes an in-depth analysis of 300 funding sources for nursing and health. $75.00.

Order the following materials from David G. Bauer Associates, Inc.

Call toll free (800)836-0732.

Grantseeking Materials

Educator's Internet Funding Guide—Techniques schools can use for obtaining funding for technology and Internet access. Includes a CD-ROM. $44.95

Grants Time Line—Pad of 25 worksheets for developing time lines and cash forecasts. $3.95 per pad. For 10 or more pads, $2.95 per pad.

Grantseeking Primer for Classroom Leaders—A systematic guide to grantseeking skills that work for classroom leaders. $24.95.

The Principal's Guide to Grant Success—Strategies principals can apply to support grantseeking at their schools. $24.95.

Project Planner—Pad of 25 worksheets for developing your work plan and budget narrative. $8.95 per pad. For 10 or more pads, $7.95 per pad.

Proposal Organizing Workbook—Set of 30 Swiss Cheese Tabs. $9.95 per set. For 10 or more sets, $8.95 per set.

Successful Grants Program Management—Practical tool for the superintendent or central office administrator to assist in developing a district-wide grants support system. $29.95.

Fund-Raising Materials

Donor Pyramid—Three-fold visual depicting various levels of donor activities and volunteer involvement. $9.95 per pyramid. For 10 or more, $8.95 per pyramid.

Fund Raising Organizer—Pad of 25 spreadsheets for planning and analyzing fund-raising events. $8.95 per pad. For 10 or more pads, $7.95 per pad.

Fund Raising Organizer Activity Cards—Package of 24 cards that summarize resource allocation, costs, and net funds. $3.95 per package. For 10 or more, $2.95 per package.

The Fund Raising Primer—112 pages that provide basic information on various fund-raising strategies. $24.95.

Fund Raising "To Do" Pad—Daily reminder to assist you in prioritizing steps to fund-raising success. $1.95 per pad. For 10 or more, $1.50 per pad.

Seminars

Public Seminars—Call for information concerning David Bauer's public seminars held in major cities throughout the United States.

In-House Seminars—David Bauer gives on-site seminars at your institution or organization to increase your staff and/or board members' skills and interests in the following areas: federal grantseeking, foundation and corporate grantseeking, fund-raising, evaluation of your grant and/or fund-raising system, and motivation/productivity.

Videotape Programs

For more information or to order call (800) 228-4630 or (619) 224-7931 Monday through Friday, 9:00-5:00 Pacific time.

Winning Grants II—Proven grant-winning system on 5 one-hour videocassettes. Produced by University of Nebraska Television in cooperation with the American Council on Education. $495.00.

Strategic Fund Raising—Five one-hour video programs designed to help nonprofit organizations increase board and staff involvement in and understanding of basic fund-raising principles and development of a funding plan. $495.00.

Software Programs

For more information or to order call (619) 224-7931 Monday through Friday, 9:00-5:00 Pacific time.

Grant Winner—Four diskettes for IBM-PC or compatible. Organizes grantseeking techniques, stores four proposals and the worksheets found in *The "How To" Grants Manual*. $215.00

Winning Links—IBM-PC or compatible software package providing a database that records the contacts of your board members, staff, and volunteers. $139.00.